A WOMANIST THEOLOGY OF WORSHIP

A WOMANIST THEOLOGY OF WORSHIP

Liturgy, Justice,
and Communal Righteousness

LISA ALLEN

Maryknoll, New York 10545

Founded in 1970, Orbis Books endeavors to publish works that enlighten the mind, nourish the spirit, and challenge the conscience. The publishing arm of the Maryknoll Fathers and Brothers, Orbis seeks to explore the global dimensions of the Christian faith and mission, to invite dialogue with diverse cultures and religious traditions, and to serve the cause of reconciliation and peace. The books published reflect the views of their authors and do not represent the official position of the Maryknoll Society. To learn more about Orbis Books, please visit our website at www.orbisbooks.com.

Published by Orbis Books, P.O. Box 302, Maryknoll, NY 10545-0302.

Manufactured in the United States of America

Library of Congress Cataloging-in-Publication Data

Names: Allen-McLaurin, Lisa, author.
Title: A womanist theology of worship : justice and communal righteousness / Lisa Allen.
Description: Maryknoll, New York : Orbis Books, 2021. | Includes bibliographical references and index. | Summary: "Examines the history of worship in the Black Church in America, the enduring effects of white supremacy on its liturgical heritage, and proffers a new liturgical paradigm, using a womanist hermeneutic"—Provided by publisher.
Identifiers: LCCN 2021016699 (print) | LCCN 2021016700 (ebook) | ISBN 9781626984448 (print) | ISBN 9781608339075 (ebook)
Subjects: LCSH: African American public worship. | Womanist theology.
Classification: LCC BR563.N4 A48 2021 (print) | LCC BR563.N4 (ebook) | DDC 264.0082—dc23
LC record available at https://lccn.loc.gov/2021016699
LC ebook record available at https://lccn.loc.gov/2021016700

In memoriam
Dr. Lynne St. Clair Darden
Dr. Katie Geneva Cannon
Dr. James Hal Cone
Dr. William B. McClain

For Kiera, Chandler, and Kaylani, my budding womanists

Contents

Acknowledgments *ix*
Introduction *xi*

Part One: Liturgical Legacy

1. The Importance of Liturgy 3
2. African Roots of the Black Church 16
3. African Liturgical Practices 32

Part Two: The Development

4. Understanding Black Liturgy 53
5. Black Liturgical Development 75
6. Double-Consciousness and Evangelical Theology 102
7. Liturgical Practice and Justice 124
8. The Unbroken Circle 142

Part Three: A New Paradigm

9. Foundations of Womanist Liturgical Theology 165
10. A Womanist Liturgical Theology 199

Epilogue 219
Index 223

Acknowledgments

This book is the product of years of research, teaching, and service in and to the Black church. I am indebted to each denomination, church, and faith community I have served during the past forty-five years, since I began playing for Sunday school at my home church, Cade Chapel Missionary Baptist Church, 1000 West Ridgeway Street, Jackson, Mississippi, thirty-nine two thirteen (you have to say the whole thing, like "A Tribe Called Quest"). I am thankful for my experiences in the Baptist and United Methodist Church denominations, as each was essential in my spiritual, worship, and pastoral formation. To my sisters and brothers in the African Methodist Episcopal Church, the African Methodist Episcopal Zion Church, the Church of God in Christ, and the Shrine of the Black Madonna, thank you for your multiple and gracious invitations to share with you as a sister sojourner. I count myself blessed to be part of your congregations. And to my beloved Christian Methodist Episcopal Church, especially the Sixth Episcopal District, who welcomed me with open arms and lifts me up in supportive, loving ways, as I do the work that the Creator has called me to do, I say an unending word of thanks.

I am also indebted to the Interdenominational Theological Center, the nexus of Black theological education that has nurtured, critiqued, challenged, supported, and propelled my work and development as a scholar and public theologian these past sixteen years. To my colleagues who have transitioned beyond the veil: Dr. Edward Smith, Dr. Michael I. N. Dash, Dr. Joseph Troutman, Dr. Wayne Merritt, and Dr. Lynne St. Clair Darden, I will always call your names and keep your memories alive. To my ITC colleagues who continue to traverse and travail with me in the theological education vineyard, especially Dr. Maisha Itia Kariamu Handy, Dr. Willie F. G-dman, Dr. Carolyn Akua McCrary, Dr. Daniel P. Black, Dr. Riggins Earl, Drs. Edward and Anne E. Streaty Wimberly, and Dr. Jacquelyn Grant, I cannot begin to express how much your love and light have buoyed and strengthened me over the years. A special word of thanks to Dr. L. H. Whelchel, my brilliant mentor and colleague, whose work helped lay a firm foundation for this and many other texts focused on African American history. To other colleagues in the academy, especially Dr. Melva Sampson Young, Dr. Roger Sneed, Dr.

Cheryl Kirk-Duggan, Dr. Emilie Townes, Dr. Kelly Brown Douglas, Dr. Shively Smith, Dr. Valerie Bridgeman, Dr. Michelle Meggs, Dr. Neichelle Guidry, Dr. LeRhonda Manigault-Bryant, Reverend Amber Lowe-Woodfork, and Minister Whitney Bond, your diligent work and enthusiastic support have been invaluable through every season of my career. To the ITC Community, especially our students and alumni, thank you for the years of thoughtful dialogue and engagement; because of you, we are.

To my pastor, Dr. Maisha I. K. Handy, my spiritual mentors, especially Dr. Daniel P. Black (Baba Omotosho Jojomani), the founder and curator of the Nation of Ndugu and Nzinga, Inc., and Dr. Will Coleman (Baba Esuyemi Ifayemi), thank you for walking with me on the journey of recovering and employing African ancestral wisdom and spirituality as a daily practice. To the Rize Community Church and the Nation of Ndugu and Nzinga, thank you for your enduring love and support; you are each a balm in Gilead, and streams in the desert of my soul and spirit.

I thank my editor, Paul McMahon, whose brilliant, insightful, meticulous work, and cheerful disposition made this process truly enjoyable. Paul is an editor par excellence, and it has been a delight to work with him. I am especially indebted to the Reverend Dr. Jermaine Jovan Marshall, an outstanding pastoral and academic colleague and son in the ministry. Without his encouragement, support, rigorous critique, and continual communication, this process would have seemed an insurmountable task.

Last, and most importantly, I want to thank my family. As always, I thank my father and mother, the late Walter and Ceaser Belle Anderson Manyfield, for their enduring love, discipline, and encouragement throughout my life, even as they now reside in the ancestral realm. I thank my extended family for their continued encouragement and support in every endeavor, especially the Anderson cousins, who started out with me all those years ago at Cade Chapel, singing "I'm a Child of the King." I am especially indebted to my loving husband, Thomas McLaurin, for his unending encouragement and support, and without whom this book's completion would have been impossible. And to my daughters, Kiera and Chandler, who may not have understood all that I was talking about when they were young girls but are now beginning to understand what it means to be a womanist, and my granddaughter, Kaylani, who I pray will live in a world that welcomes her in the fullness of her personhood. I love you all.

Introduction

Liturgy ought to reflect and relate to everyday life as Black Christians struggle to make sense of life, and worship ought to reflect a captive and alienated people in a strange land, a people in pursuit of liberation, freedom, health, and wholeness.

—William B. McClain

What has happened to Black worship in the thirty years that have transpired since McClain penned these words? There are several answers. Mainline Protestantism, whether historically Anglo or Black, is fighting for survival. Churches of every description and denomination (or non-denomination) are dying, and a divestment of meaning from liturgy—the inability of worshippers to see themselves and make sense of their lives in religious rites and rituals—is an important reason. Worshippers lament that liturgies are boring, dry, dead, or static, and in response, worship planners and leaders look to incorporate current trends in hopes for revival. Unfortunately, even if these trends bring temporary increases in attendance or participation, rarely do they lead to worship experiences that result in communal liberation and transformation, because most of these trends originate outside Black worshipping traditions. Ironically, churches that remain committed to using traditional liturgies rarely experience communal liberation and transformation for the same reason.

What theologies undergird these liturgies? Were they birthed from African cosmologies and ritual practices? Most liturgies of Black worshipping congregations are based on white supremacist evangelical models that focus on individual conversion and salvation, that promise to wash the believer "whiter than snow." There is little, if anything, communal about it, and nothing political or revolutionary, so Black communities do not benefit. And, in the last twenty to thirty years, these liturgies have become enmeshed with a prosperity gospel that contends that wealth is good all the time, and all the time, wealth is good. Historically, there have been churches and cults in the African American community that adhered to these theologies, but, even many of those also included social justice elements and communal understandings.[1]

[1]For a full discussion of Black church and cultic movements, see Gayraud Wilmore, *Black*

What is being offered in many Black churches now is a watered-down gospel that offers cheap grace—a crown without a cross, Easter without Good Friday. This is manifested through liturgies dispossessed of justice, with little communal accountability. What is needed is a new paradigm for worship, rooted in African ancestral cosmologies and communal ontologies, that recovers African and early African American liturgical practices that, for Black worshipping congregations and their communities, have proven meaningful.

A Womanist Theology of Worship examines the history of worship in the Black church in America, the enduring effects of white supremacy on its liturgical heritage, and proffers a new liturgical paradigm using a womanist hermeneutic. This paradigm seeks to dismantle problematic liturgies based in white supremacist theologies that have permeated Black worship in America from its inception through the twenty-first century.

In Part One, we examine the Black church's liturgical legacy. Nicholas Wolterstorff writes that two identifying characteristics of Christian communities are "engaging in Christian liturgy" and "embracing the writings of the Old and New Testament as canonical Scriptures."[2] In Christian worship, we engage in liturgical actions, including reading the Scripture, which calls us to practice justice and share in the struggle against injustice. The word "liturgy," itself, is from the Greek word leitourgia, which means "action of the people."[3] Therefore, liturgy, as Josef A. Jungmann tells us, "is not simply ceremonial—the ceremonies are simply the outward signs of a more profound action. Nor is liturgy merely a set of rules and regulations or an established procedure—rather it is itself the act."[4] Using these definitions, then, liturgy is action—action based on belief in God's redemptive, reconciling work in the world, both in and through Jesus Christ and through God's people.

The first chapter examines these definitions of liturgy and how they are lived out in worshipping communities composed primarily of persons of African descent living in the United States of America. What is liturgy and why is it important to Black worshipping communities? What is "the work" of its people? At the center of our discussion is the question, "Does the Black church

---

Religion and Black Radicalism, 3rd ed. (Maryknoll, NY: Orbis Books, 1998); Hans A. Baer and Merrill Singer, *African-American Religion in the Twentieth Century: Varieties of Protest and Accommodation* (Knoxville: University of Tennessee Press, 1992); Joseph R. Washington Jr., *Black Religion: The Negro and Christianity in the United States* (Lanham, MD: University Press of America, 1984); Milton Sernett, ed., *African American Religious History: A Documentary Witness,* 2d ed. (Durham, NC: Duke University Press, 1999); and Gayraud Wilmore, ed., *African American Religious Studies: An Interdisciplinary Anthology* (Durham, NC: Duke University Press, 1989).

[2]Nicholas Wolterstorff, "Justice as a Condition of Authentic Liturgy," *Theology Today* 48 (1991): 6–14.

[3]Franklin M. Segler and C. Randall Bradley, *Christian Worship,* 3rd ed. (Nashville, TN: B&H Academic, 2006), 6.

[4]Josef A. Jungmann, *The Liturgy of the Word* (Collegeville, MN: Liturgical Press, 1966), 1–2.

equate liturgy with justice?" Perhaps, more accurately, the question is: "Does the Black church still equate liturgy with justice?" It has been proposed by numerous historians, scholars, preachers, and teachers that the Black church grew out of the need for justice in worship. The "invisible institution" was created because enslaved Africans and their descendants were not allowed to worship freely; indeed, the "acceptable" worship services they were made to attend were little more than attempts to justify slavery as God's judgment on, or provision for, the inferior, enslaved African. Cosmologically, Africans knew that humans were divinely created and linked to all of God's good creation.[5] Therefore, they knew that what they were told in the "acceptable" worship services was not true. Their liturgy—the "work of the people"—required creating a sacred space where they could worship God as a God of liberation and justice, and who was keeping them and working out their liberation in God's time.

The second chapter explores how this cosmological viewpoint, and others from African ancestral traditions, continued to undergird Black worship as the "invisible institution" grew into the Black church and becoming "the center of social intercourse and the citadel of hope against the unfulfilled promises of Emancipation."[6] Contrary to prevailing, though mistaken, ideas about Africans who were immorally imported to the Americas and elsewhere, Africans worshipped God. It was not the God to whom they were introduced by their Anglo oppressors—once it was deemed necessary to proselytize them—but it was a concept of God as One who had made them as part of divine creation and to whom they were linked as creations of the Most High and part of the divine cosmological order.[7] Consequently, enslaved Africans believed that they were linked to everything in creation—human, animal, and plant—and were responsible, as much as humanly possible, for the well-being of that creation.

Other African cosmological and theological worldviews that directly impacted the understanding of the liturgy of Black worshippers were the concepts of kinship and sacred cosmos. We were kinfolk, sisters, brothers, aunts, uncles, and cousins of each other, though one may have been Fulani and the other, Ashanti, one Kamba and the other, Maasai. Our understanding of life, and subsequently, liturgy, was communal. Sacred cosmos meant there was no separation of sacred and secular because there was no secular; all of life was lived as an offering to the divine. What one did in private, one still did in the presence of God, and therefore, one was called always to live ethically.

From the "invisible institution" through the Civil Rights Movements of

---

[5]Melva W. Costen, *African American Christian Worship,* 2nd ed. (Nashville, TN: Abingdon Press, 2007), 5.

[6]Wyatt T. Walker, *Somebody's Calling My Name: Black Sacred Music and Social Change* (Valley Forge, PA: Judson Press, 1979), 20.

[7]Melva W. Costen, *African American Christian Worship,* 5–6.

the twentieth century, worship practices in the Black church were imbued with African ancestral calls for equity, justice, and communal righteousness. Inherent in these practices was a communal perspective, which had grown directly out of the African proverb: "I am because we are, and since we are, therefore, I am." Therefore, the *leitourgia* (action of the people) of the Black church, regardless of denomination, was inextricably tied to justice, for there could be no true worship of God without equity and liberation for all God's people. Chapter 3 investigates the African inheritance in liturgical practices that developed from the arrival of Africans in America through the antebellum period and how those retentions permeated Black worship through the mid-twentieth century.

McClain proclaims that "the genius of black worship is . . . the ability to create the new and fresh out of the old and stale, to lend a refulgence to the dark and somber, to create a *tertium quid* out of the coming-together of two diverse influences so distinct and different as to be called unique."[8] Part Two explores the development of this unique genius—liturgy and liturgies in the Black church—and how, particularly as denominations grew, Black congregations copied or adapted liturgies from churches of European descent for their own use. Chapter 4 examines the unique identity of Black liturgy, as it developed amid antebellum spaces and influences. How did the presentation of Anglo-Christianity become primary in the formation of Black theology? How were distinctions made between what was oppressive and marginalizing for Black skin and spirit, and what was liberative and transformative?

The fifth chapter investigates how these worship practices continued as the "invisible institution" developed into the Black church and were codified in liturgies in visible churches. Many liturgies, most often based on Calvinist, Anglican, or Puritan theologies, were not life-giving or healthy for people of African descent, as they contradicted directly African worldviews of cosmology, theology, and embodiment. Racist interpretations of the biblical text further underscored the oppressive nature of these liturgies. However, Black congregations continued, and continue, to employ these liturgies out of misguided desires to observe orthodoxy and be deemed "good" and/or "safe." As this occurred, Black worshippers often began to allow African ancestral worship traditions and heritages to be maligned, negated, and, in many contexts, disallowed. It has been well documented that, in many worship settings in mainline Protestantism, whites were against retaining any aspect of what might be considered African worship. The communal nature of call and response was deemed "disorderly," and the ecstatic nature of music, shouting,

---

[8]William B. McClain, *Come Sunday: The Liturgy of Zion* (Nashville, TN: Abingdon Press, 1990), 50–51.

and dancing was considered "heathenish."[9] What is more surprising is that, as Blacks began to establish denominations, many leaders and members echoed these sentiments. The assimilation and acculturation processes undergone by Black people in America evinced itself in worship styles in many contexts.[10] Many denied their African worship heritage, assumed a very Anglo posture in worship, attempting to remove any vestiges of Africanness, including skin color, and began to use this characteristic to draw class distinctions. Thus, as we will explore, began a *double-consciousness* in worship that has led to the dichotomy between liturgy and justice.

Chapter 6 examines the deleterious effects of *double consciousness*, the evangelical and prosperity theologies, on Black liturgy and liturgies. Regarding double consciousness, W. E. B. Du Bois articulated:

> It is described as a sense of always looking at one's self through the eyes of others, of measuring one's soul by the tape of a world that looks on in amused contempt and pity. One forever feels his or her twoness—an American, a Negro; two souls, two thoughts, two unreconciled strivings; two warring ideals in one dark body, whose dogged strength alone keeps it from being torn asunder.[11]

As Black people began to make strides in and become part of mainstream American society and, ever so slowly, became part of either Anglo churches that would accept them or those they built themselves based on Anglo liturgies, they began to abandon their own ways of being in worship. It was not merely a surface abandonment but an entire shift in the theological paradigm of worship. Prior to their inclusion in other churches, the primary focus of worship was liberation—being free to worship the God who would deliver them and working for that liberation through acts of justice in their communities.

This shift was underscored and even enhanced by the Great Awakenings of the eighteenth and early nineteenth centuries. The first was a revival movement in the colonies, focused on evangelism, personal piety, and revitalization of church worship. The second, a revival movement much like the first, was located primarily among America's frontier towns. At the center of this movement was an evangelical theology based in personal experience and responsibility for initiating one's own religious conversion. This new evangelical paradigm, coupled with the desire to assimilate into American mainstream

---

[9] Anthony B. Pinn, *Terror and Triumph: The Nature of Black Religion* (Minneapolis, MN: Fortress Press, 2003), 100.

[10] Walker, *Somebody's Calling My Name*, 25.

[11] W. E. B. Du Bois, *The Souls of Black Folk* (New York: Penguin Books, 1989), 5–6.

society, with the hopes of being accepted, served to render Africanness a liability, rather than an asset. The focus became individual conversion to the detriment of a communal understanding of salvation. As James Cone writes, "The post–Civil War black church fell into the white trick of interpreting salvation in terms similar to those of the white oppressor. Salvation became white: an objective act of Christ in which God 'washes' away our sins in order to prepare us for a new life in heaven."[12]

No matter how Black congregations may have struggled with the presence, or absence, of African retentions in worship, the ancestral call to communal justice was ever-present in the liturgy of Black protest. Chapter 7 reviews how Black worshippers continued to bind justice to liturgy through protest movements during and after enslavement through the Civil Rights Movements of the 1940s, 1950s, and 1960s. Liturgical practices in the form of resistance work centered on a theo-ethic of equity and liberation. Songs, prayers, and sermons employed during these services and events issued a communal response to the question posed by the Psalmist, "How could we sing the Lord's song in a foreign land?" (Ps 137:4). Though many may have experienced a dichotomy between liturgy and justice in formal worship on Sunday mornings, the worship that took place in brush arbors, town halls, protest meetings, marches, sit-ins, and bus rides were clearly steeped in African ancestral liturgical calls for justice.

Other religious movements impacting Black liturgy include the rise of storefront churches, the Spiritual Movement, and what E. Franklin Frazier deemed "Negro Cults in the City."[13] These new denominations and sects developed as Blacks migrated to Northern cities in response to changing economic and political climates in the South. Two of the most impactful issues arising from these new movements were the abandonment of "sacred cosmos" in favor of a dichotomy between flesh and spirit, and the promise of financial prosperity as a result of "the enactment of certain magico-religious rituals."[14] These two issues have continued to influence the development and role of Black worship and liturgy into the twenty-first century. Consequently, particularly with the advent of televangelism and social media access, a new model of worship, one that prioritizes a personal relationship with God and/or Christ over communal justice and responsibility, and "organic" worship that decries the need for a particular order or liturgy has emerged. This model has been adapted even by denominational churches as a way of attracting people, particularly younger generations. However, because of the dichotomies caused by dual

---

[12]James H. Cone, *A Black Theology of Liberation*, 40th anniv. ed. (Maryknoll, NY: Orbis Books, 2010), 134–135.

[13]E. Franklin Frazier, *The Negro Church in America* (New York: Schocken Books, 1974), 60.

[14]Hans Baer, "Black Spiritual Churches," in *African American Religious Studies: An Interdisciplinary Anthology*, ed. Gayraud Wilmore (Durham, NC: Duke University Press, 1989), 97.

consciousness and a divestment of justice from liturgy in many churches, this new model has often had the opposite effect.

Furthermore, there is the staunch adherence of many Black congregations to traditional liturgies mired in problematic theologies. Chapter 8 explores how, even as seminary-educated pastors of Black churches have matriculated in and received degrees from institutions teaching Black liberation and womanist theologies, they and the congregations they lead still insist on employing these liturgies. What prevents these congregations from revising these orders or totally rewriting their own liturgies that affirm Blackness, Black life, Black wholeness, and the link between justice and liturgy? One reason is the belief that Blackness is inferior and that anything European is better, higher, and holier. Another is the historical fear of being "wrong" in worship, of being perceived as heathenish or uncivilized. A third is a fear of liberation, itself. Doing the work of liberating liturgies from racist, sexist, white supremacist ideas and ideals is as difficult as liberating bodies, if not more so, because it is the work of liberating the mind and the spirit. To do this work requires a commitment to dismantling white supremacy, which, in itself, requires an acknowledgment that one's beloved worship is steeped in racist, sexist, and patriarchal theologies and ideologies. That is a monumental task for educated seminarians, let alone pastors and parishioners who may have never seen the inside of a seminary, let alone attended one.

Why is this work necessary? Throughout the last twenty years, the Black church as an entity has lost much of its spiritual and communal authority. The loss of African ancestral legacies has led to an unmooring of the Black church from its liturgical foundations of justice and righteousness. In Chapter 8, we reflect on how allegiance to evangelical and prosperity theologies and their problematic liturgies has caused, in part, an exodus of church members in the last twenty years. This exodus has been primarily among younger generations and is reflected in how recent protest movements, including Black Lives Matter, have declined to invite or involve the Black church on a large scale. Although other factors have certainly contributed to membership decline, a significant number of young Black people are no longer attending churches every Sunday because, as one young woman stated, "They don't have anything there for me anymore."[15] When questioned why the Black church isn't at the forefront of the Black Lives Matter movement, Rev. Watson Jones, pastor of Compassion Baptist Church in Chicago, remarked, "The church has lost some of its prophetic voice. It's lost some of its fervor."[16] "It's also lost some of its cultural status," according to Aldon Morris, Northwestern

---

[15]Melanie Eversley, "Black Millennials Dropping Out of Church, But Say It Isn't Because of Religion," *The Grio,* March 19, 2019, accessed September 10, 2020, https://thegrio.com.

[16]Kelsey Dallas, "Where Are Churches in the Black Lives Matter Movement?" *Deseret News,* July 24, 2020, accessed September 10, 2020, https://www.deseret.com.

University professor of sociology and African American studies. "Activists no longer feel like they need the power of religious institutions behind them to change the world."[17]

In 2010, Eddie Glaude Jr. penned an extremely provocative article, "The Black Church Is Dead." Rather than an epitaph, the piece reads as a call to consciousness for stakeholders. Glaude delineates reasons why the Black Church is no longer "central to black life" and "a repository for the social and moral conscience of the nation."[18] One that is central to the purpose of this book is his claim that "we have witnessed the routinization of black prophetic witness," meaning the Black Church's authority is now based simply on what happened in the past. Professor Glaude warns: "But such a church loses it power. Memory becomes its currency. Its soul withers from neglect. The result is all too often church services and liturgies that entertain, but lack a spirit that transforms, and preachers who wish for followers instead of fellow travelers in God."[19] The reason these services and liturgies lack a transformative spirit is because of decades, even centuries, of liturgies and liturgical practices that have not served Black congregations and communities well.

In a hopeful response, the final part of the book offers a new paradigm for Black worship, one that reimagines liturgy and liturgies through a womanist lens and works to dismantle white supremacy in and through the Black church. Chapter 9 examines the roots of liturgical theology—both outside and inside the Black church—and offers a framework for a womanist liturgical theology that centers on African and African-descended cosmological and theological worldviews and spiritualities; affirms full embodiment in worship; employs womanist hermeneutics in all worship elements, and womanist hermeneutics/spirituality of communal empowerment and agency. Chapter 10 outlines this new womanist liturgical theology and paradigm, exploring how womanist worship and liturgy would look and operate in praxis. The paradigm addresses how historic violence done to Black American bodies—physically, socially, politically, and religiously—over the past four hundred years has resulted in disembodied worship and liturgy in Black worshipping contexts and caused a disconnect between prophetic witness and lived protest.[20] Furthermore, the

---

[17]Dallas, "Where Are Churches in the Black Lives Matter Movement?"

[18]Eddie Glaude Jr., "The Black Church Is Dead," *HuffPost*, April 26, 2010, accessed September 11, 2020, https://www.huffpost.com.

[19]Glaude, "The Black Church Is Dead."

[20]Ethicists Katie Cannon and Riggins Earl and theologians Jacquelyn Grant, Delores Williams, and Dwight Hopkins are but a few who have explored the concept of embodiment and how it relates to the Incarnation of Jesus and Christian discipleship, viewed through Black theological and/or womanist hermeneutics. More recent works, including M. Shawn Copeland's *Enfleshing Freedom: Body, Race, and Being* (Minneapolis: Fortress Press, 2009), Anthony Pinn's *Embodiment and the New Shape of Black Theological Thought* (New York: New York University Press, 2010), and Eboni Marshall Turman's *Toward a Womanist Ethic of Incarnation: Black Bodies,*

chapter includes a broad overview of how womanist spirituality permeates this paradigm, bringing to it a holistic identity and approach. In closing, a brief epilogue offers reflections and thoughts on how the Black church might use this paradigm and research to recover and restore its full prophetic identity.

---

the Black Church, and the Council of Chalcedon (New York: Palgrave Macmillan, 2013), take the concepts of embodiment and incarnation further and offer models that prove helpful in constructing a womanist theology of worship.

Part One

LITURGICAL LEGACY

1

The Importance of Liturgy

What is liturgy and why is it important to Black worshipping communities? To answer this question, we first need to define the terms *worship* and *liturgy* and how they are related. Interestingly, both terms have secular roots. The word *worship* "comes from the Old English word *weorthscipe*, literally *weorth* (worthy) and *scipe* (-ship) and signifies attributing worth, or respect to someone."[1] *Leitourgia*, from *laos* (people) and *ergon* (work), was defined in ancient Greece as "a public work performed for the benefit of the city or state. It could involve donated service as well as taxes."[2] Edwin Womack argues that worship is the most important thing we do.[3] He also takes his definition of worship from an old Anglo-Saxon word, *woerthan,* which meant "to declare how much something is worth." Worship is whatever is at the top, whatever is most important, whatever is worth the most. Worship is also action. The Greek New Testament uses several words that are translated as worship, but they are all verbs, action words. Womack defines and describes these for us:

> The first is *sebomai,* meaning, "to lift up or exalt." The second is *proskuneo*, which means literally to kiss forward and is translated, "to bow down." In biblical times, when a person would come before the king, she or he would bow down literally, with her hands, feet, and forehead to the ground. In this position the person could not fight, was in fact, completely helpless. This position showed complete subservience and obedience. The third word is *latreuo* which means "to serve." The word refers to the hired servant who gives faithful service to her master in return for food, shelter, and money, which make it possible to live.[4]

---

[1]James White, *Introduction to Christian Worship*, 3rd ed. rev. (Nashville, TN: Abingdon Press, 2000), 27.

[2]White, *Introduction to Christian Worship*, 26.

[3]Edwin B. Womack, *Come Follow Me: A Study Book for Acolytes* (Lima, OH: CSS Publishing, 1984), 12–13.

[4]Womack, *Come Follow Me*, 13.

James White distinguishes two kinds of worship: common worship and personal devotions.[5] Personal devotions, though perhaps linked to corporate worship, generally occur separately from the physical presence of other members of the faith community. Common worship, however, "is the worship offered by the gathered congregation, the Christian assembly, also known as the *ekklesia*, 'those who are called out from the world.' "[6] Constance Cherry suggests another view of worship and asserts: "Christian worship is a God-instituted gift to the church for nurturing our relationship with God and others. Worship is above all *to* God, *with* God, and *for* God."[7]

We have described liturgy as "action," and perhaps liturgy is better described than defined, for it is a word that encapsulates several meanings. The original Greek, as stated earlier, means "work of the people," but that work can be any work, not merely religious. In English, the term *liturgy* is "used in two senses: in general, all the prescribed services of the Church, including, for example, the canonical hours, as contrasted with private devotion; and specifically, as a title of the Eucharist (as the chief act of public worship)."[8] Melva Wilson Costen asserts:

> The New Testament understanding of liturgy, which has suffered loss in translation, is that Christ's life, death, and resurrection are, in fact, the epitome of liturgy. Christians who claim that their lives are in Christ are formed and shaped by the likeness of Christ, and are an embodiment of efforts to make present this *one* liturgy in all times and places.[9]

In his book, *Liturgical Theology*, Simon Chan describes liturgy as *embodied worship*, that is, "worship expressed through a certain visible order or structure (thus the phrase, 'order of service')."[10] Gordon Lathrop agrees:

> The meaning of the liturgy resides first of all in the liturgy itself. If the gathering has a meaning for us . . . then that becomes known while we are participating in the gathering. The liturgical vision engages us while the order of actions flows over us and while we ourselves perform the patterns and crises of this public work.[11]

Indeed, *liturgy* is a word that, when viewed through the lens of faith, encompasses those acts of worship in which a community of faith participates.

---

[5]White, *Introduction to Christian Worship*, 29.

[6]White, *Introduction to Christian Worship*, 29.

[7]Constance Cherry, *The Worship Architect* (Grand Rapids, MI: Baker Academic, 2010), xii.

[8]*The Oxford Dictionary of the Christian Church*, s.v. liturgy.

[9]Melva Wilson Costen, *African American Christian Worship*, 2nd ed. (Nashville, TN: Abingdon Press, 2007), 113.

[10]Simon Chan, *Liturgical Theology* (Downers Grove, IL: IVP Academic, 2006), 62.

[11]Gordon Lathrop, *Holy Things: A Liturgical Theology* (Minneapolis: Fortress Press, 1998), 5.

Harmon Smith argues that "liturgy ineluctably reflects, indeed, that it must mirror and mediate what we believe to be true and good and beautiful if it is to be an authentic celebration. Liturgy both reflects and teaches us the kind of people we are and are meant to be."[12] Based on these definitions, liturgy can be understood as those acts in which communities of faith engage as the people of God.

Liturgy and the Black Church

What, then, does *liturgy* mean in the life and worship of the Black church? In many cases, the word itself may have little significance. In fact, when polled, about 85 percent of my students stated that the word carried negative connotations. These negative connotations are not limited to Black worshipping congregations, of course. In 1994, Don Saliers remarked that "many suspect liturgy to be a means of suppression or social imperialism of one kind or another."[13] When asked why congregations held negative views of the word "liturgy," most students stated that the application of the word to worship carried meanings such as "high church," "Anglo," and, "boring." This is not to say that liturgy does not exist in the Black church; indeed, liturgy exists wherever worship exists because it simply means whatever acts of worship take place in a given structured setting, regardless of how that structure is ordered. Costen claims that "African American congregations generally agree that corporate Christian worship is acknowledgment of and response to the presence and power of God as revealed in Jesus the Christ through the work of the Holy Spirit."[14]

Many worship contexts, particularly in non-denominational churches, pride themselves on being "contemporary," and/or non-liturgical. However, whatever is done in that context is its liturgy, whether it be the deacon's devotional for 25 minutes, singing "praise and worship" for 35 minutes, altar call for 45 minutes, or preaching for 55 minutes. That is the liturgy in that context. In fact, the misunderstanding of the word gives some indication why worship in our churches has "devolved" into its current state. Even in Black churches that have a "prescribed liturgy," it is often viewed as a necessary evil. Many people don't care for it, have very little enthusiasm when performing it, try to omit as much of it as possible, and try to find ways to adapt it—and perhaps with good reason. Nevertheless, it is not the presence of liturgy that has caused the mass exodus of our mainline Protestant churches. Rather, it

[12]Harmon L. Smith, *Where Two or Three Are Gathered: Liturgy and the Moral Life* (Cleveland, OH: Pilgrim Press, 1995), x.

[13]Don Saliers, *Worship as Theology: A Foretaste of Glory Divine* (Nashville, TN: Abingdon Press, 1994), 14.

[14]Costen, *African American Christian Worship*, 79.

has been the content of liturgies and their origins. Liturgy is not the enemy, but rather our misunderstanding of the meaning and purpose of liturgy. What is liturgy and what is it supposed to do?

The Purpose of Worship and Liturgy

Two additional perspectives on worship and liturgy, both from African American women, help us answer these questions for Black congregations. The first comes from homiletics and worship scholar Valerie Bridgeman, who states:

> Liturgy . . . is playing with God. For me, liturgy is where our playful hearts meet the creative imagination of God and God experiences worship while we experience grace, redemption, re-formation, salvation and wholeness. Worship belongs to God. It is in our play: our proclamation, our affirmations, and our repetitive recitation of the truths of our faith that we meet the God of all creation, God who spoke and still speaks. We play on the edges of eternity, seeking to know the incomprehensible, unknowable One. Worship, then, is an encounter with a playful God in a playing creation. The gathering of the people of God for this worship is an aperture, an opening in the midst of ordinary life, in which we slip the sacred completely on.[15]

The second perspective, from Melva Costen, is that worship is *empowerment*. Costen defines empowerment as "experiencing and feeling freedom as 'realized eschatology' in, but not limited to, corporate worship."[16] She notes:

> The warp and woof of African American worship is a celebration of the reality of a transformed relationship between Creator and creature. This relationship undergirds the empowerment that is expressed in freedom by the grace of God. . . . Worship can be viewed as both praise and empowerment, as it enables communities of faith to claim the "right to the tree of life" and act as agents of love and justice in the world.[17]

These two frames of reference for worship and liturgy reflect unique aspects of personhood, psychological, and sociocultural contexts of Black worshipping congregations. This speaks to different and deeper dimensions of communal

---

[15]Valerie Bridgeman Davis, "Go Play with God: Reclaiming Liturgy for Spiritual Formation," in *Companion to the Africana Worship Book*, ed. Valerie Bridgeman Davis and Safiyah Fosua (Nashville, TN: Discipleship Resources, 2007), 27.

[16]Costen, *African American Christian Worship*, 107.

[17]Costen, *African American Christian Worship*, 106.

perspectives of worship and liturgy among Black worshippers, both vertically (with God) and horizontally (with humanity).

What, then, does liturgy do in Black faith communities? Edward S. Wimberly, author and pastoral care theologian, notes that "Black worship grows out of what God has done, is doing, and will do on behalf of people of color. The quality of lived life cannot be separated from what the people do to respond to God's activity in the past, present, and in the future. The response of a community to God's activity requires work by the respondents."[18] Wimberly asserts that Black Christian communities combine work and worship through three dimensions that he calls "liturgical functions": organizing, celebrating, and mediating.[19] *Organizing* refers to the work of the Black Church centering its life on values that emerge from communal God-encounters. *Celebrating* involves participation in authentic and holistic praise of God through catharsis, a welcoming of God's presence and activity, healing, and wholeness. Finally, *mediating* requires the transmission of the community's core values and the dynamic power and properties contained therein. This transmission occurs through the community's establishment of relationships, and its efficacy is evinced in the quality of communal life.

James Cone, the father of Black liberation theology, provides another liturgical perspective of Black worshipping congregations:

> The Black church congregation is an eschatological community that lives as if the end of time is already at hand. . . . The eschatological significance of the Black community is found in the people's believing that the Spirit of Jesus is coming to visit them in the worship service each time two or three are gathered in [God's] name, and to bestow upon them a new vision of their future humanity.[20]

Echoing these sentiments, William McClain writes that "in the black church going to church is more than attending a worship service. It is a way of gathering all of what the people are. . . . Going to church offers a way of deciphering the meaning of living life in relation to God and neighbor."[21]

Essentially, both these scholars identify the core of Black worship and liturgy as communal action that is dynamically expressed in relationships between God, individuals, and neighbors; it is focused on God's activity in the

---

[18]Edward P. Wimberly, "The Dynamics of Black Worship: A Psychosocial Exploration of the Impulses that Lie at the Roots of Black Worship," in *Readings in African American Church Music and Worship*, ed. James Abbington (Chicago: GIA Publications, 2001), 342.

[19]Wimberly, "Dynamics of Black Worship," 343.

[20]James H. Cone, "Sanctification, Liberation, and Black Worship," *Theology Today* 35, no. 2 (1978): 140.

[21]William B. McClain, *Come Sunday: The Liturgy of Zion* (Nashville, TN: Abingdon Press, 1990), 37.

lives of Black people; it addresses directly the lived experiences of Black people; and it affirms God's plans for the future of Black people. Furthermore, it is the commonality of Black lived experiences that underscores these communal actions—experiences borne of collective horror, sorrow, and even joy in the face of seemingly insurmountable realities. It is not merely being Christian that joins us in fellowship; it is being *Black* and Christian. It is affirming the universal theological view of God as liberator under the particular auspices of how God's liberating justice and righteousness operate in and through the lives of Black people. As Cone stated succinctly, "Black Christians believe that the God of Moses and of Jesus is first and foremost the God of love and of justice who is 'ever present in time of trouble.' "[22]

Three Common Aspects

How is this perspective of Christianity lived out in the liturgy of Black worshipping communities in America? One of the telling aspects of Black liturgy is the *personal view of God* in all aspects of the worship service. Prayers, music, exhortations, and sermons all reflect a personal, reciprocal relationship with the Divine. God is not a cosmic watchmaker or dispassionate creator; rather, God is deeply concerned with the circumstances presently occurring in the lives of God's people and, moreover, is moved to action because of this personal, reciprocal relationship. Black worshippers take to heart biblical texts that affirm God's willingness to hear and respond to the cries of God's people, including the possibility that God might change God's mind.

A second aspect is the *communal call for justice* in liturgical documents and worship acts. Most denominational books of worship, discipline, and order in Black worshipping communities reflect a knowledge and understanding of Black history/histories that inspired the creations of Black worshipping practices, and later, denominations, in America. These books help define and structure theological, doctrinal, and liturgical tenets that inform and infuse Black worship, and underscore why Black liturgy is tied to justice in ways that are unique, distinct from other worshipping communities. Standard liturgical acts of worship such as calls to worship, prayers, responsive readings, sermons, and final blessings are often written or adapted to include direct connections to Black history and the development of faith and worship. Furthermore, in worship services, communal calls for justice occur extemporaneously through these acts of worship. Current events that highlight the ongoing fight for Black freedom are mentioned often in the aforementioned acts of worship, as well as additional acts that may be included as part of a particular call to justice.

A third aspect is the *communal identity*. The ways that Black communi-

[22]James H. Cone, *For My People: Black Theology and the Black Church* (Maryknoll, NY: Orbis Books, 1984), 10.

ties understand how they, as individuals, are inextricably linked are different from the ways other communities believe themselves to be related. Though persons in European-descended/Anglo churches or denominations may believe themselves to be "family" because they are members of the same church, it is not identical to how Black people who are members of the same church or denomination believe themselves to be "family." Other races in other churches often feel a sense of kinship, because they share common religious beliefs, values, and background. That is also true in Black churches, but with different foundations at the core of this kinship. Costen explains:

> African-American Christians share several common aspects of worship regardless of denomination. They are: 1) gathering to offer thanks and praise to God in and through Jesus Christ, and to be spiritually fed by the Word of God; 2) a common historical taproot, extending deep into the African soil; and 3) our history of struggle for survival as African people in America.[23]

This "common historical taproot" binds Black peoples together regardless of which country or region of Africa they may have been descended from. In the next chapter, I explore the roots of African cosmological worldviews that have impacted the formation of Black worship and liturgy in America. But one of these worldviews that is clearly an African understanding of kinship was and is present in Black worshipping communities and influences how they perceive themselves as family. The history of the struggle for survival that I discuss later further binds these communities in kinship and is born of a communal fight for familial preservation and a desire for justice (cf. Amos 5:24).

What we see from these definitions and descriptions is that *worship* is the inhabiting of communal space and the particular actions of the gathered community, and *liturgy* is the ordering of and participation in those actions.

Ritual

Before I discuss how liturgy and justice function together, let us consider the aspect of *ritual*. Ronald Grimes states that "ritual is as old as humanity."[24] The roots of ritual are many and varied, including "human bodies, the environment, cultural traditions, social processes. . . . Ritual itself has no single origin."[25] How does ritual function in our understanding of worship and liturgy? For the Christian community, Costen notes that ritual "is founded on

---

[23]Costen, *African American Christian Worship*, 1–2.

[24]Ronald L. Grimes, *Beginnings in Ritual Studies*, 3rd ed. (Waterloo, Canada: Ritual Studies International, 2013), 1.

[25]See Grimes, *Beginnings in Ritual Studies*, "Introduction."

actions and words of Jesus, which are imbued with hope and fulfillment."[26] White identifies ritual as a category of human behavior that includes Christian worship. As such, ritual has three definitive characteristics: (1) a form of behavior, (2) repetition, and (3) a social activity that serves some communal function.[27] McClain describes ritual as an aspect of Christian worship rooted in a common culture that is relevant to the lives of the people and serves several functions,[28] including giving people ways to explain the vicissitudes of life, opportunities to remember and re-member shared experiences within community, and spaces to express their need for identity formation through *anamnesis* (historical memory). Rituals do not develop overnight; they emerge over time as those activities and events become steeped in the community's beliefs, traditions, and practices that have lasting significance for *that* community. Importantly in the rituals of African and African-descended worshipping communities is "the presence of a Higher Being that has power over their existence and is therefore worthy of worship."[29]

Liturgy and Communal Justice

To consider liturgy fully, we must define *justice*. *Webster's Dictionary* defines *justice* as "just or right action or treatment, the carrying out of law, and the quality of being fair or just."[30] Therefore, justice is the doing of what is right, legally or in the act of fair treatment. What does justice have to do with liturgy? How does doing what is right or fair find a home in worship? The words of the prophets Amos and Micah hold an answer for us: "Let justice roll down like water and righteousness like an ever-flowing stream" (Amos 5:24); "What does the LORD require of thee, but to do justice, to love mercy, and to walk humbly with God" (Micah 6:8). These are just two of the well-known scripture passages that proclaim God as a God of justice. This concept of God permeates the biblical text and, according to Nicholas Wolterstorff, has two aspects: first, the justice that God exercises and expects God's people to enact is not retributive or punitive, but restorative, and second, there are four groups to whom justice is always due—widows, orphans, strangers (sojourners), and the poor.[31] In the biblical text, "liturgical actions

---

[26]Costen, *African American Christian Worship*, 45.

[27]White, *Introduction to Christian Worship*, 19.

[28]McClain, *Come Sunday*, 50–51.

[29]Gennifer Brooks, "The Creation of an Africana Worship Ritual: Baptism in the Shouters of Trinidad," in *Companion to the Africana Worship Book*, ed. Valerie Bridgeman Davis and Safiyah Fosua (Nashville, TN: Discipleship Resources, 2007), 67.

[30]*Webster's Student Dictionary*, s.v. "justice."

[31]Nicholas Wolterstorff, *Hearing the Call: Liturgy, Justice, Church, and World* (Grand Rapids, MI: Wm. B. Eerdmans, 2011), 42.

lose their authenticity when those who participate in the liturgy do not practice and struggle for justice."[32] Thus, we see that justice and mercy—ethics—and walking with God—liturgy, ritual, and sacraments—are inextricably tied together. As communities of faith who uphold the authority of the biblical text, we recognize that, through the canon of Scripture, we are called to walk together with God and each other, living in ways that manifest the presence of God, authentically linking liturgy and justice. Costen asserts: "In true and authentic worship of God, there is a dialectical relationship rather than a dichotomy between faith and practice, justice and ritual action (liturgy and justice), theological talk and doxological living, and sanctification and human liberation."[33] Indeed, liturgy and ethics are not separate, autonomous entities, but liturgy, which is everything the church offers to God in the name of Jesus, is authentic only when exemplified in lives lived in harmony with the ethical commands God gives and Jesus affirms. Harmon Smith notes, "The Gospel knows nothing of sundering liturgy and the moral life; or conversely, when the Gospel knows of liturgy and the moral life sundered, it calls this 'hypocrisy.' "[34] Hypocrisy, what a loaded word! And yet this is precisely why many people claim they do not attend church—because the people who *do* attend on Sunday act as though they *do not* on Monday through Saturday.

Whatever the Black church was at its inception, it was about justice and remaining true to its African heritage.[35] Gayraud Wilmore asserts:

> This black folk religion contained a definite moral judgment against slavery and a clear legitimation of resistance to injustice. White anti-slavery radicals, the precursors of Lovejoy and John Brown, contributed to the militancy of some black Christians and to the spirit that created the independent black churches. But we have made the point that there was something else that made religion among the slaves different from the Christianity of the white churches. It was the slaves' African past that did most to influence their style of religious life, their rejection of the spiritual and political despotism of the whites, and made the most important contribution to the black Christian radicalism of the nineteenth century.[36]

Indeed, the Black church was the only place for a long time, and then only one of a few places, where Black persons could go and be on equal footing

---

[32]Wolterstorff, *Hearing the Call*, 43.

[33]Costen, *African American Christian Worship*, 112.

[34]Smith, *Where Two or Three Are Gathered*, 37.

[35]See Gayraud Wilmore, *Black Religion and Black Radicalism* (Maryknoll, NY: Orbis Books, 2000), 48, and *Pragmatic Spirituality* (New York: New York University Press, 2004), 38.

[36]Wilmore, *Black Religion and Black Radicalism*, 48.

with everyone present. The Black church was the one place where a man could be "Mr. Jones," instead of "Willie" or "boy," and where a woman could be "Mrs. Jones," instead of "Mammy" or "Auntie." In the Black church, there was a focus on social justice that held out hope that God would continue to deliver us from bondage with an emphasis on the communal future for everyone assembled. Worship was not just an opportunity to come and shout or cry and then leave, content in whatever station in life one was. It was about knowing that there was a better life, not just somewhere in the sky, but in the here and now, and the Black church stood as a testament to God's faithfulness that we, as a people, could live into the fullness of our humanity.

Authentic Worship

Living into this fullness, especially in light of African ancestral worshipping traditions, meant bringing one's full self to worship. There could be no authentic worship where there was a dichotomy between sacred and secular. Even though the Black church is not a monolithic entity, its development, particularly in the United States of America, has common threads, including an understanding that one cannot worship God in spirit and truth and live two separate lives, private and public. Our worship, particularly through the mid-twentieth century, was lived out in community on a daily basis. The Black church had to work together, eat together, and live together, so when we worshipped together, we had to see the same people we saw during the week, and we knew that if we had been unethical to each other, it would be brought out "at the meeting." The Black church, therefore, was involved in every segment of life: education, health, economics, and familial concerns; indeed, there were few aspects of daily life, if any, that were not addressed by the church. Does that mean that the Black church dealt with every issue in liberative ways? No, it wrestled with issues of women in leadership, class distinctions based on skin tone and economic status, and the general non-affirmation of same-gender loving persons, just as many Black congregations still do today. Furthermore, the abandonment of the sacred cosmos as a cosmological worldview and the adoption of doctrinal beliefs based on Greek dualities of flesh and spirit led to spiritual double-consciousness and the divestment of justice from liturgy in Black worship that continues even now in many churches.[37] However, the overall focus of the Black church was on the community as a race of people seeking to survive in a society that told us all day and every day that we were "less than" because we were Black. Our liturgies reflected this commitment, requiring the presence of justice in the life-giving actions we celebrated, both within and outside of the church.

[37]The impact of dualism and double consciousness will be explored further in Chapter 7.

Does the ancestral commitment to fight for Black preservation still exist in and through the weekly worship and liturgies? If so, why has attendance among many Black congregations declined so drastically, especially in mainline Protestant churches that were founded on the principles of liberation and justice? Often, responses to this question relate to worship styles: "Worship in our church is boring." "We don't sing the type of music young people want to hear." "Why does our church have to follow the same order of worship every week?" While the issues of attendance and religious identity run deeper than mere stylistic preferences, these responses are quite revealing. Often, when people leave churches for the reasons listed, they visit, and ultimately join, churches whose worship and liturgical practices address those superficial issues and fill the unmet needs. What happens in the church that was left behind? The leaders look to what these popular churches are doing in worship. Sometimes they have added contemporary or blended worship services to their traditional service, or infused worship with contemporary or popular music adapted for sacred settings. The leaders of the initial church implement a version of what has seemed to work at the second church to make it appear more relevant, contemporary, and popular. Results, generally, are mixed. The first church may garner some new members, but often at the cost of losing the support of long-standing members. Additionally, the new worship styles and/or liturgies implemented may seem inauthentic, causing more members to lose interest and stop attending.

The core issue, here, is not the style of worship but whether members or prospective members believe the church is truly meeting their needs—and even churches with thousands of members may not be tapping into the needs of their congregants. There is a misconception in our society that the larger the crowd, the more substantive the product or presentation. That is a false equivalency that leads many astray. Often, people follow and become part of a crowd because they feel their needs are being met. This is particularly true of religious organizations where people follow crowds because they believe the organization with more people must be stronger, better, and more righteous. Otherwise, why would so many people be there? However, many Black communities are still dying, whether they reside just outside a mainline church or a non-denominational church. We still have hunger and homelessness, poverty, and COVID-19, not to mention a government that doesn't seems to care. What does it mean, then, that persons are sitting inside a ten- or twenty-thousand-member church with "lit" worship? Do these worship models and liturgies serve anyone besides the persons inside? Do they even serve the persons inside? It is important to ask these questions because many of the persons attending are still wondering how they are going to make it from day to day, paycheck to paycheck, or are in the process of finding employment. And so often, these models and resulting liturgies are focused on personal salvation and restoration; the focus is on getting healed and delivered personally, not communally, which is reflected in the liturgy—the music, prayers, scripture readings, and preaching.

These models have made their way into denominational churches because clergy and worship leaders perceive them to be successful in attracting people. Interestingly, these models do not fit the liturgies of piety and evangelicalism most often found in denominational churches, much less African liturgies based on concepts of sacred cosmos and kinship. That is why many churches in Black America are dying, because every week, attendees engage in liturgical schizophrenia. Services begin with "praise and worship" calisthenics, based on a 1980s televangelistic model that is not African or African American in origin. Services include denominational liturgies, also based on someone else's heritage, and culminate in prosperity preaching, which is not only not African in origin but is generally exegetically incorrect, and basically proof-texting in overdrive. It is easy to understand why these models and liturgies, while perhaps creating "feel-good" moments, rarely result in actual transformation, individual or communal.

The Role of Sacraments

How do congregations perceive baptism and communion? In many cases, they are afterthoughts. Although worshippers may prepare themselves personally for the events of baptism and communion—and historic churches that employ traditional liturgies generally engage in meticulous preparation for the celebration of sacraments—do worshippers truly possess a communal understanding of these acts of worship? What is African about the way we engage in these identifying marks of Christian community? In many traditional baptismal liturgies, congregants affirm that baptism is an initiation into the community of faith, the beginning of new life in Christ. But what is the understanding of being initiated into that community of faith? Is the focus on the individual believer and how that person views her or his own baptism? Is it left to them to work out their own salvation? Do congregations view communion or Eucharist as a communal act of transformation? Or is it about getting one's personal wafer or cracker and juice? Is the liturgy of Eucharist, as Harmon Smith notes, "the church's communal sacrifice, its giving itself away, its losing control in order to be faithful and obedient to the God 'who so loved the world that God gave God's only begotten Son' " and "how we become one with God, and one with one another, how the church becomes the body of Christ"?[38] Do we have an understanding of how or whether the sacraments are connected to a life ethic? Do we have an understanding of

[38]Smith, *Where Two or Three Are Gathered*, 65.

Jesus as the one "who is the bread and the wine, . . . who takes the lead, gives the command, and renews the old ways of 'doing justice, loving tenderly and walking humbly with our God' "?[39] Or is it precisely, as Ralph Kiefer suggests, "this disjuncture between liturgy and ethics-social justice that is at root an issue of the relationship of the Church to contemporary culture, particularly as the role of the Church is perceived and lived out within contemporary culture"?[40]

The majority of articles and books that deal with communal understandings about baptism and Eucharist are from Anglo writers and theologians with a dearth of African or African American sources. Is it because they are not important to Black worshippers? Or is the lack of public discussion of baptism and communion one more result of acculturation and subsequent *double consciousness*? Rites and rituals no longer prioritize the link between liturgy and justice, perhaps due to the adoption of a European/Anglo understanding of worship, a Platonized dichotomy of flesh and spirit which also imbues the partaking of sacraments. A preponderance of Black churches has abandoned ancestral perspectives that creation flowed directly from the Creator, and thus sacraments are a reminder of who the Creator has called us to be, not for ourselves, but for our communities. It was not about grace or salvation being imputed to us, solely as individuals, but a belief that, in participating in the sacraments, we celebrate the divine within us, which God placed upon conception. We further understood that to participate meant that we were called to live transformed lives that evinced themselves in our attempts to transform our world.

Liturgy, as the work, or action, of the people, is essential to worshipping communities. I have explored in this chapter the general purposes and functions of liturgy, particularly in the Black church. Common aspects of liturgy are present across a myriad of Black faith communities, including a personal view of God and an espoused communal identity. These aspects are manifested through worship rituals and practices that historically have been linked with communal calls for justice in the wider society. Elements of worship, including sacramental rituals, remind Black faith communities of the link between liturgy and justice that helps determine the authenticity of worship. In the next chapter, I explore the African roots of Black worship and how this link between liturgy and justice was born out of these roots.

---

[39]Megan McKenna, *Rites of Justice: The Sacraments and Liturgy as Ethical Imperatives* (Maryknoll, NY: Orbis Books, 1997), 3.

[40]Ralph Kiefer, "Liturgy and Ethics: Some Unresolved Dilemmas," in *Living No Longer for Ourselves: Liturgy and Justice in the Nineties*, ed. Kathleen Hughes and Mark Francis (Collegeville, MN: Liturgical Press, 1991), 76.

2

African Roots of the Black Church

What is the Black church? The Black church emerged from the *invisible institution*, which was birthed out of the necessity for enslaved persons to experience authentic worship of God. Contrary to prevailing, and mistaken, ideas about Africans who were immorally imported to the Americas and elsewhere, Africans worshipped God. Indeed, in his monumental research for *Concepts of God in Africa*, John Mbiti studied African peoples throughout the continent and reports that "in all these societies, without a single exception, people have a notion of God."[1] Though some African regions and tribes may have been aware of and/or well-versed in Christianity, most Africans who were brought to the Americas in chains were not. The gods they knew and worshipped were those to whom they were linked as creations of the Most High and part of the divine cosmological order.[2] As part of this understanding of God, enslaved Africans understood that they were linked to everything in creation, whether human, animal, or plant, and were responsible, as much as possible, for the well-being of that creation.

African Cosmology

African cosmological worldviews undergirded every aspect of the lives of the people and served as the foundation for the creation of Black worship in the New World. Scholars have noted several of these worldviews that many, if not most, African nations and peoples held in common. The first worldview is the belief in one supreme God, known across countries and cultures by many

[1]John S. Mbiti, *African Religions and Philosophy*, 2nd ed. (Portsmouth, NH: Heinemann, 1990), 29.

[2]Melva Wilson Costen, *African American Christian Worship*, 2nd ed. (Nashville, TN: Abingdon Press, 2007), 5.

names, and who serves as "the High God" in a "monarchical polytheism"[3] with lesser deities. Mbiti writes, "God is outside and beyond His creation. On the other hand, He is personally involved in His creation, so that it is not outside of Him or His reach. God is thus simultaneously transcendent and immanent."[4]

Although God may exist on the transcendental plane, Mbiti asserts that Africans believe that God is also manifested in "natural objects and phenomena, and available to them in worship."[5] In many African systems of belief, God is omniscient (all-seeing), omnipresent (simultaneously everywhere), and omnipotent (all-powerful). Again, these attributes are perceived hierarchically, with God at the top, as most powerful, with spirits or divinities underneath with lesser powers, and humanity, with little or no power. In some sense, the High God in many of these belief systems is not concerned or involved in the daily comings and goings of humanity, but delegates this work to lesser gods, each of whom has particular powers and abilities and is responsible for assisting humanity who request help in those areas. According to scholar Dwight Hopkins, other African religion practitioners do "believe in a God who cares," whom they refer to as "'the Compassionate One' or 'the God of pity' and who 'looks after the case of the poor man.'"[6] Hopkins continues, "God is a divinity of partiality to the victim; God sides with the political powerlessness of society's injured."[7] Beliefs in a God who possesses these attributes of compassion, caring, and concern for the poor would prove instrumental in the development of Black religion in the Americas.

A second worldview is communal solidarity in a system of relatedness known as kinship. The African concept of kinship does not extend merely horizontally to one's immediate family or close extended family, but also includes a vertical kinship with ancestors. Leonard Barrett notes, "The second major component of the African religious heritage in the New World is the belief that the ancestors have enormous influence over their descendants. This concept is universal among African peoples."[8] Though some have disparaged African veneration as "ancestor worship," Africans and people of African descent know that because ancestors are those who showed themselves during earthly existence to be helpful, they are still deserving of honor and respect. Moreover, Africans believe ancestors have a collective power that energizes the living and infuses daily life. Mbiti asserts that "the living-dead constitute the

[3]Gayraud S. Wilmore, *Black Religion and Black Radicalism: An Interpretation of the Religious History of African Americans* (Maryknoll, NY: Orbis Books, 1998), 20.

[4]Mbiti, *African Religions and Philosophy*, 29.

[5]Mbiti, *African Religions and Philosophy*, 33.

[6]Dwight N. Hopkins, *Shoes That Fit Our Feet: Sources for a Constructive Black Theology* (Maryknoll, NY: Orbis Books, 1993), 16–17.

[7]Hopkins, *Shoes That Fit Our Feet*, 17.

[8]Leonard E. Barrett, *Soul-Force: African Heritage in Afro-American Religion* (New York: Anchor Press/Doubleday, 1974), 22.

largest group of intermediaries in African societies," because of the "unique position" they occupy and their ability to "speak a bilingual language of human beings and spirits."[9] Hopkins states: "Oftentimes one would have to placate the ancestors in order to reach the High God. . . . Here, the cultural significance of the ancestors' role is the most relevant because the memory and presence of the ancestors help preserve and teach the cultural heritage of the community."[10]

In addition to an esteem for ancestors, kinship includes interrelatedness with all creation. Costen asserts that "humanity is part of the created order, thus human beings are to exist in unity with one another and with all of creation. To be human means that one belongs to a family or community."[11] This worldview creates a theological construct that binds humanity together out of which emerges a collective outlook for community—past, present, and future. There is a mutual interdependence that undergirds the entire structure upon which community is built. What happens to one happens to all; and what happens to all affects the one. Decisions, therefore, are not based only on individual goals, desires, or happiness but on what would benefit or harm the entire community. The principle of Ubuntu sums it up: "I am because we are; and since we are, therefore, I am."[12]

Respect for nature as God's sacred creation is a third worldview that undergirds an African way of life. Mbiti notes that African peoples associate animals and plants with the concept of God, and often consider them sacred, eating some only after they are sacrificed in religious ceremonies.[13] Furthermore, the heavens carry God-meaning, along with weather phenomena such as rain, storms, and earthquakes. In other words, the entire universe exists in witness to God's power and beauty, through sign and symbol; therefore, humanity must respect nature as God's good gift, and live holistically in harmony with it.[14]

In conjunction with this regard and appreciation for nature is the need for humanity to internalize a relevant understanding of sacred cosmos. This concept involves several facets, including the African perspective that there is no separation between sacred and secular; all of life is sacred. Indeed, as Barrett states, "Religion for Africans was, is and ever shall be the source of

---

[9]Mbiti, *African Religions and Philosophy*, 69.

[10]Hopkins, *Shoes That Fit Our Feet*, 17–18.

[11]Costen, *African American Christian Worship*, 9.

[12]Mbiti, *African Religions and Philosophy*, 141.

[13]Mbiti, *African Religions and Philosophy*, 50.

[14]Maulena Karenga, "Black Religion," in *African American Religious Studies: An Interdisciplinary Anthology*, ed. Gayraud Wilmore (Durham, NC: Duke University Press, 1989), 273.

life and meaning."[15] Here, the word "religion" does not refer to one aspect of life and is not contained in or limited to a weekly worship service, reading and observing the principles in one book, or personal adherence to a list of rules, but rather is describing the way belief systems permeate and order an individual's and a community's lives. He continues:

> The worldview of African peoples is best described as the vision of a cosmic harmony in which there exists a vital participation between animate (God, man) and inanimate things. That is to say, all Africans see a vital relationship of being between each individual and his descendants, his family, his brothers and sisters in the clan, his antecedents, and also his God—the ultimate source of being. Thus the world is not just an abstraction; it is a force field with all things interacting.[16]

Comprehension and internalization of the sacred cosmos is what gives meaning and purpose to life. One must perceive oneself as part of the divine creation that exists in the natural world and evinces itself through cosmic rhythm—what Costen asserts as "the harmonious structure of the cosmos, the foundation for the 'rhythm of life.' "[17] Mercy Oduyoye also highlights this holistic understanding of sacred cosmos: "A sense of wholeness of the person is manifested in the African attitude to life. Just as there is no separation between the sacred and the secular in communal life, neither is there a separation between the soul and the body in a person."[18] Another aspect or result of this understanding of the sacred cosmos was the role that spirit possession played in religious ceremonies.

A fourth African worldview that is both foundational and formational to Black worship is African wisdom—the creation and use of proverbs and folklore. As with the proverbs contained in the Hebrew Scriptures, African proverbs are not attributed to any one source or elder; they exist as "the wisdom of the nation." They deal with various subjects, including humanity's relationship with God, one's moral behavior, and social virtues, and are used daily in a myriad of contexts. Folktales espouse the wisdom of elders, through narratives about God, lesser deities, the universe, humanity, animals, and the environment. These narratives contain and communicate a people's traditions, belief systems, and stories of origin regarding God and creation.

---

[15]Barrett, *Soul-Force*, 16.

[16]Barrett, *Soul-Force*, 17.

[17]Costen, *African American Christian Worship*, 6.

[18]Mercy Amba Oduyoye, "The Value of African Religious Beliefs and Practices for Christian Theology," in *African Theology En Route*, ed. Kofi Appiah-Kubi and Sergio Torres (Maryknoll, NY: Orbis Books, 1979), 111.

The Development of Early Black Theology

Peter Paris asserts that "African societies on the continent have produced extremely complex cosmologies in their many and varied attempts to explain and relate the three realms of reality: spirit, history, and nature."[19] These cosmological worldviews served as broad and overarching concepts that infused and informed the daily lives of African communities. Religious and spiritual beliefs emanating from these worldviews found expression both in ritual worship and the mundane ordinariness of the workday. Mbiti declares:

> Where the African is, there is his religion: he carries it to the fields where he is sowing seeds . . . he takes it with him to the beer party or to attend a funeral ceremony; and if he is educated, he takes religion with him to the examination room . . . if he is a politician, he takes it to the house of parliament.[20]

Consequently, Africans brought these worldviews and beliefs to these shores and with their early descendants incorporated them into an ethos that would develop into what historian Albert Raboteau calls "slave religion."

How did these worldviews impact, influence, and infuse the development of theologies in African communities and those of African descent in the New World? To answer this question, we need to note that African traditional religions were just one of the sources of theological belief for enslaved Africans. There were at least three other sources that contributed to the development of these theologies and must be accounted for, as they played a key role in the evolution of African belief systems. Costen, Hopkins, Wilmore, and other scholars assert that Black worship, as it was "re-born," and developed in the Americas was influenced by traditional African religions, Western/Euro-American Christianity, and African American folk religion, which, Costen states, "emanated from world views shaped in the American context in a crisis of slavery and oppression."[21] She notes an additional thread—Judeo-Christian religion—but does not specify whether she means the more recent Western Euro-American Christianity or the Christian religion as represented by the Old and New Testaments in the formal canon of Christian scripture as it emerged and developed from the fourth century until the Protestant Reformation. Hopkins does not delineate sources of worship, but speaks rather of Black theology noting the close similarities between the streams: "Black

[19]Peter J. Paris, *The Spirituality of African Peoples: The Search for a Common Moral Discourse* (Minneapolis: Fortress Press, 1995), 34.

[20]Mbiti, *African Religions and Philosophy*, 2.

[21]Costen, *African American Christian Worship*, 10.

theology results from reflection on the Spirit's will of liberation revealed in various expressions of black folk's faith and practice within the context of Protestantism, American culture, and slave religion."[22]

For many scholars, the development of Black worship practices and the theologies that undergirded them is a syncretism of African beliefs and practices with European Christianity and folk religion that emerged out of the experience of enslavement. Raboteau has noted the differences between the two schools of thought, represented in the work of Melville J. Herskovits and E. Franklin Frazier. Though both agreed there were strong African retentions among enslaved Africans in the Caribbean, Frazier argues there was no significant African retention of culture among enslaved Africans in North America.[23] Herskovits claimed that there were African cultural retentions that remained among those brought to these shores, no matter the stripping away of heritage each endured. Raboteau cites factors that aided in some African belief systems surviving and even thriving much more readily in countries other than America; however, he readily acknowledges the presence of the African heritage in their beliefs, aesthetics, and what would become liturgical practices in the invisible institution and beyond. Moreover, this presence is not superficial or external; as Raboteau notes, "Adapting to the foreign culture of the Europeans meant for the Africans not the total abandonment of their own cosmologies but, rather, a process of integrating the new into the old, of interpreting the unfamiliar by reference to the familiar."[24]

How were these cosmologies, these primal worldviews, present in the theologies of Africans and their descendants during the antebellum period? Let us begin with how these Africans and their descendants thought about God. We turn again to Raboteau:

> It is important to observe that on a very general level African religions and Christianity (Protestant as well as Catholic) shared some important beliefs. A basic Christian doctrine which would not have seemed foreign to most Africans was belief in God, the Father, Supreme Creator of the world and all within it.[25]

And Paris:

> As have all peoples who are uprooted from their cultures and transplanted to an alien environment, African slaves brought their worldviews

---

[22]Dwight N. Hopkins, *Down, Up, and Over: Slave Religion and Black Theology* (Minneapolis: Fortress Press, 2000), vii.

[23]Albert Raboteau, *Slave Religion: The Invisible Institution in the Antebellum South* (New York: Oxford University Press, 2004), 48.

[24]Raboteau, *Slave Religion*, 126.

[25]Raboteau, *Slave Religion*, 127.

with them into the diaspora. Though different in many respects, they all shared one primary feature, namely, their belief in a sacred cosmos created and preserved by a supreme deity.[26]

God

For peoples who were steeped in beliefs of God as the "High God," all-seeing, all-knowing, and all-powerful, an introduction to the Christian God as the "Most High" would have seemed an easy concept to grasp. What would have been more difficult to grasp was why the "High God" would have allowed them to arrive at such a horrific place and under such brutal oppression as enslavement. What also would have been illogical and inconsistent was how the Christian God was presented by their white captors as one who justified their bondage and maltreatment. When the preacher in the slave master's church proclaimed, "Slaves, obey your masters," or "Don't steal your master's chicken," or when the enslaved person was reminded of how good and kind her master was, when her back was still raw and bloody from a whipping, "*AfricansinAmerica*"[27] knew that this god who was being proclaimed was not the same as the one in whom they believed. Hopkins notes that "despite the apparent immortality of the slave system, black chattel persisted in a faith in the God of freedom . . . and simply refused to accept white theology."[28] James Cone uses the descriptive theological phrases, "mighty good leader," "dying-bed maker," and "soul's emancipator," as representative of how *AfricansinAmerica* thought of God, asserting that "all these phrases point to God as the living and ever present One who grants freedom for the humiliated and stands in judgment upon oppressors who attempt to destroy black dignity."[29]

The African concept of God as "just,"[30] and corresponding beliefs that "God evens things out," rewarding or punishing rightly those who do good or evil, respectively, is seen clearly in narratives and testimonies of enslaved and formerly enslaved persons. As Julia Brown testified, "When he died we all said God got tired of Mister Jim being so mean and kilt him."[31] The paradox of the presentation of the slave master's God against what Africans

---

[26]Paris, *The Spirituality of African Peoples*, 34.

[27]"AfricansinAmerica" is my term and is based on the work of Dr. Daniel Omotosho Black, professor of English and African American Studies at Clark Atlanta University. He asserts that the word, "Black" is not truly representative of Africans and African-descended persons living in America: "Black" is a color; Africa is a continent. Therefore, those of African heritage living in America are *AfricansinAmerica*.

[28]Hopkins, *Shoes That Fit Our Feet*, 23.

[29]James H. Cone, *God of the Oppressed*, rev. ed. (Maryknoll, NY: Orbis Books, 1997), 20.

[30]Mbiti, *African Religions and Philosophy*, 37.

[31]Dwight N. Hopkins, "Slave Theology in the Invisible Institution," in *Cut Loose Your Stammering Tongue: Black Theology in the Slave Narrative*, ed. Dwight N. Hopkins and George C. L. Cummings, 2nd ed. (Louisville, KY: Westminster John Knox Press, 2003), 12.

in America knew to be the true nature of God resulted in the Christian God becoming an African God, who, according to Barrett, "if not considered more powerful than the traditional gods, was perceived to be at least as great as those in the traditional African pantheons."[32]

Therefore, in the African/African American theological construct of God from the perspective of enslaved persons was an image of One who, despite their circumstances, was still their protector, defender, judge, and potential liberator. Though the "High God" may still have been considered transcendent and "far off," in their daily struggles for humanity, God was immanent and "nearby." For enslaved Africans and their descendants, God was intimately concerned with and a major participant in their quest for justice and liberation. When the white preacher preached "salvation," enslaved persons challenged the rhetoric by asking, "Gonna give us freedom 'ong wid salvation?"[33] This challenge was rooted in what Hopkins calls a "theological debate about the nature of God."[34] For the enslaved, God was a liberator; if not, then to believe was pointless. There was no figurative liberation from the spiritual bondage of sin and metaphorical horrors of hell without literal liberation from the physical bondage of oppression and lived horrors of enslavement.

Jesus

How would *AfricansinAmerica* have perceived the notion of Jesus Christ, as Son of God? Raboteau asserts that, because of their understanding of lesser gods or divinities who worked as intermediaries for the "High God," enslaved Africans would have readily accepted Jesus as God's divine representative.[35] Furthermore, stories of Jesus as suffering servant and sacrificial lamb would have resonated deeply with those who daily bore the brunt of physical torture and suffering. Spirituals, which I examine in the next chapter, often employed themes of Jesus as suffering servant and dying lamb, a theological viewpoint that helped enslaved persons identify with One who had struggled because of the evil ways of others. Indeed, Cone asserts, "To know Jesus is to know him as revealed in the struggle of the oppressed for freedom."[36]

Just as significant is the enslaved African's understanding of Jesus as the resurrected One, victorious, not just over certain individuals who betrayed and killed him, but over systems of oppression that betrayed and killed him. The theological assertion that Jesus wouldn't "die no mo" assured the enslaved community that evil kingdoms, indeed the kingdom of Satan—as represented

---

[32]Barrett, *Soul-Force*, 96.
[33]Hopkins, *Cut Loose Your Stammering Tongue*, 13.
[34]Hopkins, *Cut Loose Your Stammering Tongue*, 13.
[35]Raboteau, *Slave Religion*, 127.
[36]Cone, *God of the Oppressed*, 31.

by white slaveholders—had been defeated by Jesus's death and resurrection. From this view, Jesus is extolled as "Conquering King," to whom "the slavery system would inevitably succumb." Hopkins also notes that enslaved Africans would have attributed a priestly role to Jesus, as one "who serves as the pastor over the Invisible Institution," and who represented new life through "deliverance from the earthly snares of sin and oppression."[37]

Holy Spirit

Though enslaved persons, particularly those who were African-born and first generation Americans, may not have understood Trinitarian concepts of God nor believed that only three gods—Father, Son, and Holy Spirit—were sufficient to carry out the Creator's plans, they would have understood the character and nature of the Holy Spirit. Once slave owners decided to proselytize their captives, they began a system of catechesis, or religious training, to make sure enslaved persons were learning the faith "correctly." For slave owners, that meant enslaved persons accepting that God had consigned them to their fate, and that they were to accept it without resistance. For the enslaved, however, this system rang hollow and led to the development of a different catechesis known as "getting religion" or the "seekin" journey or experience. Numerous personal accounts of enslaved Africans and their descendants tell of this process, which, according to Alonzo Johnson, had one goal: "being 'born again.'"[38] George Cummings notes:

> Getting religion was manifested in a variety of ways. Some slaves had visions, others shouted and walked, and still others bore witness to the creative power of the Spirit. The Spirit possessed the physical being of the slaves, and as a consequence they shouted; spoke of great visions of God, heaven, or freedom; and engaged in physical activity that manifested the Spirit's presence.[39]

Africans and their descendants familiar with spirit possession in the African sense would have perceived these experiences as authentic and normative for a worship participant. Mbiti states: "Spirit possession occurs in one form or another in practically every African society. . . . When the person is thus

---

[37]Hopkins, *Shoes That Fit Our Feet*, 30–31.

[38]Alonzo Johnson, "'Pray's House Spirit': The Institutional Structure and Spiritual Core of an African American Folk Tradition," in *Ain't Gonna Lay My 'Ligion Down: African American Religion in the South*, ed. Alonzo Johnson and Paul Jersild (Columbia: University of South Carolina Press, 1996), 26.

[39]George C. L. Cummings, "The Slave Narratives as a Source of Black Theological Discourse," in *Cut Loose Your Stammering Tongue: Black Theology in the Slave Narrative*, 2nd ed., ed. Dwight N. Hopkins and George C. L. Cummings (Louisville, KY: Westminster John Knox Press, 2003), 34.

possessed, the spirit may speak through him, so that he now plays the role of a medium, and the messages he relays are received with expectation by those to whom they are addressed."[40] Barrett notes, "Possession also has a therapeutic value. The devotee, on recovering from possession, is believed to have undergone personality transformation."[41]

The work of the Spirit in Black antebellum worship was to intensify and enhance the worship and the more-hoped-for conversion experiences of the enslaved, as well as provide a liberative sense of joy, amid unbearable sorrow. Cone notes that the Spirit "is God's way of being with the people, enabling them to shout for joy when the people have no empirical evidence in their lives to warrant happiness."[42] As to the Spirit's work of creating new personhood in the lives of those transformed, former slave Cornelius Garner testified in his narrative that slaves weren't impressed by the preaching of the white minister; rather, they desired to "sing, pray and serve God in our own way." For Garner and others who refuted mentally, emotionally, and physically, if not verbally, the theological foundations of white Christianity, "the Spirit's presence entailed the affirmation of independence and selfhood; sustained hope for freedom as embodied in their prayer life; served as the basis of love within the slave community; and even assisted slaves in their desire to escape to freedom."[43]

Cummings describes this identity and autonomy among the transformed slaves as a defiance of "dominant powers" while also serving as a "means of coping with the reality of their exploitation and suffering."[44] Mechal Sobel describes the seeking process as having a "before" and "after" dimension, one referring to the individual's life prior to conversion and the other denoting life after conversion, after "the High God gave the candidate the vision to see his inner essence."[45] Though definitely not identical to the African understanding of spirit possession, the indwelling of the Spirit in Black antebellum worship was just as efficacious and transformative for the participant and would find its way into all liturgical practices of the invisible institution, and beyond.

Kinship

How did African peoples in America live out their worldview of kinship in the antebellum period? Much has been written about the systematic strip-

---

[40]Mbiti, *African Religions and Philosophy*, 80.

[41]Barrett, *Soul-Force*, 25.

[42]James H. Cone, "Sanctification, Liberation, and Black Worship," *Theology Today* 35, no. 2 (1978): 142.

[43]Cummings, *Cut Loose Your Stammering Tongue*, 35.

[44]Cummings, *Cut Loose Your Stammering Tongue*, 35.

[45]Mechal Sobel, *Trabelin' On: The Slave Journey to an Afro-Baptist Faith* (Princeton, NJ: Princeton University Press, 1988), 116.

ping away of African heritages and customs from the enslaved Africans. Slave traffickers engaged in all manner of illegal and immoral actions to ensure that Africans and their descendants had little, if any, connection to or memory of the traditions, languages, customs, or beliefs of their ancestors. Persons from like tribes were separated from one another, in hopes this would prevent any successful attempt at communication, as well as leave the chattel in such despair that they would be too despondent to function communally. While these efforts proved effective in some ways, they did not keep the enslaved from communicating with each other completely. As Africans and their descendants became acclimated to their surroundings and began to manage their individual and collective sense of shock, dismay, and concern for what each moment might bring, they recovered and reconstituted African communal practices.

Part of the necessity for re-establishing a community came from "the environment and the ethos of black slaves . . . who had to 'feel their way along the course of American slavery,' enduring the stress of human servitude, while still affirming their humanity."[46] This understanding of humanity was not individual, but collective. Mbiti reminds us that "the kinship system is like a vast network stretching laterally (horizontally) in every direction, to embrace everybody in any given local group. . . . That means that everybody is related to everybody else."[47] Hopkins concurs with this African concept of relationship, "To be human was not to be individualistic, a casting into a non-human and non-being state. The dynamic of individual rights and familial-neighbor obligations weighed more toward the latter."[48]

Hopkins points out how this worldview differed from that of the slave traffickers/owners espousing Christianity:

> African religions gave rise to a dynamic interplay between community and individual. Whatever happened to the communal gathering affected the individual; whatever happened to the individual had an impact on the community. Such a theological view of humanity cuts across bourgeois notions of white Christianity's individualism and "me-first-isms." It seeks to forge a group solidarity and identity, beginning with God, proceeding through the ancestors to the community and immediate family, and continuing even to the unborn.[49]

Accounts of this relational way of being are present throughout slave narratives, particularly in testimonies about worship in the invisible institution, where we hear the collective calls to brush arbor worship that were made

---

[46]Cone, *God of the Oppressed*, 10.
[47]Mbiti, *African Religions and Philosophy*, 102.
[48]Hopkins, *Down, Up, and Over*, 111–112.
[49]Hopkins, *Shoes That Fit Our Feet*, 17.

surreptitiously for fear of being caught, the communal cries for deliverance, not primarily from personal sin, but from the sin of oppression and brutality exacted upon them, and the joy manifested on the whole group of gathered worshippers when the Spirit descended. As enslaved Africans were being introduced and/or catechized into white Christianity, this framework of kinship may have provided "a foundation for relatedness in the household or family of God in Jesus Christ."[50] According to George Offori-Atta-Thomas, "strengthening spiritual kinship ties in the connecting relationships of church, family and community" was one of several congregational objectives in worship.[51] He refers to the importance of corporate worship experiences in creating "a collective social consciousness." Community events such as naming ceremonies, marriages, births, and funerals provided opportunities to "solidify the communal-kinship system while serving as a "process of incorporation," reflecting both African ancestral rites and rituals and the newly adopted syncretized Christianity.

Sacred Cosmos

The sacred cosmos worldview is grounded in a "relational and communal" ontology. Humanity is not merely one aspect of creation, but is "divinely linked, related to, and involved with all of creation."[52] This results in (w)holistic relationships and responses that honor, respect, hear, and acknowledge the entire universe as the Creator's handiwork and how one is called to "be" as a part of that. Internalizing this worldview resulted in a self-affirmation that flew in the face of white, hegemonic opinions about Black people. Hopkins states:

> Building on top of the foundation made up of ingredients from African indigenous religions, common sense folk wisdom, and a reinterpretation of the Christianity forced upon them by their slave masters, the constitution of the African American self as creatures of God involved knowing about oneself and taking care of oneself. To know oneself as both an object of and co-laborer with divine initiative emboldened one to act in a self-initiating manner.[53]

Living with this knowledge would have empowered enslaved Africans with a different focus for their lives—one that would not be the "slave ship, auc-

[50]Costen, *African American Christian Worship*, 9.

[51]George Ofori-Atta-Thomas, "The African Inheritance in the Black Church Worship," in *The Black Christian Worship Experience*, ed. Melva Costen and Darius Leander Swann (Atlanta: ITC Press, 1992), 69.

[52]Costen, *African American Christian Worship*, 5.

[53]Hopkins, *Down, Up, and Over*, 115.

tion block, and plantation regime," but the potential for freedom, whether literal or figurative. Paris asserts, "Everything they thought and did reflected the sacred nature of the cosmos . . . their songs, music, dances, stories, art—transcended any secular-sacred dichotomy."[54] Again, narratives of worship experiences in the invisible institution exhibit this expression of personal and communal freedom, self- and communal-affirmation, and cosmic rhythm—the "embodiment of divine order and the foundation for the 'rhythm of life.' "[55] This sense of freedom emerged from a "divine grace," which, as Hopkins proclaims, "made them free to pursue their holistic liberation—both incremental and complete, both spiritual and material—signifying theological acts of free self-care wherever black folks found themselves. To know oneself and to take care of oneself was to release the enthusiasm in determining how one wanted to be in the world along with a God who liberates one from an old self and frees one to a new self."[56]

Such freedom, Cone asserts, is "an eschatological freedom, beyond the historical context . . . a vision of a new heaven and a new earth."[57] It would not be limited to one's personal attainment of physical freedom nor the ending of the period of enslavement. Rather, it would be the coming of God's kingdom/reign on earth, where creation would be redeemed back to its original intent and humanity would participate in communal salvation by practicing justice and liberation for all creation. The ability of *AfricansinAmerica* to manage daily horrors of slavery without losing ultimate hope or a sense of purpose could be attributed to the incorporation of this ancestral sense of sacred cosmos—working and worshipping while awaiting this freedom.

Folklore

Finally, what was the gift of folklore—wisdom literature—to the theological development of enslaved Africans during the antebellum period? In her ground-breaking text, *Katie's Canon: Womanism and the Soul of the Black Community*, ancestor Katie Geneva Cannon discusses the cultural inheritance of Black folklore, including spirituals, which she describes as, "the indispensable device that slaves . . . used to transmit a worldview fundamentally different from and opposed to that of slaveholders."[58] Cannon describes folklore as "a strategy for coping with oppression,"[59] a method of using coded language

[54]Paris, *The Spirituality of African Peoples*, 34.
[55]Costen, *African American Christian Worship*, 6.
[56]Hopkins, *Down, Up, and Over*, 115.
[57]Cone, *God of the Oppressed*, 11.
[58]Katie Geneva Cannon, *Katie's Canon: Womanism and the Soul of the Black Community* (New York: Continuum, 1995), 35.
[59]Cannon, *Katie's Canon*, 33.

to communicate messages that would have been dangerous to state openly. Author Richard Wright contends that "it was, however, in a folklore moulded out of rigorous and inhuman conditions of life that the Negro achieved his most indigenous and complete expression."[60] Through stories, children's rhymes, games, and music, *AfricansinAmerica* talked and sang about how the supposedly stronger, smarter character in a story was constantly bested by the weaker, ignorant one. This was a way to launch a direct attack on their oppressors without suffering retaliation. Cannon notes that "folklore was the essential medium by which the themes of freedom, resistance, and self-determination were evoked, preserved, and passed by word of mouth from generation to generation. . . . By objectifying their lives in folktales, Afro-American slaves were able to assert the dignity of their own persons and the invincibility of their cause."[61] Folklore was one device that spoke of African cosmological ideas and beliefs, particularly regarding justice and the treatment of others. Two genres of African and African American folklore that clearly evince the development of Black theologies in the antebellum period are folktales and spirituals.[62]

Scholars have written extensively about the impact and influence of "trickster" folktales that extolled the exploits of Brer Rabbit, High John the Conqueror, Stagolee/Stagger Lee, and other protagonists who, for the most part, stand in the place of the powerless and outwit their oppressors through cunning and deception. While some characterize these tales as "amoral,"[63] others, including folklorist William J. Faulkner, believed that these tales "symbolize the struggle between good and evil, in which Brer Rabbit's 'antagonists were wicked, on the side of the Devil. As the slaves identified with the Rabbit, they felt themselves to be allied with God, and their white adversaries to be henchmen of the Devil.' "[64] In portrayals of High John the Conqueror, John represents "African Americans' contribution of hope through laughter and song to those facing hardship."[65] For this Black character, the ability to laugh and sing was a source of hope, a refuge in the face of relentless death-dealing evil, which, for Hopkins, served the theological role of "passageway

[60]Richard Wright, "Introduction: Blueprint for Negro Writing," in *The Black Aesthetic*, ed. Addison Gayle (Garden City, NY: Anchor Books, 1972), 317.

[61]Cannon, *Katie's Canon*, 34.

[62]*Spirituals* as a theological genre and liturgical element are examined in more detail in Chapter 3.

[63]See Lawrence Levine, *Black Culture and Black Consciousness: Afro-American Folk Thought from Slavery to Freedom* (New York: Oxford University Press, 1977); Stanley Elkins, *Slavery: A Problem in American Institutional and Intellectual Life* (Chicago: University of Chicago Press, 1976); and Charles Joyner, *Down by the Riverside: A South Carolina Slave Community* (Urbana: University of Illinois Press, 1984).

[64]William J. Faulkner, *The Days When the Animals Talked: Black American Folktales and How They Came to Be* (Chicago: Follet, 1977), 6.

[65]Hopkins, *Shoes That Fit Our Feet*, 112.

from divine certainty in future 'conquering' to the lowly 'Johns' all over the world."[66] Whether portrayed by animals or humans, the trickster figure serves as an intermediary of the Divine, having human qualities while possessing a measure of supernatural power. This power was most often employed by the figure to overcome the malicious actions of others, for self, as well as for communal benefit.

Another figure in African American folklore whose tales exemplify theological development of enslaved persons was that of the Way Maker, which was regarded as "the ultimate power in African American folk culture, a being so infinite in abilities that anything is possible."[67] The Way Maker works in the lives of Black folk to make crooked places straight, rough places plain, with the ultimate goal being self-acceptance and a sacred space of personal and communal fulfillment, known as the Way Made.

Folktales about the attributes and accomplishments of the Way Maker became part of Black wisdom literature in the works of Zora Neale Hurston, Langston Hughes, James Weldon Johnson, and others, testifying to the enduring ancestral legacy of this God-character and the genre as a whole. Again, the theme of God as voice for the voiceless, defender, and protector of the oppressed comes through in stories of how the Way Maker delivers and empowers marginalized peoples and breaks the power of evil as it functions to hinder true followers of the Way. Important theologically is that the Way Maker does not grant the oppressed great wealth, equal status with whites or any others in power, or significantly change their social standing. Hopkins reveals:

> The Way Maker delivers us back to itself (our creator) without preconditions or petty pretensions. Rather, a major criterion for emancipation is the poor's acceptance of their own identities regardless of how the larger society grades acceptable or non-normative behavior. Self-acceptance and self-naming, both cultural questions, have an impact on one's liberating return to the Way Maker.[68]

What we see happening theologically in these folktales is a conversion process, similar in ways to worship experiences in the invisible institution. In both events, the telling and re-telling of these stories and the immediate, cathartic experience of brush arbor worship, African ancestral cosmological beliefs are re-membered, fused with the slaves' perceptions of Christianity, and re-enacted to form a unique theological amalgam that has the power to transform.

[66]Hopkins, *Shoes That Fit Our Feet*, 112.
[67]Hopkins, *Shoes That Fit Our Feet*, 84.
[68]Hopkins, *Shoes That Fit Our Feet*, 95.

Certainly, African roots are infused within the theological and liturgical foundations of Black worship. Cosmological views of God, Jesus, and the Holy Spirit that reflect African ancestral beliefs and practices helped shape and form the inception of Black religion in North America. Concepts of kinship, sacred cosmos, and folklore permeated the communal world of enslaved Africans and were evinced in the development of religious traditions during the antebellum period. The following chapter explores how these ancestral traditions and rituals became liturgical practices in the invisible institution—the first iteration of communal Black worship in the New World.

3

African Liturgical Practices

How did burgeoning theological beliefs about the Christian god and Christianity itself influence the development of liturgical practices in antebellum America? Were these practices direct descendants of African rites and rituals, and if so, how did they change because of new or syncretized beliefs? Moreover, how did the environment in which they emerged impact how they were practiced? Gayraud Wilmore asserts that "the religious beliefs and rituals of a people are inevitably and inseparably bound up with the material and psychological realities of their daily existence. Certainly the realities of this world for the slaves were vastly different from those of the slavemasters."[1]

Worship in the Invisible Institution

The emergence of the invisible institution had the most impact on the development of Black worship and liturgical practices during the antebellum period. Although E. Franklin Frazier is credited with coining the term, he offered no definition of it. Rather, as a key to understanding the term, he recalled the words of Robert Anderson, a self-professed "ex-slave":

> Our preachers were usually plantation folks just like the rest of us. Some man who had a little education and had been taught something about the bible would be our preacher. The colored folks had their code of religion, not nearly so complicated as the white man's religion, but more closely observed. . . . When we had our meetings of this kind, we held them in our own way and were not interfered with by the white folks.[2]

---

[1]Gayraud S. Wilmore, *Black Religion and Black Radicalism*, 3rd ed. (Maryknoll, NY: Orbis Books, 1998), 22.

[2]E. Franklin Frazier, *The Negro Church in America* (New York: Schocken Books, 1974), 23.

Furthermore, Alonzo Johnson asserts:

> It was in the context of their brush arbor meetings on plantations that slaves first began to forge from the crucible of their African experience and the terrors of their inservitude a vision of Christianity that would be distinctively their own. In the night, out of sight and hearing of the big house, the brush arbors were the sacred spaces, the holy ground upon which slaves stood as they sang, prayed, shouted, testified, preached, planned their escape, and otherwise did what they felt spiritually led to do. The key to the brush arbor tradition was its relative secrecy and its being in the control of the slaves themselves.[3]

Dwight Hopkins concurs, stating, "Enslaved Africans took the remnants of their traditional religious structures and meshed them together with their interpretation of the Bible. All this occurred in the Invisible Institution, far away from the watchful eyes of white people. Only in their own cultural idiom and political space could black slaves truly worship God."[4] As a way of countering the hypocritical, and thus, inauthentic, messages and mold of white Christianity they experienced in slave owner churches, enslaved *AfricansinAmerica* held their own secret gatherings, where they did not have to subscribe to the white man's god or his beliefs of Black inferiority. They could incorporate aspects of their African heritage and belief systems into the Christian worship they had witnessed in the white man's churches. Thus an Africanized Christianity was born, "a unique interaction between the white Baptist world view and the black African/American world view, resulting in a new black or Afro-Baptist Sacred Cosmos."[5] The daily experiences of *AfricansinAmerica* led them to develop a holistic religious consciousness that included all they had seen and heard, both past and present, good and bad. Dr. Robert Franklin tells us that the worship experience for slaves was "multisensory." He states, "Given the difficulty and dehumanizing nature of their work, slaves created sacred space as a zone of ultimate freedom. In worship, the mind, emotions, and other sensory capacities were engaged in transcending the banality of evil."[6] For the slave, worship was a time of liberation, when they could praise the Creator for sparing them one more day, a day closer to freedom, either in this life or the next. This led to a

---

[3]Alonzo Johnson, "Pray's House Spirit," in *Ain't Gonna Lay My 'Ligion Down* (Columbia: University of South Carolina Press, 1996), 10.

[4]Dwight N. Hopkins, *Shoes That Fit Our Feet: Sources for a Constructive Black Theology* (Maryknoll, NY: Orbis Books, 1993), 18.

[5]Mechal Sobel, *Trabelin' On: The Slave Journey to an Afro-Baptist Faith* (Princeton, NJ: Princeton University Press, 1988), 80.

[6]Robert Franklin, *Another Day's Journey: Black Churches Confronting the American Crisis* (Minneapolis: Fortress Press, 1997), 30.

worship experience that transcended the horrific consequences of their lives and, subsequently, gave many a will to live, to "run on and see what the end's gon' be." George Ofori-Atta-Thomas notes that "the indigenous Black Church, coming out of the Black Religious Experience and worship heritage transposed the Africanisms of spirituality into new forms of expressions in modes of worship, music and movement."[7]

Liturgical Elements

According to W. E. B. Du Bois, "Three things characterized the religion of the slave—the preacher, the music, and the frenzy."[8] He describes these elements as "born on American soil," but "sprung from African forests." While he does not focus here on the development of liturgy in Black religious spaces, Du Bois provides the ground on which other scholars begin to build a foundation of Black liturgical practice. Preaching, music, and ecstatic expressions of the Spirit in antebellum Black worship environments emerged from the common historical taproot of African consciousness and cosmology and were forged in the fires of daily experiences of inhumanity endured by the enslaved. Melva Costen and James H. Cone explicitly delineate almost identical lists of elements of worship in the invisible institution: *praying*, *preaching*, *singing*, and *shouting* being the four elements that both name; Costen adds *call to worship*, and Cone combines *conversion* with *shouting* and *testimony* with *prayer*.[9] I will first examine *call to worship*, followed by the four common elements of *prayer*, *preaching*, *music*, and *shouting*, and also consider how each is a product of and functions as a theological development in antebellum Black worship spaces.

Call to Worship

The call to worship as an element of worship in the twenty-first-century church is considered part of the Gathering—one of the five categories of worship acts. It may begin the worship service or follow introductory musical selections such as a prelude, introit, or praise and worship. In many

---

[7]George Ofori-Atta-Thomas, "The African Inheritance in the Black Church Worship," in *The Black Christian Worship Experience*, ed. Melva Costen and Darius Leander Swann (Atlanta: ITC Press, 1992), 51.

[8]William Edward Burghardt Du Bois, *The Souls of Black Folk* (New York: First Vintage Books/The Library of America Edition, 1990), 138.

[9]See Melva Costen, *African American Christian Worship*, 2nd ed. (Nashville, TN: Abingdon Press, 2007), 28–37; and James H. Cone, "Sanctification, Liberation, and Black Worship," *Theology Today* 35, no. 2 (1978): 139–152.

churches, the call to worship consists of a scripture recitation ("The Lord is in his holy temple, let all the earth keep silence," "I was glad when they said unto me, 'Let us go into the house of the Lord' "), a standard scripture dictated by denominational or church worship order, or an extemporaneous offering by the worship leader. Often, the call to worship is printed in church bulletins and may include congregational participation. But in the invisible institution, the call to worship occurred before the people gathered. Because enslaved persons were not often free to worship as they chose, brush arbor worship could not be announced publicly. It had to be communicated throughout the week, by symbols, codes, signs, and physical clues. The times and places were determined by the community, and worship did not begin until the community assembled. People would answer the call that had gone out hours or days before, and sneak off from slave quarters or plantation homes, travel through forests, bushes, and woods, hoping to "steal away to Jesus."

Prayer

John Mbiti tells us that historically, prayer has been "the commonest act of worship" for African peoples.[10] He states:

> It is evident that African peoples communicate with God through prayer, pouring their hearts before Him, at any time and in any place. The prayers are chiefly requests for material welfare, such as health, protection from danger, prosperity and even riches. Some prayers express gratitude to God; and in a few cases the people dedicate their belongings or activities to Him.[11]

We immediately see parallels between the prayers of Africans and *AfricansinAmerica*. Just as Africans pray for material welfare, so too did their descendants on these shores. Enslaved Africans also expressed gratitude in prayer, gratitude often being included in the first words of the prayer. They prayed throughout the day and evening with no set time officially allotted, but as deemed necessary by the individual or community. Regarding communal prayers, *AfricansinAmerica* incorporated prayer in worship in the forms of invocation—what became known after Emancipation as the deacon's prayer.

Mbiti notes that "invocations show a spontaneous response to God,

[10]John S. Mbiti, *African Religions and Philosophy,* 2nd ed. (Portsmouth, NH: Heinemann, 1990), 61.

[11]Mbiti, *African Religions and Philosophy*, 64.

asking God to intervene for a particular purpose. They show that people consider God to be ever close to them, ready to respond to their need, and not subject to religious formalities."[12] The deacon's prayer tends to follow a pattern, "in which many of the attitudes toward God and the present world-order are recurrent."[13] This attitude reflects the belief that God is omnipotent, omniscient, and omnipresent and that God was present in their worship spaces. The foundation for these prayers comes out of the African experience of and response to God and exemplified a theological understanding, for in these prayers *AfricansinAmerica* approached the throne of grace with holy boldness, seeking to know what they could understand of God's will for their lives and trusting God to handle that which they neither understood nor could change. Costen asserts that, especially during the communal *prayer event*:

> Rather than passively listening to a prayer, the gathered community becomes involved with the prayer leader, using a variety of responses . . . verbal "witnessing" to what is being prayed, such as "Amen!" . . . or "Yes, Lord!" There are often injections of admonitions to God to "Come by here". . . or "Help us now, Lord!" Some participants moan or hum in perfect cadence with the prayer leader. Some rock, sway, cry softly, or merely nod their heads in assent. The "prayer event" often reaches full intensity as the leader and congregation, filled with the Spirit, demonstrate that everyone's heart is spiritually "in tune."[14]

One of the main themes of prayer in the invisible institution was, of course, liberation. *AfricansinAmerica* appealed to the gods of their ancestors, as well as the Christian God, to deliver them from bondage. Dwight Hopkins recounts the way enslaved Africans co-opted the biblical story of Exodus:

> African American bondsmen and bondswomen discovered their own predicament and deliverance in the story of the Old Testament Israelites who fled into the wilderness to escape bondage in Egypt.
>
> All us had was church meetin's in arbors out in de woods. De preachers would exhort us dat us was de chillen o'Israel in de wilderness an' de Lord done sent us to take dis land o' milk and honey.[15]

---

[12] Mbiti, *African Religions and Philosophy*, 65.

[13] Benjamin Elijah Mays and Joseph Nicholson, *The Negro's Church* (New York: Institute of Social and Religious Research, 1969) 145.

[14] Costen, *African American Christian Worship*, 30–31.

[15] Hopkins, *Shoes That Fit Our Feet*, 23.

Albert Raboteau recounts a similar testimony:

> Mingo White remembered: "Somehow or yuther us had a instinct dat we was goin' to be free," and "when de day's wuk was done de slaves would be foun' . . . in dere cabins prayin' for de Lawd to free dem lack he did chillun of Is'ael."[16]

Those *AfricansinAmerica* who had heard the biblical account of the Exodus story would have used the language of Exodus in their prayers, making sure that they, like ex-slave Henry Bibb, "never omitted to pray for deliverance."[17] Hopkins asserts that in this text, "slaves directly experienced for themselves the mighty words of Yahweh," as they evolved theologically from the Old Testament—and, I would add, from their remembrance of African gods—to their "current religious life with God."[18] In the liturgical practice of prayer, they would have exercised a "rejection of white people's value system," and "the religious outlook of the white master"[19] in favor of a view of God as "the One who sees the afflictions of the oppressed, hears their cries, and delivers them to freedom."[20]

James Cone adds testimony to prayer, a way of "bearing witness to one's determination to keep on the 'gospel' shoes."[21] Slave narratives about prayer in the invisible institution were testimonial accounts of their theological beliefs in a God who would hear and answer their pleas for freedom and justice. Though their theological perceptions about God were evolving through the passage of years, their collective belief that God was a God of justice and liberation was an African retention that remained steadfast, fed their faith, and "kept hope alive . . . under the heel of a stultifying existence."[22]

Preaching

As W. E. B. Du Bois is often quoted: "The Preacher is the most unique personality developed by the Negro on American soil. A leader, a politician, an orator, a 'boss,' an intriguer, an idealist—all these he is."[23] Like prayer, Black preaching and the role of the Black preacher in the antebellum period

---

[16]Albert Raboteau, *Slave Religion: The Invisible Institution in the Antebellum South* (New York: Oxford University Press, 2004), 219.

[17]Hopkins, *Shoes That Fit Our Feet*, 23.

[18]Hopkins, *Shoes That Fit Our Feet*, 23.

[19]James H. Cone, *God of the Oppressed*, rev. ed. (Maryknoll, NY: Orbis Books, 1997),19.

[20]Hopkins, *Shoes That Fit Our Feet*, 23.

[21]James H. Cone, "Sanctification, Liberation, and Black Worship," *Theology Today* 35, no. 2 (1978): 146.

[22]Hopkins, *Shoes That Fit Our Feet*, 24–25.

[23]Du Bois, *The Souls of Black Folk*, 138.

grew out of an inherently African perspective about God and life. Ofori-Atta-Thomas references Mbiti's descriptions of religious specialists who serve as "gifted custodians in the knowledge, practice and mystical roles of linking the natural and the supernatural worlds in the worship moment."[24] According to Ofori-Atta-Thomas,[25] African retentions are clearly present throughout the six roles or offices occupied by the Black preacher in the invisible institution and, subsequently, the Black Church:

1. *The Diviner-Inheritance of the Black Preacher: Preaching and Questing for Spiritual Fulfillment*—the Black preacher becomes reincarnated as an ancient African custodian of the worship experience. Before they can assume this leadership role, priests/preachers must have received the "mantle of ancient 'diviner'" through rites of initiation and/or spirit possession.
2. *The "High Office"-Inheritance of the Black Minister: Administrating Authority and Sharing Power*—the Black preacher assumes the role of religious leader in the community, as one anointed by the power of the Spirit, and occupies the "high office" or seat of spiritual authority ("golden stool," altar, or pulpit).
3. *The Griot (Storyteller)-Inheritance of the Teaching Ministry: Teaching and Nurturing for Holistic Growth*—the Black preacher serves as the "Griot of the Oral Tradition, Master-Communicator, continuing the African tradition by 'telling' and 'teaching' the Story."[26] Preachers, even those who could not read, had to be proficient in presenting the Word of God from the biblical text in a way the community could receive it readily. In this office, preachers inhabited the teaching role that informed social obligations and relationships, and shaped and nurtured personal and interpersonal relationships.[27]
4. *The Priest-as-Medicine Man-Inheritance in the Black Church: Pastoring and Shepherding for the Care of Souls*—the Black preacher followed the African tradition of serving as priest, performing rites, rituals, and other religious duties in the community. In this role, the preacher was also called to serve as medicine man, caring therapeutically for those who were physically, mentally, emotionally, and spiritually sick. Ofori-Atta-Thomas recalls one of the most significant actions by this pastoral care provider, "to lead the events of worship whereby the ritualistic mood, moment and method of cleansing took place to

[24]Ofori-Atta-Thomas, "The African Inheritance in the Black Church Worship," 53.
[25]Ofori-Atta-Thomas, "The African Inheritance in the Black Church Worship," 52–72.
[26]Ofori-Atta-Thomas, "The African Inheritance in the Black Church Worship," 59.
[27]Ofori-Atta-Thomas, "The African Inheritance in the Black Church Worship," 59.

absolve impurities and resolve harmful effects from the negative forces in sickness, disease or misfortune."[28]

5. *The "Rites of Passage"-Inheritance of the Black Pastor-Priest: Ritualizing and Celebrating in Rite of Incorporation*—Here, Ofori-Atta-Thomas notes how communal incorporation, such as rites of passage, "mediates a connecting linkage between the African inheritance and the Black Church Worship Heritage." He delineates three ways the pulpit preacher approaches this connection:
    a. The "continuities" in communal rites, including baptism, initiation, marriage, and funerals, that Ofori-Atta-Thomas states are "invisible linkages from Africa to the New World [America]."
    b. The double meanings of certain practices that emerged from a syncretism of New World religion with creative innovations birthed from situational necessity (i.e., the invisible institution). Ofori-Atta-Thomas cites secret meetings of insurrectionists as an example, stating that they served both as a way of recovering the African cult mystique and as an opportunity to plan revolt.
    c. Tracing the roots of Africanism through the "beliefs and practices of the Black worship experience" throughout the Christian year.
6. *The "Prophetic"-Inheritance in the Black Church: Prophesying and Advocating for Transformation*—Ofori-Atta-Thomas recounts how this specialist was active in Africa before the slave trade occurred and how Black religious leaders in the invisible institution continued to occupy the role of prophet. However, he notes, "the function of the prophet changed" as these persons assumed leadership in the struggle for liberation from enslavement in America. Again, they were called to integrate the traditional African prophetic role with the religious and contemporary context in which their community lived.

Other scholars echo Ofori-Atta-Thomas's descriptions of the slave or antebellum Black preacher as prophet, diviner, storyteller, medicine man, and holder of "high office" authority. Wilmore describes these "so-called conjure-men and 'voodoo doctors,' " as "men of ability and integrity who took their vocations with the utmost seriousness," and were "sought out for spiritual counsel and healing by both blacks and whites."[29] Costen notes that "the roles of priest as leader, diviner, seer, and medium," as well as *griot*, "were rooted in African traditions."[30] Like Ofori-Atta-Thomas, Costen points out

[28]Ofori-Atta-Thomas, "The African Inheritance in the Black Church Worship," 65.
[29]Wilmore, *Black Religion and Black Radicalism*, 40.
[30]Costen, *African American Christian Worship*, 35.

that "in a new Christian environment, African American 'prophets' combined the African and Judeo-Christian roles as charismatic leaders called of God to hear and then make forthright pronouncements as divine proclaimers."[31] Costen quotes Ofori-Atta-Thomas in her assertion, "Invisible Institutions, and later free churches, were greatly influenced by prophetic preachers 'who would use their spiritual powers and charisma to struggle against oppression and for liberation.' "[32] Frazier concurs with Ofori-Atta-Thomas that the Negro preacher was "called to his office" from "some religious experience which indicated that God had chosen him as a spiritual leader."[33] Further, Frazier has similar sentiments regarding the Black preacher's required abilities when he states, "His knowledge of the sacred scriptures had to be combined with an ability to speak and communicate his special knowledge to the slaves. Preaching meant dramatizing the stories of the Bible and the way of God to man."[34] Cone also notes that the Black preacher inhabits a prophetic role to which s/he must be called by the Spirit. Indeed, for Cone, the roles of prophet and storyteller are conflated, as Cone declares, "In the black tradition, preaching as prophecy essentially is telling God's story, and 'telling the story' is the essence of black preaching. It is proclaiming, with appropriate rhythm and passion the connection between the Bible and the history of Black people."[35] The "rhythm" and "passion" to which Cone refers is part and parcel of Black preaching, an interactive style, rooted in African culture. Henry Mitchell states:

> The Black style, which includes the pattern of call and response, is very easily traceable to Black African culture. Black preaching has had an audience from the beginning. Black preachers must say something to the congregation; they must address the ills of society and the oppressive nature of African American life. However, in this address, they offer hope. There must be a "word from the Lord."[36]

Further, Black preaching is part of an oral tradition. Even if a preacher uses notes, and even if the message has been fully transcribed, the preacher will often depart from the notes during the sermon and may abandon them altogether if the Spirit speaks to her or him before or during the message. Homiletical scholar Olin Moyd states that "the African American theology

---

[31]Costen, *African American Christian Worship*, 35.
[32]Costen, *African American Christian Worship*, 35.
[33]Frazier, *The Negro Church in America*, 24.
[34]Frazier, *The Negro Church in America*, 24.
[35]Cone, "Sanctification, Liberation, and Black Worship," 143.
[36]Henry Mitchell, *Black Preaching* (New York: J. B. Lippincott, 1970), 47.

of preaching is the acknowledgment and affirmation that preaching is the divine mandate and medium for communicating, elucidating, and illuminating God's revelation for the people."[37] It is doubtful that any antebellum Black preacher would have used notes, as it was illegal for the enslaved to read, but even after Emancipation, most Black preachers preached extemporaneously or memorized their messages. They were expected to be able to communicate the sacred witness of the lived Word of God, as they served in the role of "prophetic mouthpiece."[38]

Music

Before I discuss music of the Black antebellum worship experience, I must first mention what preceded it. Mbiti asserts that "music, singing and dancing reach deep into the innermost parts of African peoples."[39] Costen links this to religious practices of *AfricansinAmerica*:

> Africa is the anchor that holds music as the theological thread that runs through the fabric of African American existence. . . . The musical anchor begins in rites and rituals of the community. . . . In traditional African cultures, music and dance play an active role in religious and healing rites, and in rites of passage in the "rhythm of life" of individual members of the community.[40]

Leonard Barrett observes that the two elements of African religion transplanted in the New World were dance and the use of drums.[41] He calls dance "the soul of the religious life of Africa" and states that "the drum is Africa"[42] itself. Dance was part of spirit possession; this was primarily how dance functioned in religious practices during the invisible institution.

According to Mechal Sobel, "Africans recognized the drum beat as a form of symbolic language, and many believed their sound was given to man by God as the *third word*. The rhythm of the primal smithy, hammering out consciousness, shook and reverberated in the earth, transforming being."[43]

---

[37]Olin P. Moyd, *The Sacred Art: Preaching and Theology in the African American Tradition* (Valley Forge, PA: Judson Press, 1995), 57.

[38]Costen, *African American Christian Worship*, 35.

[39]Mbiti, *African Religions and Philosophy*, 67.

[40]Melva Costen, *In Spirit and in Truth: The Music of African American Worship* (Louisville, KY: Westminster John Knox Press, 2004), 3.

[41]Leonard E. Barrett, *Soul-Force: African Heritage in Afro-American Religion* (New York: Anchor Press/Doubleday, 1974), 82–83.

[42]Barrett, *Soul-Force*, 83.

[43]Sobel, *Trabelin' On*, 140.

The drum provided rhythms, specifically African rhythms, which were unique to and among African peoples. Even though particular tribes may have used differing types of drums, various materials indigenous to their land, and even particular beat patterns that may have been heard only in their area, there were common religious and musical aspects of rhythm shared among African societies. These include "the sense of sacrality; and . . . multimetricity, cross-rhythms, asymmetrical patterning, and call and response."[44] Jon Michael Spencer asserts the importance of the drum to African culture, stating, "In many traditional African societies the drum is a sacred instrument possessing supernatural power that enables it to summon the gods into ritual communion with the people."[45] Even drums that were not perceived in this manner were still regarded as necessary for performance in ritual action. In his groundbreaking novel, *The Coming*, Daniel P. Black cites the voices of captured African elders recounting the pervasive use and remembrance of the drum in African society:

> And of course we heard the drums. Everyone. Everywhere. In every village. They beat with the regularity of the heart itself. Deep rhythms reverberated across the plains, through trees, and into the heavens. It was the language of our gods, the collective voice of a people. The drum's polyrhythmic repertoire surpassed the number of hairs on our heads. Even on rainy days, it rumbled praises, far in the distance, to the Great God who'd sent nourishment to the earth. It also admonished and celebrated us. One studied many years before mastering the drum. Most never played it, but we understood its message loud and clear.[46]

Spencer and other anthropologists and ethnographers posit that, because the drum was such an important element in African cosmology and communication, its use was "disallowed" by enslaved Africans in North America, as slave owners recognized and feared its ability to "talk."

Though the drum was "theologically pertinent to African ritual,"[47] its absence did not prevent certain rituals of African heritage from continuing to be observed on North American shores. Enslaved *AfricansinAmerica* compensated for the lack of drum-induced African rhythms by reproducing them physically, clapping, tapping their bodies, or stomping their feet. This physical reenactment developed into one of the three main genres of music

---

[44]Jon Michael Spencer, "The Rhythms of Black Folks," in *Ain't Gonna Lay My 'Ligion Down* (Columbia: University of South Carolina Press, 1996), 39.

[45]Spencer, "The Rhythms of Black Folks," 39.

[46]Daniel P. Black, *The Coming* (New York: St. Martin's Press, 2015), 48.

[47]Spencer, "The Rhythms of Black Folks," 39.

sung and/or performed by *AfricansinAmerica* in Black antebellum religious spaces, and was known as the *shout*, or *ring shout*.[48] Costen makes a distinction between "shouting" as an element of worship and the "ring shout" which she describes as "a ritualized, group activity clearly of African origin."[49] Shouting is "an ecstatic moment" where "the Holy Spirit fills and empowers the worshipers so that they are unable to remain still."[50] Though similar in essence to the spiritual origin of the *ring shout, shouting* is an individual physical reaction to being indwelt by the Holy Spirit, neither a ritual nor a group activity. Du Bois's description of the frenzy in Black worship seems closer to Costen's description of shouting than the *ring shout*: "It varied in expression from the silent rapt countenance or the low murmur and moan to the mad abandon of physical fervor—the stamping, shrieking, and shouting, the rushing to and fro and wild waving of arms, the weeping and laughing, the vision and the trance."[51]

The *ring shout* was a "type of dance done to the cadence of a favorite shout song or running spiritual, and began with a slow, syncopated shuffling, jerking movement bumped by the handclapping or body slapping of those waiting on the sidelines."[52] The movements increased in speed until those involved were worked into a frenzy, often collapsing from exhaustion, only to be replaced instantly by others. Because of its perception as "heathenish," most whites disapproved of the *shout*. However, ethnomusicologist Eileen Southern suggests that they did not understand the *shout*'s significance as both communication with and worship of God.[53] Sobel also comments on the *shout*, stating that it found "an integral place in black Baptist ritual on the South Carolina Sea Islands. The *shout* moved beyond the islands during the Civil War and remnants can be found in Virginia, Alabama, Florida, and Georgia."[54] It was accepted in many Black churches but rejected and denigrated by some as being vulgar, including African Methodist bishop Daniel Payne and Black Methodist Richard Allen.[55]

One of the most well known African American song forms is the *Spiritual*. Costen states that "the earliest Spirituals emerged during the antebellum slave period and have been identified as the first authentic American folk

[48]Costen, *African American Christian Worship*, 36, 41–43.
[49]Costen, *African American Christian Worship*, 36.
[50]Costen, *African American Christian Worship*, 36.
[51]W. E. B. Du Bois, *The Souls of Black Folk*, 138.
[52]C. Eric Lincoln and Lawrence Mamiya, *The Black Church in the African American Experience* (Durham, NC: Duke University Press, 1996), 352.
[53]Eileen Southern, *The Music of Black Americans, A History*, 2nd ed. (New York: W. W. Norton, 1983), 170.
[54]Sobel, *Trabelin' On*, 141.
[55]Sobel, *Trabelin' On*, 143.

song form."[56] Some scholars debated whether spirituals emerged as a faith response in worship or simply as a cry for communal freedom from oppression. Historian Joseph Washington argues that spirituals were an expression of religion rather than faith because "they expressed religious fervor related to situations of struggle which ended in 1890. Negro spirituals represent the spirit of the *invisible institution*, a spirit born of aspiration but not of faith."[57] Spirituals were folk songs in that they expressed the longings, experiences, and values of African Americans. Washington suggests that spirituals—"songs of protest, defiance, revolt, and escape"—grew out of an independent theology born of an independent Black religious movement following the Civil War and Reconstruction.[58] However, Frazier contends that spirituals were "shout songs," that contained or characterized the content of the Black preacher.[59] They grew out of Old and New Testament narratives ("Go Down, Moses," "Ride On, King Jesus") and the slaves' experiences of oppression and despair ("Sometimes I Feel Like a Motherless Child," or "I've Been 'Buked and I've Been Scorned"). Lincoln and Mamiya argue, like Frazier, that spirituals were "a spontaneous creation during the preaching event," as a congregational response to the sermon, and the Black preacher was also the one responsible for them being passed down orally.[60] Southern records the first acknowledgment of the spiritual as a distinctive form of Black "spiritual song" at revival camp meetings of the Second Great Awakening.[61] Costen also acknowledges that camp meetings promoted the growth and spread of spirituals as an original genre. She cautions, however, that, in their original form and intent, spirituals belong to a classification of song form that defied solely religious appropriation; other nascent forms of this type of spiritual song included "African chants, field hollers, work songs, and personal and communal cries of liberation."[62] However, Lincoln and Mamiya contend that "whatever its origin, it seems clear that it was the 'Negro Spiritual' which first developed as the signature of serious Black involvement in American Christianity."[63]

Spirituals emphasized the slave's belief that all would be made right in heaven; however, this was an eschatology "anchored firmly in this world" with both an actual and a coded meaning.[64] Therefore, "Steal Away" was not only a song about stealing away to be with Jesus, but stealing away to

[56]Costen, *African American Christian Worship*, 83.
[57]Joseph Washington, *Black Religion* (Boston, MA: Beacon Press, 1974), 206–207.
[58]Washington, *Black Religion*, 206–207.
[59]Frazier, *The Negro Church in America*, 25.
[60]Lincoln and Mamiya, *The Black Church in the African American Experience*, 348–350.
[61]Southern, *The Music of Black Americans*, 85.
[62]Costen, *In Spirit and In Truth*, 36.
[63]Lincoln and Mamiya, *The Black Church in the African American Experience*, 350.
[64]Lincoln and Mamiya, *The Black Church in the African American Experience*, 351–352.

freedom in the North, or stealing away to the woods to worship.[65] These songs emphasized the interrelatedness of the individual's and community's struggles against oppression and evil.

Spirituals became less popular after the end of slavery as blacks began to embrace their new status as freed people, but they enjoyed a resurgence in the late nineteenth century. This was due in part to the Fisk Jubilee Singers who toured throughout the country performing spirituals while raising money for the school. They enjoyed a renewed popularity during the Civil Rights Movement of the 1950s and 1960s when they were once again employed as protest songs that demanded liberation of a people.

In the Northern colonies, Africans, or "Negroes," as they were called, were allowed to worship in Anglo churches, singing from designated pews, separate from whites. The churches of this time, primarily Presbyterian, Reformed, or Congregationalist, engaged in psalm singing or psalm-lining, a style of singing that also came across the waters, but from England. Psalm singing required a song leader, the precentor, to tune the psalm, chanting one or two lines at a time, ending on a definite pitch, and the congregation responding with the singing of the same line. Though they sat in separate pews, Blacks learned the tunes and lyrics together with whites, and sang them together at many communal events, such as weekly prayer meetings, weddings, funerals, and public ceremonies such as Election Day. Organizations such as the Society for the Propagation of the Gospel in Foreign Parts and the Established Church of England sent clergy to convert enslaved Africans to Christianity and, in some sense, educate them, particularly in religious instruction. Psalm singing was part of the catechetical enterprise. Eileen Southern notes, "In 1726, the rector of Trinity Church observed that over one hundred English and Negro servants attended the catechism on Sundays and sang psalms at the close of instruction."[66]

The 1730s brought the First Great Awakening, a revival movement in the colonies focused on evangelism, personal piety, and revitalization of church worship. With this revitalization came the need for livelier music, as many felt the common way of singing psalms was grave and too slow. Reformers advocated for "regular singing" using established rules of Western classical music. Many songs used for camp meetings were written by Dr. Isaac Watts, an Anglican cleric who, in 1707, had published the book *Hymns and Spiritual Songs*, which had gained great popularity with Black and whites. Part of the appeal of these arrangements, Costen tells us, was attributed to the use of uncomplicated metrical systems, simplicity of vocabulary, and frequent use of repetition.[67] Also appealing was Watts's concept of hymnody and congregational praise, which

---

[65] Lincoln and Mamiya, *The Black Church in the African American Experience*, 352.

[66] Southern, *The Music of Black Americans*, 38.

[67] Costen, *In Spirit and in Truth*, 44.

called for "original expressions of praise, thanksgiving, devotion, and desire for spiritual renewal."[68] This philosophy of hymnody allowed Blacks and whites to feel freer in worship and thus more emotionally connected.

In the South, some enslaved Africans were allowed to worship in slaveholders' churches, sitting in balconies or on the floor, or holding separate services at the church. They, too, were instructed in the singing of psalms and adapted this genre for use in their separate worship services, albeit often with a different tune and understanding of meter.[69] This style became known as *hymn lining*.[70] Though psalm singing involved lining out a hymn, the precentor lined out the written or remembered tune and the congregation repeated what had been sung. Because this call-and-response style mirrored African retentions of call and response, Blacks adapted psalm lining in their own contexts, but with decidedly different African melodic and harmonic tones. Named Dr. Watts's hymns in homage to the hymn writer, this style of singing was performed without accompaniment and required a song leader who lined out the hymn, but in a vocal recitation rather than melodic line. The congregation surged in to respond with a lengthy melodic line, generally employing the pentatonic scale of African chant and harmonies on the fourth or fifth note of that scale. Using the terms *common meter, long meter*, and *short meter*, which meant something different in this context than originally intended, Blacks added their own melodies and harmonies to the psalm-lining tradition, creating a new musical and liturgical form and style that exists to this day.

Though not an original African song genre, hymnody, particularly as it evolved in revivals of the Second Great Awakening of the late 1700s and early 1800s, was greatly influenced by African music and rhythm. At the center of this campaign was the camp meeting, "a continuous religious service spread out over several days, often an entire week, taking place in forests or woods under large tents."[71] James Goff records:

> No camp meeting achieved a greater legacy than the Cane Ridge Camp Meeting begun in 1801 in Bourbon County, Kentucky. Planned by Presbyterians as a communitywide communion service, it drew crowds of over 10,000 attendees, and became famous for the emotional freedom that many worshippers demonstrated as they shouted and danced under the influence of religious power.[72]

---

[68]Costen, *In Spirit and in Truth*, 44.

[69]Costen notes that once enslaved Africans were given freedom to hold their own worship meetings, psalm singing was a requirement, *African American Christian Worship*, 86.

[70]See Costen, *In Spirit and in Truth*, 44–51; Southern, *Music of Black Americans*, 30–42; and Portia K. Maultsby, "The Use and Performance of Hymnody, Spirituals, and Gospels in the Black Church," in *The Black Christian Worship Experience* (Atlanta: ITC Press, 1992), 143–147.

[71]Southern, *The Music of Black Americans*, 82.

[72]James Goff, *Close Harmony: A History of Southern Gospel* (Chapel Hill: University of North Carolina Press, 2002), 17–18.

Southern records that "the camp meeting was primarily an interracial institution; indeed, sometimes there were more black worshipers present than white,"[73] although seating was often segregated. John Goff notes that some camp meetings established segregated services, but even in segregated meetings, Blacks and whites in the South greatly influenced each other, in embracing a more unrestrained worship style and sharing the enthusiastic singing of common hymnody.[74] Also shared between Black and white attendees were the African retentions of syncopated rhythms, melodies, and call-and-response styles which would thread their way into future music genres of both races.

Another influence of Blacks, perceived negatively by some white attendees, was the addition of refrains and choruses to the orthodox hymns, some almost sounding like the tunes of jubilee dance melodies. This would grow into a new form of music known as the "camp-meeting hymn," inspired by the extemporaneous singing of Black attendees, called *spiritual songs*, distinguishing them from psalms and hymns, and constructed from popular folk melodies already well known to many in the audience, solving the "dual problem of illiteracy and a shortage of songbooks."[75]

Consequently, the rich musical heritage of *AfricansinAmerica* was founded on African rhythms and chants based on drumbeats as a form of symbolic language and singing as a method of God speaking and the believer responding. Indeed, one well-known African proverb states, "The Spirit cannot descend without a song." As Costen has asserted, music is not merely a means of expressing feelings. It evokes the reciprocal activity of imagination and understanding of the soul. The sound of music born of human breath bore witness to the presence and love of God in the being of Black folks from the beginning of time.[76] As W. E. B. Du Bois describes it, music is the soul of Black folk.[77]

Shouting

As mentioned previously, *shouting* as an element of worship is more closely identified with the phenomenon of "frenzy." Dwight Hopkins recalls the experience of "ex-slave Emily Dixon," who explains how the Spirit "made one 'jist turn loose lack.' "[78] The common thread of ecstatic religious experience runs through her narrative and other narratives of enslaved worshippers, tying together African retentions of spirit possession with this new faith tradition.

---

[73]Southern, *The Music of Black Americans*, 83.
[74]See Goff, *Close Harmony*, 19–20.
[75]Goff, *Close Harmony*, 18.
[76]Costen, *African American Christian Worship*, 32.
[77]Du Bois, *The Souls of Black Folk*, 180–190.
[78]Hopkins, *Shoes That Fit Our Feet*, 19.

What is unique in this element as expressed in the invisible institution and beyond is that one may be indwelt by the Holy Spirit without necessarily serving as an intermediary for God. Most often, in the African experience of spirit possession, one is acting in a specialized role as a medium or diviner, to bring a message to the gathered community on behalf of God, and thus must be acted upon by the deity after a "conjuring-up" of the spirit.[79] As noted by Ofori-Atta-Thomas in the section on preaching, this role was often assumed by the Black preacher in the invisible institution. Ordinary members or lay folk did not perceive someone "shouting" necessarily acting as a medium or diviner. That does not mean a person experiencing the Holy Spirit could not receive a message from God, but that was not the intent of the experience. Shouting occurred within the context of a worship experience, often after a similar *conjuring up* of the Spirit (a phrase which fell into disuse or was replaced with "working-up," because of its association with and negative view of African traditional religions). Communal prayers, singing, exhortations, and preaching were all part of the experience that led to "all holy hell breaking loose."[80] Cone states that this results in "'the shout', which refers not to sound but to bodily movement" in response to the Spirit's presence in worship.[81] Cone also links conversion to shouting, because in the experience, "God's Spirit visits their worship and stamps a new identity upon their persons, in contrast to their oppressed status in white society. . . . This experience is so radical that the only way to speak of it is in terms of dying and rising again."[82]

Again, note that Cone does not explain conversion as solely or even primarily receiving a new spiritual identity, but a new personal and psychological identity as a full human in society. This is another reference to the liberative nature of the Black antebellum worship experience, the purpose of which was to connect with God, divinities, ancestors, and oneself in order to receive, if only for a moment, a sense of full freedom and humanity.

Liturgical practices of *AfricansinAmerica* in the invisible institution were born of African ancestry and evolved in the crucible of antebellum enslavement. The overarching elements of indigenous Black worship included call to worship, prayer, preaching, music, and shouting, each saturated with the religious legacies of ritual practices from the Continent and rebirthed in a new experiential context. Daily encounters with racism, violence, and brutality

---

[79]Mbiti, *African Religions and Philosophy*, 167–174.

[80]Brenda Eatman Aghahowa, "Definitions of Praising and a Look at Black Worship," in *Readings in African American Church Music*, ed. James Abington (Chicago: GIA Publications, 2001), 364.

[81]Cone, "Sanctification, Liberation, and Black Worship," 142.

[82]Cone, "Sanctification, Liberation, and Black Worship," 146.

imbued *AfricansinAmerica* with communal needs for spiritual engagement that offered some affirmation of Black humanity and vision of eschatological hope. The next chapter examines how this spiritual engagement produced meaning-making liturgies in the nascent Black church.

Part Two

THE DEVELOPMENT

4

Understanding Black Liturgy

I have examined African cosmological worldviews and how these were present in retentions that influenced the development of the theological beliefs of *AfricansinAmerica* during the antebellum period. Now, I explore how these retentions and resulting theological beliefs led to the development of a particular form of worship, first, in the invisible institution and later, in praise houses.

What would have made enslaved Africans decide to worship or engage in a religious practice in a particular way? Despite the circumstances in which they found themselves, *AfricansinAmerica* still believed in the power and efficacy of their gods and held enough experiential memory of rites and rituals to summon their presence and assistance. Through successive generations, those who were still arriving from African countries would have shared their religious practices, as best they could, in hopes that their ritual remembrances and honoring of their gods would have effected the end of their suffering. Even after the so-called death of the African gods,[1] *AfricansinAmerica* continued to infuse their worship with practices steeped in African traditions and retentions. Though many of them accepted Christianity (sometimes begrudgingly), slaveholders would have been surprised to know that *AfricansinAmerica* conflated this Christian god with the identities and attributes of African gods, particularly the "High God," and that Jesus and the Holy Spirit were viewed as intermediaries, tasked with serving as the immanent and very real presence of the "High God" and doing God's work in the world. Further, many enslaved persons developed and celebrated the existence of an entire mediating system of saints, known to them as African and African-descended ancestors. The religious practices, in which they engaged, were imbued with Africanisms that survived across continents and centuries—Africanisms that lived and live within African and African-descended rituals and liturgical practices in North America.

[1]See Albert J. Raboteau, *Slave Religion: The "Invisible Institution" in the Antebellum South* (New York: Oxford University Press, 2004), 43–94.

African and African-Descended Rituals

Religious rituals and worship experiences of *AfricansinAmerica*, no matter how extemporaneous or planned, followed certain African ritual and worship patterns. Theophus Smith defines ritual and its prominent place in African and African-descended cultures in North America as "a primal, and primary, mode of social interaction and performance. In operation it either precedes ideation, articulation of concepts, and symbolic expression (as in myth, poetry, or theatre) or subordinates these as means in its patterning of action."[2] Smith notes ecstatic worship or spirit possession and conjure as two ritual strategies of Black people in North America. The understanding of ritual as strategy in African culture is affirmed by Nya Taryor who states, "Rituals also help the Africans to accept the claims of society in the new state. The individual can express his conflicts and tensions through ritual and resolve them. Africans use rituals of life's crises to provide them with needed emotional support."[3]

The legacy of African ritual as a practice was evinced in the ways that enslaved Africans and their descendants developed worship practices in the invisible institution. Homiletical theologian Gennifer Brooks attests, "The hiddenness of the worship rituals of the captive people, exiled and enslaved far from mother Africa, was in direct response to the environment of slavery that had become their societal norm."[4] The use of ritual by *AfricansinAmerica* underscored the African cosmological worldview of sacred cosmos, which helped to identify and communicate "the reality of existential situations."[5] According to Melva Costen, "Rites and rituals are forms of communication with the creator who established the cosmos, and a means of reactualizing the paradigmatic act of creation."[6] The development of brush arbor or "hush" arbor worship, which became identified as the invisible institution, grew out of the enslaved Africans' insistence on worshipping in ways that re-membered African rites and rituals. Even though they were initially forbidden to worship, even in the slaveholders' churches, and their drums taken away, in the invisible institution, *AfricansinAmerica* performed what they remembered of African ritual, or what had been passed down orally, and eventually formed

[2]Theophus Smith, *Conjuring Culture: Biblical Formations of Black America* (New York: Oxford University Press, 1994), 56–57.

[3]Nya Taryor, *Impact of the African Tradition on African Christianity* (Chicago: Strugglers' Community Press, 1984), 78.

[4]Gennifer Brooks, "The Creation of an Africana Worship Ritual: Baptism in the Shouters of Trinidad," in *The Companion to the Africana Worship Book* (Nashville, TN: Discipleship Resources, 2007), 63.

[5]Melva Costen, "African Roots of Afro-American Baptismal Practices," in *The Black Christian Worship Experience* (Atlanta: ITC Press, 1992), 23.

[6]Costen, "African Roots of Afro-American Baptismal Practices," 24.

and observed new rituals from the syncretization of African traditional religions and Christianity.[7] Costen asserts:

> Slaves who embraced Christianity, deeply rooted in an awareness of the importance and necessity of community rituals, found new meaning in familiar social behavior. Continuity and identity with the ancient past and the present, prevalent in African rituals, were preserved in the light of God's action in Jesus the Christ. A hermeneutic of hope in a liberated future became the good news from God, who sides with the oppressed. Rituals of eating, drinking, and washing and rites of passage were imbued with the essence of the gospel message. The gathered African American church community, which already embraced the African ancestors (living dead) and the unborn, was extended to include those considered outside the immediate societal group as understood in the African world view.[8]

The continuation of ritual practices in Black antebellum worship experiences also evinced the retention of Africanisms (African roots of contemporary practices) even as enslaved persons espoused certain tenets of a new belief system.[9] Inherent in and infused throughout these worship events were signs, symbols, and testimonies of God-consciousness—an acknowledgment and internalization of sacred cosmos, expressions of kinship vertically and horizontally, spirit possession, melodic and rhythmic aspects of music, and prayer. The music, preacher, and frenzy that W. E. B. Du Bois references and that slave narratives testify to experiencing provide a consistent picture of the survival and preservation of African retentions in worship. These retentions signify a spiritual inheritance that George Ofori-Atta-Thomas notes is "an authentic and integral part of the Black Religious Experience and the Black Church Heritage."[10]

Part of this spiritual inheritance is what Costen refers to as "key characteristics" of worship in the invisible institution, which I outline below.[11] These characteristics also testify to the presence and power of African heritages, including the importance of private, divine space where persons were free to worship, freedom of the Spirit to indwell those gathered and permeate the space with divine, transformative power, communal affinity and care for one

---

[7]Brooks, "The Creation of an Africana Worship Ritual," 64.

[8]Melva Wilson Costen, *African American Christian Worship*, 2nd ed. (Nashville, TN: Abingdon Press, 2007), 45.

[9]George Ofori-Atta-Thomas, "The African Inheritance in the Black Church Worship," in *The Black Christian Worship Experience*, ed. Melva Costen and Darius Leander Swann (Atlanta: ITC Press, 1992),68.

[10]Ofori-Atta-Thomas, "The African Inheritance in the Black Church Worship," 48.

[11]Costen, *African American Christian Worship*, 26.

another, and preaching that was both inspiring and sensitive to the fragile, fledgling community.

Jon Michael Spencer argues that African rhythm was "the essential African remnant—the acme of Africanism."[12] He references the *ring shout*, as well as secular dances such as the *itch*, the *wringin'* and *twistin*,' the *black bottom*, and the *camel walk* that demonstrated the presence of "African movement motifs" that could be traced back to specific countries on the Continent. Spencer argues that African drumbeats survived the *Maafa*, the auction block, urbanization, and industrialization, because they were creolized and corporealized, meaning they were mixed with creole Africanisms and concretized through body movement.[13]

Though scholars debated whether and to what extent the African heritage was preserved and present in Black antebellum worship, there was and is clearly a link between African traditional religions and the syncretized Christianity they practiced. Gayraud Wilmore contends that *AfricansinAmerica* brought their traditional religions with them to these shores and that "it was from within an African religious framework that the slaves made adjustments to Christianity after hearing the gospel."[14] Indeed, Ofori-Atta-Thomas directly refers to African religion as "an 'invisible link,' a modification or complement to the 'invisible institution' to become expressed in time in the institutionalization of the 'church visible' from the 'invisible institution.' "[15]

Underlying Themes

Scholars and historians have identified four main themes that informed the development of Black antebellum worship in the invisible institution: survival; resistance; deliverance and liberation; and affirmation and joy.

Survival

Each day during the antebellum period was an exercise in survival for *AfricansinAmerica*. Who could know whether a particular day would be one in which an enslaved person displeased those in charge, and was thus subject to severe, life-threatening punishment? Enslaved women enduring

[12]Jon Michael Spencer, "The Rhythms of Black Folks," in *Ain't Gonna Lay My 'Ligion Down* (Columbia: University of South Carolina Press, 1996), 39.

[13]Spencer, "The Rhythms of Black Folks," 41.

[14]Gayraud S. Wilmore, *Black Religion and Black Radicalism: An Interpretation of the Religious History of African Americans* (Maryknoll, NY: Orbis Books, 1998), 50.

[15]Ofori-Atta-Thomas, "The African Inheritance in the Black Church Worship," 51.

pregnancy and childbirth under the most inhumane conditions were not given special consideration; they still had to complete their daily workload. Insufficient clothing, food, and health care were constant realities for *AfricansinAmerica*. Along with physical challenges, enslaved persons had to deal with the mental, emotional, and spiritual burdens of being enslaved. Slaveholders perpetrated constant psychological warfare on enslaved persons, first, by isolation from tribe and family, then, by stripping them of everything deemed African, and finally, through a sustained program of devaluation and dehumanization. Until the inception of the invisible institution, there was nowhere the enslaved African or her descendants could go to be affirmed as a human being, not even the slaveholder's church. Countless slave narratives note how white preachers continuously reminded enslaved persons that they were to obey their masters, making sure enslaved persons knew they were not viewed as human. Jenny Proctor, born into slavery in Alabama, recalled one such sermon:

> Now I takes my text, which is Nigger obey your master and your mistress, 'cause what you git from them here in this world am all you ever going to git, 'cause you just like the hogs and the other animals—when you dies you ain't no more, after you been throwed in that hole.[16]

The invisible institution arose out of the need for *AfricansinAmerica* to experience a safe, divine space that signified freedom amid oppression. Wilmore addresses this:

> The overarching question was one of survival—mental and physical—and whatever slaves could appropriate from the conjurer, or later from the charismatic Christian preacher . . . was seized upon as a gift from "de Lawd" who had not seen fit to extricate them from their plight, but nevertheless provided some means of preserving health and sanity in the midst of it.[17]

The theme of worship as survival in the invisible institution also can be affirmed when one considers the sacrifices made to participate in the experiences. First, the only free time enslaved persons had was after the workday, most often after dark, and on Sundays. During these times, enslaved persons tended to a myriad of personal tasks or tried to enjoy what little rest they could

[16] B. A. Botkin, ed., *Lay My Burden Down: A Folk History of Slavery* (New York: Dell, 1973), 101.

[17] Wilmore, *Black Religion and Black Radicalism*, 33.

before the workday began again, often before the sun rose.[18] To participate in a secret worship gathering would have required time and energy that could have been spent in these other pursuits, pursuits which some might deem more urgent. Second, enslaved persons risked discovery and punishment for surreptitiously leaving their quarters and gathering in this way. More will be said about this below. Though the ability to worship freely meant sacrificing one's time and taking serious risks to personal well-being, *AfricansinAmerica* were determined to engage space and place that affirmed their humanity and connections with the Creator and each other.

Resistance

A second theme of worship in the invisible institution was that of resistance. The fact that enslaved persons gathered secretly, even illegally, evinces what Hopkins calls "virtual political guerrilla warfare."[19] Slaveholders who caught wind of these secret meetings sent "paddy-rollers" or "patrollers" to check slave quarters and search forests for the offenders. If found, worshippers were beaten severely to discourage continued meetings. As part of their resistance, enslaved worshippers engaged in secret calls to worship and employed several means of containing sounds produced during their worship gatherings.[20] One particular strategy was to invert big iron wash pots and prop them up slightly to "catch the sound." Raboteau notes the testimony of ex-slave Patsy Hyde, who testified that enslaved worshippers "*would tek dere ole iron cookin' pots en turn dem upside down on de groun' neah dere cabins ter keep dere white folks fun herein' w'at dey waz sayin'. Dey claimed dat hit showed dat Gawd waz wid dem.*"[21]

Others would engage in physical resistance against those who sought to disrupt or disband the worship experience, as Rev. Ishrael Massie reports:

> *Lemme tell ya dis happenin' at a meeting'. Ole preacher would come in bringing . . . a long knot of lightwood. . . . When de paterrolers knock at de dow . . . dis preacher would run to de fiah place, git him a light an' take dat torch an' wave hit back and fo'th so dat de pitch and' fiah*

[18]Henry Mitchell, *Black Church Beginnings: The Long-Hidden Realities of the First Years* (Grand Rapids, MI: Wm. B. Eerdmans, 2004), 34.

[19]Dwight N. Hopkins, "Slave Theology in the Invisible Institution," in *Cut Loose Your Stammering Tongue: Black Theology in the Slave Narrative*, ed. Dwight N. Hopkins and George C. L. Cummings, 2nd ed. (Louisville, KY: Westminster John Knox Press, 2003), 7.

[20]See Raboteau, *Slave Religion*; Dwight N. Hopkins, *Shoes That Fit Our Feet: Sources for a Constructive Black Theology* (Maryknoll, NY: Orbis Books, 1993); Costen, *African American Christian Worship*; Melva Costen and Darius Leander Swann, eds., *The Black Christian Worship Experience* (Atlanta: ITC Press, 1992); and Lawrence Levine, *Black Culture and Black Consciousness: Afro-American Folk Thought from Slavery to Freedom* (New York: Oxford University Press, 1977).

[21]Raboteau, *Slave Religion*, 216.

would be flyin' every which a way in dese paterrolers faces—you know dat burnt 'em.[22]

This commitment to resistance was a mode of survival for *AfricansinAmerica.* Hopkins names it a "culture of resistance," which provided enslaved persons "an ethic of survival in the grip of white supremacy."[23] Of the three instances he notes of this ethic, one speaks directly to the development of and engagement with the invisible institution—"a duality of survival."[24] This required duplicity on the part of the enslaved person. One had to behave and perform in a certain manner in the presence of whites, while allowing oneself to function authentically among one's own people. Presenting a façade (literally, false front) was often the difference between life and death, and success necessitated daily deception. Enslaved persons who worshipped in slaveholder churches could not reveal their true feelings about what was being preached, taught, or sung, and often had to produce evidence that they understood and agreed with the catechism being taught. But in the worship of the invisible institution, they were able to shed these masks and worship authentically, calling on the names of their gods, singing ancestral-inspired songs, and engaging in practices that allowed them direct communion with the Holy. These acts of resistance spoke to and affirmed their humanity, giving them the strength to continue pressing on in the face of unrelenting inhumanity.

Deliverance and Liberation

Deliverance and liberation constitute a third theme of worship in the invisible institution. These two concepts, though slightly different in definition—performed/behaved—almost identically in Black antebellum worship. The spiritual experience of "getting religion" or being converted resulted in the transformation of hearts, souls, and minds of enslaved persons, if not their bodies. There was an empowerment that occurred through the worship experience, particularly the event of being indwelt by the Spirit. Not only were persons assured of their humanity in these moments, but they felt a kind of freedom from the daily persecutions they endured, which remained with them after the initial event ended. Mechal Sobel refers to this experience as "*trabelin' on*," a concept "characteristic of the African religiocultural worldview."[25] Sobel suggests that "in traveling to a Christian heaven, while yet

---

[22]Ishrael Massie, quoted in Charles L. Perdue Jr. et al., eds., *Weevils in the Wheat: Interviews with Virginia Ex-Slaves* (Bloomington: Indiana University Press, 1980; originally published by the University Press of Virginia in 1976), 208.

[23]Hopkins, *Shoes That Fit Our Feet*, 41.

[24]Hopkins, *Shoes That Fit Our Feet*, 41.

[25]George C. L. Cummings, "The Slave Narratives as a Source of Black Theological Discourse," in *Cut Loose Your Stammering Tongue: Black Theology in the Slave Narrative*, ed. Dwight Hopkins and George Cummings, 2nd ed. (Louisville, KY: Westminster John Knox Press, 2003), 35.

alive, Afro-Americans made the future into the past, into an event that had already occurred. Thus, they used the African sense of time—of present and past—to encompass the Christian's messianic sense of time future to make it real."[26] Prayers during worship in these secret meetings were most often centered on deliverance and liberation. The results of these prayers were also not limited merely to figurative freedom. While many prayed for mental and emotional escapes from servitude and the painful injustices that came with it, others prayed for successful efforts at achieving actual freedom, knowing that they or someone they knew was planning to flee the plantation. Some prayed that they would be liberated from evil slaveholders by the deaths of those who imprisoned them. Whatever the subject of the prayer, the focus centered on apprehending freedom, in whatever forms the Creator would grant.

Brush arbor worship experiences also empowered enslaved persons to participate in freedom movements. Slave revolts, uprisings, and insurrections often came on the heels of ecstatic worship services where persons received prophetic visions, particularly after reading or hearing certain biblical passages preached, that demanded armed response to the institution of slavery. The leaders of these revolts often claimed prophetic or religious status, as did Gabriel Prosser, Nat Turner, and Denmark Vesey. Each of these men believed that certain biblical texts applied directly to them and called for drastic actions in the cause of Black liberation.[27] Wilmore shares the following insights about the catalyzing forces of religious knowledge and experience in their lives:

> Turner . . . was a representative of an important group of slave preachers who discovered something white Christians had attempted to conceal from the slaves for more than two hundred years. Nat Turner, like others . . . discovered that the God of the Bible demanded justice, and to know God's son, Jesus Christ, was to be set free from every power that dehumanizes and oppresses. Turner discovered his manhood in the conception of the Christian God as one who liberates.[28]

Cone asserts that "black people needed liberating visions so that they would not let historical limitations determine their perception of black being."[29] As *AfricansinAmerica* were exposed and introduced to the biblical canon of scripture, they did not gravitate to every story they heard preached or read

---

[26]Mechal Sobel, *Trabelin' On: The Slave Journey to an Afro-Baptist Faith* (Princeton, NJ: Princeton University Press, 1988), xxiii.

[27]See Gayraud Wilmore, "Three Generals in the Lord's Army," in *Black Religion and Black Radicalism*, 77–98; Juan Williams and Quinton Dixie, *This Far by Faith* (New York: William Morrow, 2003), 15–41.

[28]Wilmore, *Black Religion and Black Radicalism*, 88.

[29]James H. Cone, *God of the Oppressed*, rev. ed. (Maryknoll, NY: Orbis Books, 1997), 55.

themselves. They were drawn to stories with which they shared commonalities, stories that gave them hope of a "better day a-coming"—stories that carried the overarching theme of liberation.[30] The late Samuel Dewitt Proctor, former president of Virginia Union University, affirms the unique prevailing presence of the deliverance and liberation theme in Black worship. He asserts:

> Therefore, the deliverance and liberation themes have always accompanied Black worship, And when these are absent, it is because Blacks have turned away from their true and basic spiritual need and taken on the world-view, the Zeitgeist, of others, chanting their themes and following their patterns of worship. Granted, there are common spiritual needs that all persons must address in worship, but the uniqueness of the Black experience, and the pervasiveness of the liberation theme in Black worship cause Black worship to be distinctive.[31]

Affirmation and Joy

The fourth prevailing theme of worship in the invisible institution was affirmation and joy. This may seem inappropriate, given their circumstances, but *AfricansinAmerica* found in the worship experience, among other events, an opportunity to exult, to celebrate, to rejoice, not only in the acts of prayer, singing, preaching, and shouting, not only in conversion or "getting religion," but in the affirmation of their humanity within community. Michael Battle states, "Christianity developed in a different way among enslaved Africans, a way in which community meant survival."[32] Here Battle brings to bear all the themes of worship—survival, resistance, deliverance and liberation, and affirmation and joy—because within the communal worship experience, all these were present. Wilmore asserts that "the dominant motif of slave religion was affirmation and joy . . . a way of feeling into life . . . of being more deeply nourished by the power of the inscrutable and tragic in life, without . . . which human beings cannot fully realize themselves and their place in the mysterious womb of the universe."[33] How is it that *AfricansinAmerica* could face the difficult and ever-present realities of enslavement and survive, even *sur-thrive*[34] in its midst? Wilmore notes: "The preachers could never understand the humor and light touch with which the slaves handled sacred

---

[30]Cone, *God of the Oppressed*, 55.

[31]Samuel Dewitt Proctor, "The Theological Validation of Black Worship," in *The Black Christian Worship Experience*, 220.

[32]Michael Battle, *The Black Church in America: African American Christian Spirituality* (Malden, MA: Blackwell, 2006), 58.

[33]Wilmore, *Black Religion and Black Radicalism*, 34.

[34]*Surthrival* is a term coined by Lynnette Briggs, founder and curator of an online ministry, *The Proverbial Experience.*

things. . . . How could one exult so vociferously over the ritual and ceremony of Christianity, on the one hand, and, on the other, take the solemn moral requirements of the faith with such lightheartedness?"[35]

Wilmore, himself, answers the question rather succinctly, "Slave religion was partly a clandestine protest against the hypocrisy of a system that expected blacks to be virtuous and obedient to those who themselves lived lives of indolence and immorality in full view of those they purported to serve as examples."[36] Part of this clandestine protest was the decision to be joyful in the face of horrific oppression. Those who had experienced the indwelling of the Holy Spirit, and who had been converted or simply continued to believe in the gods of their ancestors, while making room for the god of the Israelites and Mary's little *boy-chile*, Jesus, navigated life by a new star—that of incandescent hope, which glowed deep inside, despite the mundane gloom. This gave light and life and helped produce an ironic joy that the world didn't give and couldn't take away.

Three other concepts help to demonstrate the unique genius behind the development of Black liturgy: Black aesthetics, performative dualities, and dialectical tensions within the Black experience.

Black Aesthetics

Theophus Smith[37] claims that a "distinctive black aesthetic in America" first emerged as an artistic tradition out of folk and popular culture. Harlem Renaissance theorist and critic Alain Locke[38] and other collaborators of the time were able to demonstrate that Black culture was not merely derivative of other traditions, but was, indeed, original and composed of expansive resources and particular characteristics. The Black Arts Movement of the 1960s and 1970s continued pressing this claim and, as Smith asserts, "successfully articulated and popularized the concept of a black aesthetic tradition that is distinguishable from Euro-American or Western values and artistic conventions."[39]

The sources of what we are identifying as the Black aesthetic have their roots in an African aesthetic orientation, which is grounded in the expression of *Ubuntu* ("I am because we are; and since we are, therefore I am.")[40] At its core, aesthetics is the appreciation of beauty; as a philosophy, it is the study of

[35]Wilmore, *Black Religion and Black Radicalism*, 34.

[36]Wilmore, *Black Religion and Black Radicalism*, 34.

[37]Theophus Smith, *Conjuring Culture: Biblical Formations of Black America* (New York: Oxford University Press, 1994), 117.

[38]Alain Locke, ed., *The New Negro: An Interpretation* (1925; New York: Simon and Schuster, 1992).

[39]Smith, *Conjuring Culture*, 117.

[40]John S. Mbiti, *African Religions and Philosophy*, 2nd ed. (Portsmouth, NH: Heinemann, 1990), 141.

beauty, particularly through artistic and sensory expressions and experiences. An African aesthetic perceives beauty as multidimensional and concrete, rather than transcendent, and its appreciation can be apprehended through multiple aspects, including mathematical, ethical, and metaphysical.[41] Factors that influence the development of aesthetics in any culture include environment, experience, tradition, and associations.[42] Often, an unfortunate and misleading presumption made when evaluating Black aesthetics is that its sole—and perhaps most influential—source of origin was the North American experience of enslavement. Certainly, enslavement as environment and experience made an impact on the development of Black religion and liturgy, but Africans and their descendants were shaped and formed by many other cultures and traditions prior to arriving on these shores. The African inheritance and heritage that infused and informed every part of life on the continent came across the waters with its citizenry, and, as scholars, historians, and primary witnesses have testified and shared, this orientation was continued and maintained throughout the development of what is now referred to as the *Black Aesthetic*.

Darius L. Swann[43] offers several characteristics of the Black aesthetic, which he refers to as "soul." These, together with Nathan Jones's aspects of Black religious experience, provide a primary framework for exploring the concept. The characteristics that Swann offers "shape Black perceptions of human life, the world, history, reality and a sense of desired objectives."[44] These characteristics include:

> (a) Black people are a "spiritual" people, meaning Black people prefer and place a higher value on empathetic feelings than objective analyses. This arises from the collective experience of suffering, as well as a personal commitment to hold space for others in suffering, and to the struggle for justice.[45]

This spirituality, particularly as it is lived out in communal relationships, is a direct descendant of African understandings of divine relationality, sacred cosmos, and kinship. The fervent and ecstatic expressions present in "official"

---

[41]See Harris Memel-Fotê, "The Perception of Beauty in Negro-African Culture," in *Colloquium on Negro Arts* (Dakar, Senegal: Society of African Culture, 1966), 63–64.

[42]Darius L. Swann, "Black Aesthetics and Black Worship," in *The Black Christian Worship Experience* (Atlanta: ITC Press, 1992), 121.

[43]Dr. Darius L. Swann was a Presbyterian minister and missionary to India in the 1950s and 1960s. He served on the faculties of Johnson C. Smith University, George Fox University, and the Interdenominational Theological Center between 1964 and 1993, when he retired. He is perhaps best known as a plaintiff in the 1965 landmark civil court case against the Charlotte-Mecklenburg School System which resulted in court-ordered desegregation of the school system and court-ordered busing to enforce it. Dr. Swann transitioned on March 8, 2020 at the age of 95.

[44]Swann, "Black Aesthetics and Black Worship," 122.

[45]Swann, "Black Aesthetics and Black Worship," 122.

Black worship and the refusal to dichotomize sacred and secular clearly reflect what Wilmore calls "the creative residuum of the African religions."[46] Furthermore, the struggle for justice reflects the African concept of liberation as a required result of spirit possession. *AfricansinAmerica* worshipped not as a way of experiencing escapist, feel-good moments; authentic worship resulted in liberation—personal and communal, figurative, and literal.

Three of Jones's nine descriptive phrases correspond with this aesthetic. The first is, "I Have Come to Feel God's Presence Near."[47] While Black worship is not mindless, it does emphasize feeling over knowing. Worshippers in the invisible institution certainly gravitated toward the intuitive as a way of apprehending the Spirit's presence. Many slave narratives reference their difficulty in perceiving any spiritual connection while worshipping in slaveholder churches, particularly during the sermon.

The second phrase that complements Black spirituality is "Let Go and Let God."[48] This aspect of worship notes that much of Black religious experience is circular rather than linear in its approach to communication. Black spirituality comes forth through spontaneity, as evidenced in extemporaneous, creative expressions of singing, dancing, praying, preaching, and shouting. Black antebellum worship experiences exhibited other aspects of this descriptive phrase in the freedom of order of worship acts—they were truly led by the Spirit, praying, singing, and so on, as the Spirit led. Furthermore, the length of worship services was dictated by the Spirit (within the parameters of their work obligations, and considering risks involved in gathering) with the intent being the ability to tarry long enough for attendees to experience presence of the Divine.

Jones's third descriptive phrase referencing spirituality is "God's Not Finished with Us Yet!"[49] Here Jones highlights that Black worship is process-oriented rather than static. God is perceived as always moving, and the Christian life reflects this movement. This process orientation is clear within the Black antebellum religious experience, as each iteration of worship was unique and reflected how God had moved within the community since their last gathering and/or how recent events affected how they wanted God to move. Prayers, in particular, reflected the immediacy of situations and present needs, acknowledging God's ability to work secretly and silently on the behalf of those affected.

---

[46]Wilmore, *Black Religion and Black Radicalism*, 49.

[47]Nathan Jones, *Sharing the Old, Old Story: Educational Ministry in the Black Community* (Winona, MN: Saint Mary's Press, 1982), 35.

[48]Jones, *Sharing the Old, Old Story*, 35.

[49]Jones, *Sharing the Old, Old Story*, 36.

(b) Black people, historically, have not participated in rigidly accepted patterns of society, what is now termed, *respectability politics*.[50]

According to Evelyn Brooks Higginbotham,

> The politics of respectability emphasized reform of individual behavior and attitudes both as a goal in itself and as a strategy for reform of the entire structural system of American race relations . . . such a politics did not reduce to an accommodationist stance toward racism, or a compensatory ideology in the face of powerlessness. Nor did it reduce to a mindless mimicry of white behavior. Instead, the politics of respectability assumed a fluid and shifting position along a continuum of African American resistance.[51]

AfricansinAmerica in the antebellum period were generally not interested in or affected by white mores or values, especially since these mores and values rang hollow and were hypocritical in the light of the brutal treatment suffered at the hands of whites. Moreover, the African inheritance of communal existence and belief in the constant abiding presence of the Holy provided a sense of authenticity required for living as a true community member. Hopkins refers to this "dynamic interplay between community and individual":

> Whatever happened to the communal gathering affected the individual; whatever happened to the individual had an impact on the community. Such a theological view of humanity cuts across bourgeois notions of white Christianity's individualism and "me-first-isms." It seeks to forge a group solidarity and identity. . . . One cannot be a human being unless one becomes a part of, feels a responsibility to, and serves the community.[52]

In the Black antebellum aesthetic, this came forth in the full appreciation of all manner of creative expressions, "holy and profane, good and evil, the

---

[50]The concept of the "politics of respectability" and the term "respectability politics" were coined by Evelyn Brooks Higginbotham in her influential text, *Righteous Discontent: The Women's Movement in the Black Baptist Church, 1880–1920* (1993; Cambridge, MA: Harvard University Press, 2002). She devotes a chapter to this phenomenon, which, in the context Higginbotham relates, was a "religious-political message drawn from biblical teachings, the philosophy of racial self-help, Victorian ideology, and democratic principles of the Constitution of the United States" (186). The prevailing motive for this response was to "assimilate to the dominant society's norms of manners and morals" (187). Also see Swann, "Black Aesthetics and Black Worship," 123.

[51]Higginbotham, *Righteous Discontent*, 187.

[52]Hopkins, *Shoes That Fit Our Feet*, 17.

beautiful and dreadful."[53] Resisting and/or rejecting performative *respectability politics* of white church worship, *AfricansinAmerica* gave themselves up "with shouts of joy and 'singing feet' to this wholeness of being, to the ecstatic celebration of one's creaturehood, and to experience that creaturehood taken up and possessed by God in a new state of consciousness."[54] As one enslaved worshipper exclaimed (after being promised boots as a reward for not shouting in worship), "*boots or no boots, I gwine to shout today.*"[55]

> (c) Black people prefer honesty over flattery. Well-aware of the fleeting nature of fame and status, *AfricansinAmerica* would rather hear hard truths about themselves or situations than empty praise or flowery rhetoric designed to pacify or appease and mollify.[56]

Enslaved persons endured bitter hardships, pains, and trials each day. When they were able to experience some alleviation, whether in brief rest, recreation, or worship, they knew their troubles were not over in those moments. Even when persons managed to escape or buy their freedom, they knew because of their status as fugitives, or simply, as Black people, life would not become magically easier. In fact, many were wary of those who preached freedom and liberation too loudly, because they were not sure what freedom or liberation meant practically. After Emancipation, many enslaved persons remained on farms and plantations because they were unsure of where to go, and the promise of a land flowing with milk and honey was merely an eschatological dream. Adversity was here and now, and most enslaved persons would rather face the truth of that, even while thanking God for the prospect of freedom. Moreover, enslaved persons realized and recognized that to be free, even in worship, they would have to fight in the physical and spiritual realms. Dwight Hopkins asserts:

> Like their self-expression in the cultural sphere, slaves acknowledged that their religious worship and theological development meant a political fight to preserve the Invisible Institution. . . . The Invisible Institution symbolized both a cultural statement of slave theology as well as a liberated space in which slaves controlled the political power to develop their theology.[57]

---

[53]Wilmore, *Black Religion and Black Radicalism*, 34.
[54]Wilmore, *Black Religion and Black Radicalism*, 34.
[55]Botkin, ed., *Lay My Burden Down*, 36.
[56]Swann, "Black Aesthetics and Black Worship," 123–124.
[57]Hopkins, *Shoes That Fit Our Feet*, 19.

Jones's phrase, "Everybody Talkin' 'bout Heaven Ain't Goin' There,"[58] speaks to this liberated space where what is preached and taught gets reflected in communal action. A main reason that enslaved Africans did not accept or espouse the catechesis missionaries taught was because of the inherent hypocrisy within white Christianity. The spiritual, "I Got Shoes," where Jones's phrase originates, reflects the enslaved community's awareness of slaveholders' bastardization of scripture, and how those who preached heaven were destined instead for hell, because of their maltreatment of Black humanity. Through the use of wisdom sayings and folklore, *AfricansinAmerica* told the truths of their circumstances to each other and, surreptitiously, to whites.

> (d) Black people appreciate creative expression and place a hallmark on those who can "say it" with vivid imagery and rhythmic intensity.[59]

The African cosmological worldview of cosmic rhythm, as well as the gifts of proverbs and folklore bespeak innate abilities of Black peoples—on the continent and in the Diaspora—to tell stories and "tell the story" that liberate through "conjuring-up" freedom. Henry Louis Gates refers to this literary device as "signification/signifying."[60] Employing coded language, reversal of word meanings, and repetition were all methods of self-preservation for *AfricansinAmerica*; a "particular rhetorical strategy . . . which prevented African Americans from being totally dominated and/or destroyed."[61]

The most visible representation of verbal linguistics was the Black antebellum preacher. Raboteau shares a glimpse into the sermonic discourse of this historical figure:

> The style of the folk sermon . . . was built on a formulaic structure based on phrases, verses, and whole passages the preacher knew by heart. Characterized by repetition, parallelisms, dramatic use of voice and gesture, and a whole range of oratorical devices, the sermon began with normal conversational prose, then built to a rhythmic cadence, regularly marked by the exclamations of the congregation, and climaxed in a tonal chant accompanied by shouting, singing, and ecstatic behavior. The preacher, who needed considerable skill to master this art, acknowledged not his own craft but, rather, the power of the spirit which struck him and "set him on fire."[62]

---

[58]Jones, *Sharing the Old, Old Story*, 36.

[59]Swann, "Black Aesthetics and Black Worship," 124.

[60]Henry Louis Gates Jr., *The Signifying Monkey: A Theory of Afro-American Literary Criticism* (New York: Oxford University Press, 1988), 46.

[61]Gates, *The Signifying Monkey*, 74–77.

[62]Raboteau, *Slave Religion*, 236–237.

African traditions of oratory, including folklore and wisdom sayings, were present and even foundational to the development of the Black antebellum preacher's oratorical skills. Costen reminds us that those who had been entrusted with oral histories and keeping the traditions on the continent "functioned as the 'voice from God,' *a griot*"[63] on American soil.

Jones employs the phrase, "Make It Plain, [Rev]!" to highlight the preference for inductive, rather than deductive learning in Black religious spaces.[64] According to Silver, Dewing, and Perini, "Inductive Learning is a powerful strategy for helping students deepen their understanding of content and develop their inference and evidence-gathering skills. In an Inductive Learning lesson, students examine, group, and label specific 'bits' of information to find patterns."[65] Black antebellum religious experiences gave worshippers opportunities to navigate the meanings and significance of acts of worship for their unique life situations. Again, the use of wisdom sayings and folklore, as well as signification, reflected the power of *AfricansinAmerica* to discover and create patterns of language and other modes of expression necessary for interpreting their world.

> (e) Black people perceive life in strongly communal terms. Swann lists three particular ways Black people function communally: 1) they seek out places where "things are happening;" 2) they become part of a group unit while dancing; and 3) Black men create and congregate around meeting places.[66]

We have covered fully the African cosmological worldview of kinship and communal ethos. Though Swann is referring primarily to contemporary Black life, here, the three ways mentioned of functioning communally could also refer to Black antebellum life, particularly during times, albeit brief, of rest and recreation.

Related closely to this aspect of Black aesthetics is Jones's descriptive phrase, "We Want Some of the Action."[67] Noting Black religious experience as communal rather than hierarchical, Jones speaks to the ways Black people engage in worship primarily through group participation. Singing, praying, dancing, and the dialogical nature of preaching are all perceived as group

---

[63] Costen, *African American Christian Worship*, 35.

[64] Jones, *Sharing the Old, Old Story*, 35.

[65] Harvey Silver, R. Thomas Dewing, and Matthew J. Perini, *The Core Six: Essential Strategies for Achieving Excellence with the Common Core* (Alexandria, VA: Association of Supervision and Curriculum Development, 2012).

[66] Swann, "Black Aesthetics and Black Worship," 124.

[67] Jones, *Sharing the Old, Old Story*, 36.

(congregational) worship activities. This would have been no different in the Black antebellum worship experience. Enslaved persons gathered, not to experience individual meditation, mystical visitations, or conversions, but so that the entire community might be indwelt and transformed together.

> (f) Black people, generally, are fully attuned to their bodies. Movement, whether in worship, dance, or exercise, was and is part and parcel of the Black aesthetic, rooted in an African heritage. Swann notes African attributes of this distinctive, including strong communal instinct, poetic and rhythmic qualities of speech, movement and dance, and the integration of the physical and spiritual.[68]

During the antebellum period, *AfricansinAmerica* were viewed primarily as inhuman. Ironically, this view did not extend to physical attributes for which they were prized, priced, and sold. Each person's worth was measured by the ability to perform intensive manual labor all day long without sufficient rest, clothing, food, or water. Despite backbreaking toil, however, *AfricansinAmerica* still found energy to express themselves physically. During the few times of rest and, perhaps, recreation they had each week, some would participate in dancing, individually and in groups. In worship, as already noted, enslaved Africans would engage body movement, as they swayed, moaned, lamented, shouted, clapped their hands, stomped their feet, and participated in ring shouts, which could go on for hours, as they became indwelt by the Spirit.

Jones's phrases, "Reach Out and Touch Your Neighbor"[69] and "My Soul's So Happy I Can't Sit Down,"[70] address the relational and physical nature of worship, as well as the eschatological character of Black worship. Black worshippers are asked often to shake hands with or hug those sitting near them. During times of greeting, they may walk around the sanctuary and welcome each other, sharing brief conversations of general well-being. During processionals, sung benedictions, and recessionals, worshippers may stand, sway, clasp or lift hands, or march down church aisles. Furthermore, during ecstatic expressions of worship, they may shout, cry, wave holy hands, walk or run around the sanctuary. These acts are not seen as individual expressions but part of the collective nature of a charismatic outpouring of the Holy Spirit. The participative nature of Black worship evinces these physical elements, and this was no less part of the Black antebellum religious experience. Movement, verbal exultations, and ecstatic indications of spirit/Spirit possession

---

[68]Swann, "Black Aesthetics and Black Worship," 124–126.

[69]Jones, *Sharing the Old, Old Story*, 35.

[70]Jones, *Sharing the Old, Old Story*, 36.

occurred throughout worship in the invisible institution. These reflect the immanence, or closeness, of God, and the belief that in these moments, Jesus has indeed returned to visit the gathered believers, providing a glimpse of the new heaven and new earth.[71]

Performative Dualities and Dialectical Tensions

There are several dualities and dialectical tensions that impact the performative nature of Black worship. I will examine four that are particularly germane to the discussion regarding the Black aesthetic. The first is what Ofori-Atta-Thomas names the "dynamic dialectics of spiritual interactions."[72] This dialectic is initiated between the pulpit and the pew—the preacher and the people—and involves the interchange between the mystery of supernatural expectation and response of human anticipation. What happens as the worship experience moves from inception to spiritual peak? How does the sermon, and more precisely, the preacher's performance of the sermon, influence and impact the congregation and vice versa? Ofori-Atta-Thomas notes that the dialectical dynamic that occurs within this dialogical movement results in a "complementary creativity, experienced by all as 'having church.' "[73] The apex of this movement is a spiritual integration characterized by communal wholeness.

The second dialectic that has implications for worship aesthetics is Ofori-Atta-Thomas's concept of "conflict between the Christian ideal of 'being love' and 'doing love.' "[74] Here Ofori-Atta-Thomas references the struggle for Black Christians to reconcile their confessional creeds of forgiveness with the actual acts of forgiveness and reconciliation. In Black antebellum worship spaces, enslaved persons disobeyed slaveholders' commands and legal restrictions to gather. Doing so did not render them arrogant or willful; rather, it reminded them of the One to whom true obeisance was due. Coming together with those who might have been untrustworthy, enslaved worshippers decided to trust, anyhow, and serve each other in a sense of spiritual and social hospitality. As Ofori-Atta-Thomas asserts, "Being there for the other and being recognized by the other in Jesus' name became the means of collective and individual empowerment. It provided the space for unlimited growth."[75]

Smith examines how the wisdom tradition of Black North American folk culture differs from Western modes of thinking. Whereas the latter consid-

---

[71] Jones, *Sharing the Old, Old Story*, 36.
[72] Ofori-Atta-Thomas, "African Inheritance in the Black Church Worship," 52.
[73] Ofori-Atta-Thomas, "African Inheritance in the Black Church Worship," 52.
[74] Ofori-Atta-Thomas, "African Inheritance in the Black Church Worship," 182.
[75] Ofori-Atta-Thomas, "African Inheritance in the Black Church Worship," 185.

ers most concepts from an "'either/or' . . . univocal meaning for things," the former prefers a "both/and" view "in which ambiguity and multivocity are taken for granted."[76] Rather than refer to this as a dialectic, Vernon Dixon uses the term "diunital." He states: "American Blacks rather than Whites are more deeply attuned to a diunital [both/and] existence for two reasons. First, we live in a dual existence. We are American citizens, yet we are not. . . . Secondly, we may embody a predisposition to diunity that arises from our African identity."[77] This "diunital" way of being does not function in a typical binary fashion, but is an affirmation of opposites, which Smith asserts is "the crucial aspect of wisdom traditions that feature conjunctive forms of cognition" and "readily conjoins categories such as the visible and invisible, everyday and immemorial, ethos and cosmos."[78] Evidence of this dualism is present in the wisdom tradition through conjure in Black antebellum ideologies. Raboteau notes:

> The conflict between Christianity and conjure was more theoretical than actual. Moreover, among black folk there was a refusal to dichotomize power into good and evil—a refusal which Herskovits and others see as African. Conjure could, without contradiction, exist side by side with Christianity in the same individual and in the same community because, for the slaves, conjure answered purposes which Christianity did not and Christianity answered purposes which conjure did not.[79]

Further performative dualisms exist in "a profound sense of the pervasive reality of the spirit world above and beneath the artefactual world; the blotting out of the line between the sacred and the profane; the practical use of religion in all of life,"[80] that has its origins in African cosmology. These dualisms that Morton Marks terms "style-switching"[81] are evident in Black culture "in virtually every sphere of human activity,"[82] including religious and aesthetic domains. "'Style-switching' is the alternating of patterned expression from the forms of one culturally identified style system to those of another," which, Marks notes, is "always from a 'white' style to a 'black' style, from

[76]Smith, *Conjuring Culture*, 143.

[77]Vernon J. Dixon and Badi G. Foster, *Beyond Black or White: An Alternate America* (Boston, MA: Little, Brown, 1971), 64.

[78]Smith, *Conjuring Culture*, 143.

[79]Raboteau, *Slave Religion*, 287–288.

[80]Wilmore, *Black Religion and Black Radicalism*, 280.

[81]Morton Marks, "Uncovering Ritual Structures in Afro-American Music," in *Religious Movements in Contemporary America*, ed. Irving I. Zaretsky and Mark P. Leone (Princeton, NJ: Princeton University Press, 1974), 67.

[82]Marks, "Uncovering Ritual Structures in Afro-American Music," 64.

a European to an African one."[83] Music and ritual spirit possession are two activities of the Black antebellum religious tradition where "style-switching," also called "code-switching," would have been prevalent. This dualism "provides a kind of record or deposit of culture contact between Africans and Europeans, on the one hand, and a record of mutual acculturation between them on the other."[84] Raboteau, Wilmore, Smith, and others indicate the use of codes within the language, music, and folklore and continuities between African and Christian spiritualities of Black peoples in the Americas.[85]

Smith notes that "this Black aesthetic duality is not limited to style but indicates deeper dimensions of cultural existence."[86] In his treatment of "ecstatics," Smith explores the dualities present in Black cultural perceptions of spirituals and blues. Spirituals were considered both "sorrow" and "jubilee" songs, allowing for the expressions of melancholy and joy. The blues, while demonized by many in Christian religious traditions and spaces, were infused with spirituality. James Cone, who credits C. Eric Lincoln with coining the phrase, "blues are *secular spirituals*,"[87] asserts:

> Black church people . . . did not understand them rightly. If the blues are viewed in proper perspective, it is clear that their mood is very similar to the ethos of the spirituals. Indeed, I contend that the blues and the spirituals flow from the same bedrock of experience, and neither is an adequate interpretation of black life without the commentary of the other.[88]

Cone claims that blues are spirituals, "because they are impelled by the same search for the truth of black experience."[89] Both genres certainly had the power to conjure, both employed coded meanings and modes of "style-switching," both shared melodic and rhythmic Africanisms, and both were part of the religio-cultural world of Black antebellum worship spaces.

Worship Characteristics in the Invisible Institution

As I conclude the discussion on the origins and development of Black liturgy, there is one other source of Black aesthetics I need to explore—that of

[83]Marks, "Uncovering Ritual Structures in Afro-American Music," 64.

[84]Marks, "Uncovering Ritual Structures in Afro-American Music," 61–62.

[85]See Raboteau, *Slave Religion*; Wilmore, *Black Religion and Black Radicalism*; Smith, *Conjuring Culture.*

[86]Smith, *Conjuring Culture*, 120.

[87]James H. Cone, *The Spirituals and the Blues* (Maryknoll, NY: Orbis Books, 1992), 140.

[88]Cone, *The Spirituals and the Blues*, 100.

[89]Cone, *The Spirituals and the Blues*, 100.

characteristics of worship in the invisible institution. According to Costen, the invisible institution provided "an affirmation of the clandestine or 'invisible' nature of events where mutual relationships, worldviews, behavior patterns, and social and political actions were 'officially constituted' by the slaves."[90] Several characteristics, commonly noted among slave narratives and other historical writings, were descriptive of the environment:

- The importance of private, divine space where freedom could be sought and experienced;
- Ownership of a Christian belief system and code of religion that they could call their own;
- The uncomplicated manner of worship, conducted in the way of the folks, without outside interference;
- The divinely inspired, minimally educated but biblically articulate preachers, called from among the plantation folks, with a sensitivity to the plight of the folks;
- Freedom of the Spirit to enable the preaching, singing, praying, shouting, and responsive listening of the Spirit-filled congregations;
- Freedom to worship at a time that slaves would determine for themselves;
- Mutual community affinity where "everybody's heart was in tune, so when they called on God, they made heaven ring"; and
- With the support of the community, slaves could experience and be sustained with new life and move with hope into the future.[91]

While these certainly fit within the aesthetic categories established by Swann, Ofori-Atta-Thomas, Wilmore, and others, they are unique because they predate and are foundational to the formation of those categories. Furthermore, some of the former categories, as Smith and Marks note, could be applied just as easily to non-religious events and experiences. What Costen describes here, however, are characteristics experienced and expanded within the actual framework of religious services in the invisible institution. Though enslaved persons may have been feeling "blue," or struggling with whether or not to "put a root" on someone, they did not come to worship in the invisible institution to sing the blues or learn how to "work roots." They came to those spaces with one centralized focus: the unadulterated worship of their God/s. Here, they worked through the meshing together of religious beliefs and systems; they syncretized African ritual practices with what they agreed was true and good about Christianity. They listened to the Word, both bibli-

[90] Costen, *African American Christian Worship*, 25.
[91] Costen, *African American Christian Worship*, 26.

cal and extra-biblical, and preached full and free, affirming their humanity and empowering them to seek liberation in whatever ways they could risk. They conjured-up the trance of spirit-induced possession, trusting that their God/s would still find them worthy of indwelling, even on these shores, and let the creative ecstasy that emerged sing circumspectly into the night, the furtive sounds diminished only by ferrous pots and curtains of dampened quilts draped over tree branches.

In tandem with these key characteristics, Costen notes melodic and rhythmic Africanisms that imbue Black performative culture.[92] These include:

- Call-and-response dialogical participation
- Extemporaneous singing
- Storytelling in song or storytelling linked with song
- Communal involvement in the shaping of songs
- Improvisation of texts and melodies
- Embellishing of melodies and rhythms
- Highly intensive singing with special vocal effects such as falsetto, ululation, groans, shouts, and guttural tones
- Rhythmic complexities in the music and in the manner of delivery
- Extended repetition of short melodic phrases
- Handclapping and other bodily percussion rhythms

These key characteristics of the invisible institution together with the African melodic and rhythmic retentions help to form Black aesthetics at its core and are what make Black worship and liturgy unique.

Understanding Black liturgy requires acknowledging and appreciating its unique components. Essential to comprehending its fullness and diversity is the active awareness of the presence of African retentions, Black aesthetics, performative dualities, and dialectical tensions. The development of these components and characteristics of Black worship into distinctive liturgical practices and how these practices are employed in differing denominational traditions will be examined in the next chapter.

[92]Melva W. Costen, *In Spirit and in Truth: The Music of African American Worship* (Louisville, KY: Westminster John Knox Press, 2004), 32.

5

Black Liturgical Development

As the invisible institution grew into the Black church, how were the elements of worship—call to worship, praying, testimony, singing, preaching, shouting, and conversion—codified into liturgies? What we find, historically, is that these elements of worship became ritualized/formalized as particular acts of worship concomitantly with the development of visible worship, first in praise/pray's houses and then larger, formal church edifices.

Praise/Pray's Houses

Praise/pray's houses originated on the Sea Islands, off the coasts of Georgia and South Carolina. What is unique about these locales is that, prior to the Civil War, they were overwhelmingly populated by Africans and their descendants, thus African and early African American worship practices were preserved. These spaces were provided, most often, by slaveholders, and whenever enslaved persons would gather, either the plantation owner, overseer, or some other official designee was required to be in attendance. Gayraud Wilmore expounds on this requirement, referring to it as a "matter of prudence on the part of planters":

> There was interracial worship before the Civil War, but it was never intended to suggest equality. Even if a few pious slaveholders sincerely believed that they benefited from worshiping with blacks, and were willing to be reminded of their sins by black preachers, they were wise enough to appreciate the fact that their presence in the services had a restraining effect upon black religion. . . . The possibility of slave uprisings was invariably associated with religion, despite the pains that had been taken to make the faith an instrument of compliance and control. . . . Slaveholders and overseers knew that rebellion inspired by religion was always a possibility.[1]

[1]Gayraud S. Wilmore, *Black Religion and Black Radicalism: An Interpretation of the Religious History of African Americans* (Maryknoll, NY: Orbis Books, 1998), 99–100.

Because praise/pray's houses were approved by slaveholders, there was no need for secrecy concerning worship practices. Enslaved persons could pray, sing, shout, exhort, and experience conversion freely. However, because they were no longer in a space where discovery could bring punishment, the performance of these worship acts took on a more ordered form. According to Melva Costen, praise/pray's house worship begins with a "warming-up" period.[2] The worship leader—female or male—is known as a "foreman" and serves as a guide or facilitator of the service. Rhythmic tapping of feet on wood floors accompanies songs and prayers and is used to indicate approval of testimonies and other commentary during worship. Spoken acts of worship such as prayers and testimonies were still extemporaneous but spaced out between congregational singing and readings or recitations of scripture. Spirituals may still have been sung, but congregational singing most often took the form of hymns, sung in the *Dr. Watts*' long-metered style. Preaching took place when the congregation seemed "ready" and was provided by a preacher or exhorter. Though white preachers officiated services for some of the earliest congregations, others had been served by black preachers before the Revolutionary War. After preaching, worshippers engaged in the ring shout, "that counterclockwise, shuffling dance which frequently lasted long into the night."[3] While Costen does not address conversion in her exploration of praise/pray's house worship, we can surmise that, in response to these congregational worship acts, including the ecstatic experiences involved in the ring-shout event, worshippers engaged in the spiritual process of conversion.

During the mid-eighteenth century, Black congregations became visible in both the southern and northern American colonies. Their existence is well documented by historians but I will refer to a few here, to provide some historical foundation for the types of worship and liturgy that developed within common congregational contexts.

Independent Black Churches

According to several scholars, the first Black congregation on record was Bluestone African Baptist Church, organized in 1758 in Mecklenburg, Virginia.

---

[2]See Melva Wilson Costen, "Praise House Worship," in Melva Wilson Costen, *African American Christian Worship*, 2nd ed. (Nashville, TN: Abingdon Press, 2007), 39–43. Henry Mitchell also refers to a similar type of "warm-up" practice in a "Shango Baptist" worship he observed in Trinidad (Henry Mitchell, *Black Preaching* [New York: J. B. Lippincott, 1970], 8), and Albert Raboteau references a Spiritual Baptist worship in Trinidad where Christian hymnody seems to serve as a "warm-up" to the preparation for spirit possession (Albert Raboteau, *Slave Religion: The Invisible Institution in the Antebellum South* [New York: Oxford University Press, 2004], 35–36).

[3]Lawrence Levine, *Black Culture and Black Consciousness: African American Folk Thought from Slavery to Freedom*, 13th anniv. ed. (New York: Oxford University Press, 2007), 38.

Wilmore notes that it was constituted by followers of Shubal Stearns, "the separatist Baptist missionary who was more responsible—directly and indirectly—than any other white preacher for bringing Christianity to the slaves of North Carolina, South Carolina, and Georgia."[4] Other Black Baptist churches of note in the South included one founded by David George and George Liele, the Silver Bluff Baptist Church in Beech Island, South Carolina; the Savannah, Georgia, First Colored Church, started by Liele and reestablished by Andrew Bryan; the Black Baptist Church at Williamsburg, Virginia; and the Harrison Street Church of Petersburg, Virginia. Sobel points out that these congregations, like most early Black congregations in the South, began, not as offshoots of mixed churches, but independently.[5] Black Baptist churches in the North, conversely, grew out of mixed churches with whom *AfricansinAmerica* had grown dissatisfied. Sobel cites Joy Baptist in Boston, Abyssinian Baptist in New York, and First African Baptist in Philadelphia among these. The rise of Black independent congregations did not mean the end of mixed churches; however, as I examine the impact and influence of white supremacy on the development of worship practices and liturgies in Black churches, I will show that interracial worship was a major factor in this development. Before that, though, let us first consider worship and liturgical practices in independent, predominantly Black congregations and denominations.

Black Baptist and Afro-Baptist Churches

Baptist and Afro-Baptist worship and liturgical practices, both in the antebellum period (1619–1863) and following Emancipation, evinced strong African heritages and retentions. Walter Pitts Jr. cites studies, including one by John Gumperz, that link the origins of the Black preaching style to West African forms of public declamation and recitation.[6] John Gumperz notes that "Afro-American preaching is more similar to the transplanted African religious rites found throughout the Caribbean and in Brazil."[7] One of the characteristics of Black preaching, along with prayer, is the musical chant in the oral presentation. Chant is a type of musical intonation and is employed in the worship rituals and practices of many African religions, including the Yoruba, the Dogon, and the Malinke. Pitts notes Gilbert Rouget's description of African poetry as one that offers "a viable explanation of the development of the Afro-Baptist preaching and praying styles."[8] Rouget notes the perfor-

---

[4]Wilmore, *Black Religion and Black Radicalism*, 104.

[5]Mechal Sobel, *Trabelin' On: The Slave Journey to an Afro-Baptist Faith* (Princeton, NJ: Princeton University Press, 1988), 188.

[6]Walter F. Pitts Jr., *Old Ship of Zion: The Afro-Baptist Ritual in the African Diaspora* (New York: Oxford University Press, 1993), 59.

[7]John Gumperz, *Discourse Strategies* (New York: Cambridge University Press, 1982), 189.

[8]Pitts, *Old Ship of Zion*, 60.

mative aspects of Dogon dynastic poems, which he states are "a mixture of recitation and music," and the Yoruba prayers to the *oriki*,[9] which he calls "praise poems," "a mixture of monotonic chant and melodious refrain."[10] Another tradition reminiscent of Black preaching and prayer styles is the *griot*. Musical characteristics common between the two are the use of *portamento* (embellishment of a vocal phrase by sliding between pitches), falsetto, shrieks, and high, forced tones, and the return to regular speech patterns at the conclusion of the presentation. Portia Maultsby also references these characteristics: "Elements that characterize this dramatic and intense style of Black preachers include . . . the use of vocal inflections, which produced a type of musical tone or chant, and facilitated the dramatic and climatic style of preaching."[11] The Reverend Dr. Charles G. Adams, often called the "Dean of Preaching" in Black Baptist circles, concurs with this assessment:

> The most unique quality of Black preaching is its becoming artfully intensified into music and rhythm. As the discourse develops, and the congregation enters into a rhythmic dialogue with the preacher, answering him with emotional fervor, the spoken discourse begins to boil into an opera-like musical dramatization of the Gospel. The language become rhythmically poetic, the tune becomes evident, and the speech fulfills itself in song.[12]

The musical chant in prayers was most often employed in what is known in Black Baptist churches as "deacon's devotional." As someone who grew up in a Black Baptist church where deacon's devotional was a part of every Sunday's worship liturgy, I am well acquainted with this act of worship and its musical style. It began with a *Dr. Watts* hymn, led by a deacon and chanted congregationally, and included at least two verses of the hymn. During the last verse, the deacons and mothers of the church would stand and shake hands, and at the conclusion, one deacon would bring out a folding chair and place it in the middle of the aisle. He would kneel before the chair, place his arm on the chair, hold his head in his hand, and begin to pray. His prayer would be delivered in the sung-speech cadence referenced by Rouget, while the congregation continued to moan the melodic chant of the previous hymn.

---

[9]*Oriki* are prayers to the *orisha*—"supernatural intercessors between mortals and God." Pitts, *Old Ship of Zion*, 61.

[10]Gilbert Rouget, "African Traditional Non-prose Forms: Reciting, Declaiming, Singing and Strophic Structure," in *Conference on African Language and Literature*, ed. Jack Berry, Robert Plant Armstrong, and John Povey (Evanston, IL: Northwestern University, 1966), 48–51.

[11]Portia K. Maultsby, "Hymnody, Spirituals and Gospels," in *The Black Christian Worship Experience*, ed. Melva Costen and Darius Leander Swann (Atlanta: ITC Press, 1992), 148.

[12]Charles Gilchrist Adams, "Some Aspects of Black Worship," in *Readings in African American Church Music* (Chicago: GIA Publications, 2001), 311.

When he finished praying, another deacon would raise a second *Dr. Watts* hymn, and the process would begin again. The musical chant never ceased during these prayers and often, one could not hear the entire prayer clearly for the chanting.

Prayer in Black Baptist and Afro-Baptist churches also evinced African heritages. Pitts contends that prayer texts in these churches were drawn from African prayers that "resembled scriptural phrases heard in praise house and camp meeting spirituals and sermons."[13] Lines within prayers included phrases such as "a rock in a weary land," "crossing over Jordan," "over in Beulahland or Canaanland," which referenced spiritual or hymn lyrics. Paraphrases or portions of biblical texts were also sources of prayer texts, particularly from well-loved Psalms or Gospels. Frequently used phrases such as "crying out to you, oh God," "won't you have mercy, oh Father," "leaning and depending on you, Master," and "we know you're the Good Shepherd, Jesus," punctuated and permeated these communal prayers. During prayer, particularly during deacon's devotional, congregants would restate these phrases following the prayer leader, and add others of their own, as the Spirit gave utterance. It is important to note here that prayer in the eighteenth, nineteenth, and early twentieth centuries in most Black Baptist churches, especially in the South, would have been extemporaneously delivered. That said, historians have noted the presence of a particular formula or pattern in prayers of Black worshippers during these historical periods.

Music in the worship of Black Baptist and Afro-Baptist churches during these periods was classified in several genres. Spirituals were still performed, although not as regularly as during worship in the invisible institution. More prevalent was English psalmody, which many *AfricansinAmerica* in the North learned from attending Puritan services, and Protestant hymnody. Black Baptists rarely sang these tunes in the manner taught by the Puritans, which was exceedingly slow and without musical accompaniment, choosing instead their own form of psalm or hymn-lining, using African pentatonic scales and modalities. *AfricansinAmerica*, along with white colonists, were introduced to Protestant hymnody by Isaac Watts, who published his own hymnal, *Hymns and Spiritual Songs*, superseding the popularity of the Puritans' *Bay Psalm Book*. Further introduction to this new song form came through the First and Second Great Awakenings. The camp-meeting revivals of the First Great Awakening caused many worshippers to abandon the dull psalmody of Puritanism for the freedom of Watts's hymnody. The Second Great Awakening moved worshippers even further toward a much livelier hymnody than that of Watts. As noted, during both events, *AfricansinAmerica* contributed musical Africanisms that permeated the hymnody, popularizing it

---

[13]Pitts, *Old Ship of Zion*, 69.

with Black and white worshippers, and creating new song forms that would be added to the hymn genre, namely the spiritual song and the gospel hymn.

One result of the development of spiritual songs in these camp meetings was the rise of white and Black singing schools to train singers in the standard Western musical tradition, using a system of letters called *solfege*, *solmization*, or *fasola*. The shape-note singing system made note reading easily attainable by the masses. There were even Black singing-school masters, including Newport Gardner, who founded the African Benevolent Society for the education of Black children and was one of the founders of the Colored Union Church in Newport, Rhode Island.[14]

The teaching of shape-note singing offered the opportunity for average, everyday rural people to sing hymns and brought yet another air of revival and, some argue, a third Great Awakening, while creating a new market for instructional manuals, songbooks, and other printed music. Collections of these songs met with some immediate commercial success, particularly the most popular collection, *The Sacred Harp*, published in 1844 by Benjamin Franklin White. Some music teachers rejected the shape-note system, deeming it a "dumbing down" of the traditional Western choral tradition, At the root of some of the criticism of shape-note singing was its association with rural or common folk, evidenced in a class conflict between them and the educated elite, who felt a need for acquiring traditional music training and skills.

Though Sacred Harp and other singing school traditions were frequented by predominantly white crowds, Blacks also participated where racial segregation allowed, and some created their own communities, such as the "Wiregrass Singers" in southeast Alabama. Judge Jackson, a Black self-educated Alabama farmer compiled and published the book, the *Colored Sacred Harp*, which he patterned after the original *Sacred Harp* and used to incorporate a cultural expression of his own making.

Shape-note singing was not typical of the weekly Sunday worship liturgy. The gospel hymn, however, quickly gained popularity and was used widely in worship, particularly among Black Baptist and Afro-Baptist congregations. This genre arose from the camp meetings of the Second Great Awakening and conventions designed to highlight the development of folk music. Gospel songs were not traditional or orthodox hymns, but like the spiritual songs of camp meetings, gospel song writers added new choruses to established hymns or created completely new gospel hymns by borrowing melodies from popular songs and tunes of the day, giving them sacred lyrics and adding catchy refrains.

Three of the most significant proponents of this new music were Dwight Lyman Moody, a layman associated with the YMCA in Chicago, Ira Sankey,

---

[14]Eileen Southern, *The Music of Black Americans: A History*, 2nd ed. (New York: W. W. Norton, 1983), 70.

and Mrs. Alexander Van Alstyne, better known to the public as Fanny Crosby, who wrote "Blessed Assurance," "I Am Thine, O Lord," "Near the Cross and Pass Me Not," and "All the Way My Savior Leads Me." A singer/songwriter from Pennsylvania, Moody felt his calling was to preach the gospel, and Sankey felt his to sing the gospel. In fact, Sankey is generally credited for linking the term "gospel" to religious music because of the popularity he and Moody enjoyed in England and because of Sankey's 1875 publication, *Gospel Hymns and Sacred Songs.*[15] Other composers, such as Philip Bliss, James Rowe, and William Bradbury wrote enduring favorites such as "Wonderful Words of Life," "It Is Well with My Soul," "'Tis So Sweet to Trust in Jesus," "Love Lifted Me," "Jesus Loves Me," "This I Know," "Just As I Am," "Sweet Hour of Prayer," and "On Christ the Solid Rock I Stand." An even more important contributor to Black gospel hymnody was the musical evangelist Homer A. Rodeheaver, who traveled as a song leader with Billy Sunday at the turn of the twentieth century.[16] His gospel music collections included many hymns popular with Black congregations, including Charles Gabriel's "His Eye Is on the Sparrow" and George Bernard's "The Old Rugged Cross." Linking the new music with conversion theology and evangelicalism, these gospel hymns became extremely important to the congregational music of both white and Black denominations.

Black Methodist Churches

Black Methodism erupted in Philadelphia in 1787, after Richard Allen and Absalom Jones were pulled from their knees at the altar of St. George's Methodist Episcopal Church. Though Allen affirmed the evangelical theology and polity of Methodism, he desired a church "that would combine secular relevance with deep spirituality in a context of simplicity and spontaneity."[17] Interested neither in a legalistic nor socially fashionable church, Allen was aware of how Methodism was becoming identified as a denomination of formal churchmanship, which he perceived was not for poor Blacks.[18] Historian Dennis Dickerson notes that "Allen, in reinventing Methodism through the AME Church, created an institution that advocated and facilitated the furtherance of black freedom despite the forces of empire that promoted the slave trade and slavery."[19] While Wilmore maintains that Allen "wanted spirited preaching and

---

[15]James R. Goff Jr., *Close Harmony: A History of Southern Gospel* (Chapel Hill: University of North Carolina Press, 2002), 25.

[16]Southern, *Music of Black Americans*, 445.

[17]Wilmore, *Black Religion and Black Radicalism*, 105.

[18]Wilmore, *Black Religion and Black Radicalism*, 105–106.

[19]Dennis Dickerson, *The African Methodist Episcopal Church: A History* (Cambridge: Cambridge University Press, 2020), 24.

singing, with congregational participation and the freedom of black worship evolving out of its African background,"[20] the latter portion of his claim is not supported by other scholars, including Wendell Whalum, who notes Allen's disdain for "shouting Methodists"[21] and Melva Costen, who asserts that he "was highly critical of African carryovers in Christian worship, including the ring shout."[22] Whalum and Costen also note the negative reaction of Bishop Daniel Payne to the ring shout, which he referred to as "heathenist,"[23] and Praying and Singing Bands, whose music he called "cornfield ditties."[24]

Before the African Methodist Episcopal (AME) Church was officially recognized, Allen and Jones started the Free African Society, whose gatherings followed the pattern of class meetings, the regular assembly of Methodist members, for the purpose of "nurturing a deeper love of God which members would manifest in 'the practice of Christian love in the world.' "[25] Class meetings were designed to examine how following the rules or disciplines of holiness were impacting the personal and communal lives of members. Attendees availed themselves of "the practices of prayer, 'searching the Scriptures,' fasting, and 'Christian conversation,' together with the sacrament of the Lord's Supper available in the parish churches."[26]

That Allen and Jones continued these practices even after leaving the Methodist Episcopal Church is significant, because it conveys their intentions to continue subscribing to Methodist polity, doctrine, and order. Methodist bishop Francis Asbury, who volunteered to come to British North America in 1771, apparently met with "the African people every morning between five and six o'clock at his lodging with singing, reading, exhortation and prayer, the precise ritual of secret meeting."[27] It is possible that many *AfricansinAmerica* gravitated toward Methodism because the worship practices, both visible and invisible, were similar to those they had practiced in the invisible institution, and because many Methodist leaders who proselytized Black worshippers followed John Wesley's staunch abolitionist stance. Dickerson notes, "Far more than their Caucasian counterparts, African Methodists adhered to John Wesley's unyielding opposition to slavery and found within his 'practical theology' a moral warrant to challenge sinful societal structures that sustained and perpetuated racial oppression."[28] Indeed, the push for abolition was, in

---

[20]Wilmore, *Black Religion and Black Radicalism*, 106.

[21]Wendell P. Whalum, "Black Hymnody," in *Readings in African American Church Music*, 170.

[22]Costen, *African American Christian Worship*, 43.

[23]Costen, *African American Christian Worship*, 43.

[24]Whalum, "Black Hymnody," 172.

[25]Henry H. Knight, III, *The Presence of God in the Christian Life: John Wesley and the Means of Grace* (Metuchen, NJ: Scarecrow Press, 1992), 12–13, 192.

[26]Cf. John Wesley, *Works*, 8:301.

[27]Miles Mark Fisher, *Negro Slave Songs in the United States* (Ithaca, NY: Cornell University Press, 1963), 75.

[28]Dickerson, *The African Methodist Episcopal Church*, 3.

some ways, a catalyzing factor of the worship practices of Black Methodism, leading Allen, for example, to compile hymnals specifically for worship in the AME tradition as early as 1801, as well as tailor Methodist orders and acts of worship to meet the needs of those seeking full liberation.[29]

Two other Black Methodist denominations were formed during the nineteenth century, both also committed to the cause of abolition and the liberation of Black humanity. The African Methodist Episcopal Zion (AMEZ) Church was formed in New York after Black members withdrew from the predominantly white John Street Methodist Church over issues of segregated seating. Though Wilmore notes that "the situation in New York was somewhat less hostile than in Philadelphia,"[30] these members wanted to inhabit worship spaces that were welcoming, not merely tolerant, of their total personhood, and to be able to ordain their ministers without having to seek approval by white authority.[31] Following the Civil War and the birth pangs of Reconstruction, The Colored (now Christian) Methodist Episcopal Church was formed when forty-one former enslaved members of the Methodist Episcopal Church, South, petitioned that denomination for dismission, in order to form "a separate religious organization patterned after their ideas and notions."[32] The approval of this petition held tremendous implications, as those forty-one women and men represented 40,000 Black members of what then became the third largest Black Methodist denomination in the United States.[33]

The worship in these denominations also followed the doctrine, polity, and worship order of Wesleyan Methodism, but, as with the AME Church, the acts of worship were adapted to the styles and characteristics common to Black worship, which arose from African beginnings.

Black Pentecostal, Holiness, and Sanctified Churches

Dr. Charles Adams notes that "already in 1845 certain Blacks had identified intelligence and refinement with European culture and thereby became aliens to the peculiarity of Black experience."[34] Though wanting to keep some of the hymns and choruses of African and Black traditions, the hymnody of

---

[29]Costen, *African American Christian Worship*, 97.

[30]Wilmore, *Black Religion and Black Radicalism*, 110.

[31]Writing about the founding of the AME Zion Church, the Reverend B. F. Wheeler declared, "Methodists did not persecute colored people but simply denied them certain privileges." Benjamin F. Wheeler, *The Varick Family* (Mobile, AL, 1906), 7. For a detailed history of the AME Zion Church, please see David Henry Bradley Sr., *A History of the A.M.E. Zion Church, Part I, 1796–1872* (Eugene, OR: Wipf and Stock, 1956), and *A History of the A.M.E. Zion Church, Part II, 1872–1968* (Nashville, TN: Parthenon, 1970).

[32]Othal Hawthorne Lakey, *The History of the CME Church*, rev. ed. (Memphis, TN: CME Publishing House, 1996), 189–190.

[33]Wilmore, *Black Religion and Black Radicalism*, 117.

[34]Adams, "Some Aspects of Black Worship," 298.

several Black denominations, particularly the Methodist bodies, steered clear of emotional and ecstatic expressions in worship. Many congregations, especially those deemed "silk stocking" churches, worshipped in the more austere, demure style of the white congregations in which they had previously been members. Some protested this highbrow style and created or joined Sanctified churches, sometimes identified with the phrase "Holiness-Pentecostal." Wilmore affirms that Black Holiness and Pentecostal denominations were two of the "many forms of black religion in the United States and Africa that challenged the bourgeoisification of the mainline denominations."[35]

Cheryl Sanders states that "the Sanctified church is closely related to three distinct Old and New World religious traditions: African religion, White "protest Protestantism," and Haitian *vaudou*."[36] The label *Sanctified church* distinguished these congregations of saints from other Black Christians, especially those identified as Baptist or Methodist who assimilated and imitated the cultural and organizational models of European-American patriarchy.[37] Two distinct characteristics of Pentecostal worship made it attractive to Blacks: the emotional nature of worship and that it was essentially a religion of the socially underprivileged.

One of these denominations, the Church of God in Christ, started by Charles Harrison Mason and Charles Price Jones, experienced phenomenal interracial growth after the Azusa Street Revival of 1906, when scores of white ministers joined Mason's church. It remained interracial from 1907 to 1914. William Seymour, a Black minister and student of white minister and holiness proponent Charles Parham, initiated the historic nine-year revival attended weekly by thousands of people from across the country. Historian Vinson Synan records:

> By the summer of 1906 people of every race and nationality in the Los Angeles area were mingling in the crowds that pressed into the mission from the street. There was a total absence of racial discrimination. Blacks, whites, Chinese, and even Jews attended side by side to hear Seymour preach. Eventually what began as a local revival in a local black church became of interest to people all over the nation, regardless of race. In a short while the majority of attendants were white, but always there was complete integration of the races in the services, one man exclaiming, "The color line was washed away in the blood."[38]

[35]Wilmore, *Black Religion and Black Radicalism*, 181.

[36]Cheryl J. Sanders, "In the World, but Not of It," in *Readings in African American Church Music*, 99.

[37]Sanders, "In the World, but Not of It," 100.

[38]Vinson Synan, *The Holiness-Pentecostal Tradition: Charismatic Movements in the Twentieth Century*, 2nd ed. (Grand Rapids, MI: William B. Eerdmans, 1997), 99.

This interracial distinction would not last forever, but even after many Pentecostal bodies separated by race, interracial worship in revivals, tent meetings, camp meetings, and pulpit exchanges were the rule rather than the exception among the Pentecostals of the South. Interracial worship and even congregations continued into the 1960s among the divine healers in large urban areas. By the end of the 1900s, it was not uncommon to see large racially integrated churches in cities across the land.

Like Baptist and Afro-Baptist religious traditions, worship practices in Pentecostal, Holiness, and Sanctified churches evinced strong connections with African worship and ritual practices. Author and anthropologist Zora Neale Hurston in her book *The Sanctified Church* notes the Africanism of spirit possession present in the shouting and dancing of worshippers.[39] James S. Tinney cites three African themes that permeate Black Pentecostalism: spirits, magic, and eschatology. In his description, good spirits are angels that function under the Holy Spirit; evil spirits are demons that serve the Devil or Satan; magic refers to African practices that tap and harness spiritual power in order to benefit the believer; and the African understanding of eschatology claims rewards in this life that other religions promise in the next.[40] Sanders asserts that what Pentecostal, Holiness, and Apostolic churches have in common is "an emphasis on the experience of Spirit baptism," and all "adhere to some form of doctrine and practice of sanctification."[41]

Sanders offers a composite portrait of worship from several descriptions of worship services in the Sanctified church tradition that have at least eight basic elements in common, with some variation in order: (1) call to worship, (2) songs and hymns, (3) prayer, (4) offerings, (5) scripture reading, (6) preaching, (7) altar call, and (8) benediction; the recitation of the Lord's Prayer and the reading of announcements are in three of these descriptions.[42] Though these acts of worship are not significantly different from those of other Protestant traditions mentioned here, what is different is the improvisational atmosphere, set in part by the distinctive sound of musical instruments. The Pentecostal church is one of the first to allow a full complement of instruments within the worship service context. Piano, keyboard synthesizers, guitars, drums and other percussion instruments, and especially the Hammond B3 organ set an especially lively, charismatic atmosphere, and undergird all aspects of the worship service.

Prayer in the Sanctified tradition is not generally scripted, but is extempo-

---

[39]Zora Neale Hurston, *The Sanctified Church* (Berkeley, CA: Turtle Island, 1981), 104–107.

[40]James S. Tinney, "A Theoretical and Historical Comparison of Black Political and Religious Movements" (PhD dissertation, Howard University, 1978), 232–233.

[41]Cheryl J. Sanders, *Saints in Exile: The Holiness-Pentecostal Experience in African American Religion and Culture* (New York: Oxford University Press, 1996), 5.

[42]Sanders, *Saints in Exile*, 53.

raneous and may be chanted in a manner akin to the preached sermon. The sermon is also delivered in a charismatic style and has a unique performative aspect in the addition of adjutants who assist the preacher in various ways, including holding the Bible, reading texts for the preacher, providing liquid refreshment, and wiping sweat from the brow, as needed.

The prevailing genre of music utilized in worship of the Sanctified tradition was and is gospel. Two Black gospel hymn writers whose music would be essential to the development of the gospel tradition in these denominations were Charles A. Tindley and Thomas A. Dorsey. Tindley, a Methodist minister, composed songs for Sunday schools, prayer meetings, and social gatherings.[43] His style of writing formed the foundation for this new gospel music genre being developed in Black churches. His hymn collections, *Soul Echoes* and *New Songs of Paradise*, were first published in 1905 and 1916, respectively. Thomas A. Dorsey, a former blues and honky-tonk piano player, brought his playing and singing style to compositions of religious music he called the "gospel blues." He would go on to be a prolific composer of gospel hymns and songs, creating the National Convention of Gospel Choirs and Choruses Workshop of America, which continues to this day. Hymnals such as the ones mentioned above and the groundbreaking *Gospel Pearls* included many of the traditional Protestant hymns popular in Black congregations, with *Gospel Pearls* including gospel hymns of white composers including Moody and Sankey, jubilee songs, and arranged spirituals, as well as the gospel hymns of the two Black composers, and also those of Lucie Campbell.

While white Methodist and Presbyterian denominations rarely sang these songs or sang in this new style, both white and Black Holiness-Pentecostal congregations sang and worshipped in this style.[44] "Many writers have speculated that the Holiness-Pentecostal connection flourished because of an increased openness in worship style that allowed the innovative, often upbeat, performance of commercial gospel music. This influence was felt and retained by both Black and white Baptist and Pentecostal communities in the South."[45] John Philips believes that it is not easy to distinguish uniquely African elements of Holiness-Pentecostal worship practices because much that is often considered peculiarly Black about Black churches is often equally characteristic of white churches. The characteristic features of Pentecostal churches that are demonstrably African in origin include possession trances, ritual dancing, drumming, and ecstatic speech, and indeed, as much African culture survives now among whites as among Blacks.[46] Indeed, Wilmore notes

---

[43]Southern, *Music of Black Americans*, 450.
[44]Goff, *Close Harmony*, 6.
[45]Goff, *Close Harmony*, 5.
[46]John Edward Philips, "The African Heritage of White America," in *Africanism in America*

that "the most direct influence of the Black church upon white Christianity may well have come through the Black Pentecostal churches that emerged during this period."[47]

Ritual and Rituals

We have addressed the development of worship and liturgical practices from the antebellum period through the late nineteenth and early twentieth centuries. Here, we need to distinguish between actual acts of worship and the African concept of ritual, including the rituals that emerge from this conceptualization. Although the aforementioned acts of worship (as they were codified and formalized through independent churches and denominations) became regular parts of worship services, individually and distinctly they do not constitute ritual because, individually and distinctly, they do not produce transformation. Rather, the communal agreement and engagement of those participating in these acts in a worship service—as an entire event—are what have the power to produce ritual. This understanding of ritual is crucial to my argument regarding the infiltration of white supremacist theological thought into Black worship spaces and practices.

Several definitions and descriptions of ritual undergird this discussion of ritual. Smith states:

> It appears that rituals are intended to be transformative more than representational. . . . Rituals need not be limited to religious performances but can also include secular transformations. Neither need they be rigidly fixed by the invariant repetition of particular patterns, although continuity and conserving of similarities undergird their authoritative power to bond participants and indue their adherence.[48]

Dona Marimba Richards asserts, "A ritual is a happening; an event. It is a moment of eternity in which the right set of circumstances combines to create a transcendental experience."[49] *How* does this mean for the African? I use this phrase intentionally to clarify that ritual for African cultures cannot be expressed merely as a list of ceremonies or limited to tangible, empirical actions. Perceiving and engaging in ritual are not matters of "what," then,

---

Culture, ed. Joseph E. Holloway (Bloomington: Indiana University Press, 1990), 231.

[47]Wilmore, *Black Religion and Black Radicalism*, 181.

[48]Smith, *Conjuring Culture*, 56–57.

[49]Dona Marimba Richards, *Let the Circle Be Unbroken: The Implications of African Spirituality in the Diaspora* (Trenton, NJ: Red Sea Press, 1989), 31.

but "how." The concept of ritual is so pervasive in African cultures that the word "ritual" in John Mbiti's book, *African Religions and Philosophy*, is referred to on almost every page. Molefi and Kariamu Asante share this: "The ultimate expression of the African world view is the phenomenon of ritual. Only through ritual can death be understood as rebirth. It is through ritual that new life was given to the African spirit."[50]

The concept and habitation of ritual, by nature, are performative and dramatic. As Asante and Asante state:

> Ritual drama in African society is a multidimensional mechanism of cultural expression. It can be understood on metaphysical, religious, communal, and psychological levels simultaneously. Ritual drama involves the repetition of a sacred act performed in a prescribed manner. It is religiously understood, therefore, as an imitation of divine beings or of our revered ancestors. Events are placed within the context of a harmonious order and so are sacralized. . . . African ritual drama is used to make transitions smooth, so that they will not disrupt the continuity of personal and communal life. . . . African ritual is a statement of continuity, unity, and community.[51]

The transmittal of African ritual and ritual practices on American soil, though unorganized and scattered, still managed to pervade and infuse Black antebellum worship. I have referred numerous times in this text to Africanisms and retentions present in these worship spaces, and their impact on the development of liturgical acts that arose and live, even today. Dona Richards offers insight into this presence: "Black life abounds with rituals through which we redefine ourselves as Black life by giving group expression to the African ethos."[52] *What* does this mean for *AfricansinAmerica*? Asante and Asante refer to the continuation of African ritual in the colonies, noting that

> spontaneous ritual drama was foreign to the Euro-American ethos and therefore could not have come from that source. We performed the "ring shout" in the "hush harbors," the night sings, and the "prayer meetin's." . . . We would form a circle, each touching those next to us so as to physically express our spiritual closeness. Through our participation in these rituals, we became one. We became again, a community.[53]

[50]Molefi K. Asante and Kariamu W. Asante, *African Culture: The Rhythms of Unity* (Trenton, NJ: Africa World Press, 1990), 218.

[51]Asante and Asante, *African Culture*, 218.

[52]Richards, *Let the Circle Be Unbroken*, 30.

[53]Asante and Asante, *African Culture*, 217.

How did the perpetuation of ritual, even in abbreviated or syncretized form, help *AfricansinAmerica* navigate their existence and humanity in the New World? Carlyle Fielding Stewart contends that "through ritualization the unfamiliar becomes familiar; the unknown becomes known; that which alienates and dislocates being and spiritual vitality becomes harmonized and ordered through the ceremonial invocation of the spirit and power of divine reality."[54] The ability to practice even a modicum of one's communal activities can precipitate *anamnesis*, and perhaps, transformation. Ritual practices, such as water baptism, conversion, spirit possession, funerals, and marriages helped enslaved Africans and their descendants connect with the Divine and make meaning of their circumstances. Engaging in these practices, both in the invisible institution, and later, in independent church congregations, aided *AfricansinAmerica* in bringing some semblance of self-ordering to their lives, and "codifying the structures of belief into stabilizing patterns of human existence."[55]

As enslaved persons were introduced to and catechized into Christianity, rituals they may have remembered and practiced in Africa were syncretized and synthesized into similar Christian practices. Whereas the practices and purposes of African rituals may have centered on the "High God," intermediaries, and/or ancestors, and may have been used to achieve some particular tangible sign, message, or reward, the "ritual action in the Christian community of faith is founded on actions and words of Jesus, which are imbued with hope, fulfillment . . . and the essence of the gospel message."[56]

Baptism

For many enslaved, baptism served as a reminder of African rites of passage, making it one of the more easily adapted rituals for *AfricansinAmerica*. A similar understanding existed between Africans and Christian missionaries of water immersion as dying or "disintegrating" the old self and coming out of the waters as a new self—a re-birth. For the African, water symbolizes cleanliness and re-creation and is used as a purifier and regenerator;[57] these understandings of water would have complemented the Christian notion of water baptism symbolically cleansing and purifying soul and spirit. More will be said about the irony of baptism affecting freedom of the soul but not the body of enslaved *AfricansinAmerica*. Many enslaved persons were baptized

[54]Carlyle Fielding Stewart, *Black Spirituality and Black Consciousness: Soul Force, Culture and Freedom in the African-American Experience* (Trenton, NJ: Africa World Press, 1999), 23.

[55]Stewart, *Black Spirituality and Black Consciousness*, 25.

[56]Costen, *African American Christian Worship*, 45.

[57]Melva Costen, "Roots of Afro-American Baptismal Practices," in *The Black Christian Worship Experience* (Atlanta: ITC Press, 1992), 28.

during the camp meetings of the Great Awakenings and other mass revivals. Some who attended denominational churches that practiced infant baptism brought their babies to be baptized. Costen notes that in baptism there was "an obvious assimilation of the African kinship system-fellowship, with an understanding of the theological themes of covenanted family, a sign and seal of incorporation in the mystical body of Christ and with one another."[58]

Conversion

One of the most significant texts regarding slave conversion is *God Struck Me Dead*, a collection of personal narratives of those who had experienced conversion during the antebellum period.[59] These narratives, according to Will Coleman, "blend both archetypal and biblical imagery . . . and contain many allusions to biblical symbolism," while expressing a "radical encounter with spiritual beings."[60] Sobel describes several stages of the conversion ritual experience: the person is experiencing a "low" state of mind and cries out to God for mercy; the person sees herself as two, the "little me" in the "big me" throughout the vision structure; the person's soul takes a detailed journey from Hell to Heaven; a little white man appears to guide the person on the journey; and the person experiences a vision of God and/in Heaven, enveloped in whiteness.[61] Significantly, Sobel's explanation of the conversion experience is that black and white visions of death and rebirth, while sharing certain elements, are different. The Black experience was not simply a case of integrating a Black ethos into a Euro-Christian one; rather, it was an integration of African soul and spirit into a Black Baptist rebirth, which helped create an Afro-Baptist Sacred Cosmos.[62] Whelchel argues that the assertion of enslaved persons' perceptions of conversion as deliverance from physical bondage only is an "oversimplification of their desires." He maintains instead that "conversion for African Americans was a holistic change. It included physical and spiritual rebirth. 'Being born again' was the conversion language best suited to the African-American religious experience. The new birth meant more than being liberated from slavery and physical bondage, as important as that was."[63]

---

[58]Costen, *African American Christian Worship*, 51

[59]Clifton H. Johnson, ed., *God Struck Me Dead: Religious Conversion Experiences and Autobiographies of Ex-slaves* (Philadelphia: Pilgrim Press, 1969).

[60]Will Coleman, "'Coming Through 'Ligion': Metaphor in Non-Christian and Christian Experiences with the Spirit(s) in African American Slave Narratives," in *Cut Loose Your Stammering Tongue: Black Theology in the Slave Narrative*, ed. Dwight N. Hopkins and George C. L. Cummings, 2nd ed. (Louisville, KY: Westminster John Knox Press, 2003), 60.

[61]Sobel, *Trabelin' On*, 109.

[62]Sobel, *Trabelin' On*, 109.

[63]Love Henry Whelchel Jr., *Hell without Fire: Conversion in Slave Religion* (Nashville, TN: Abingdon Press, 2002), 40.

Shouting/Spirit Possession

According to Raboteau, the style of performance in ritual action is perhaps the most obvious continuity between African and Afro-American religions.[64] He notes that "drumming, singing, and dancing are essential features of African and Afro-American liturgical expression and are crucial to the ceremonial possession of cult members by their gods."[65] Sobel affirms that shouting was a retention of the spirit possession ritual. In many worship services, the shout (*ring-shout*) was a separate part of the worship ritual, "separating the Baptist and African aspects and yet exhibiting the interpenetration of the two aspects."[66] Will Coleman refers to this phenomenon as a "blending of ancient West African techniques for inducing spirit possession and the new African American method of 'shouting' under the power of the Holy Spirit."[67] Participating in this work was known as "laboring in the spirit," a behavior that closely resembled West African spirit possession, just as the "holy dance" performed in conversion experiences in Baptist and Pentecostal worship services mirrored the "ring-shout" of West African novitiate rites.[68] Therefore, it was again this ability to syncretize the new tradition of Christianity with African traditional religious heritages that made conversion to Christianity palatable to *AfricansinAmerica*. The work of the Holy Spirit could be conflated with and identified with conjure work and spirit possession of ancestral religions.

Funerals

During the antebellum period, funerals were some of the most publicly visible rituals that evinced connections between Africa and *AfricansinAmerica*.[69] When a person transitioned, certain procedures were followed as closely as possible. The body was laid out on a cooling board—female bodies being wrapped in a winding sheet, male bodies in a black shroud—as a way of helping the soul "lie-easy," so it would not return to haunt anyone. Those who came to mourn spoke as though the deceased could hear them and touched the body. Sometimes, if the burial were held quickly, there would be a second burial so the entire community could participate, thereby ensuring proper rest for the spirit of the "living dead." The procession of mourners from the deceased person's house, accompanying the body carried by pallbearers, mirrored the African understanding of a shared journey between the living

---

[64]Raboteau, *Slave Religion*, 35.

[65]Raboteau, *Slave Religion*, 35.

[66]Sobel, *Trabelin' On*, 144.

[67]Will Coleman, *Tribal Talk: Black Theology, Hermeneutics, and African/American Ways of "Telling the Story"* (University Park: Pennsylvania State University Press, 2000), 50.

[68]Coleman, *Tribal Talk*, 51.

[69]See Sobel, *Trabelin' On*, 197–200; and Costen, *African American Christian Worship*, 55–63.

and the dead. The grave was dug in an east to west direction, and the coffin positioned with the head west and the feet east, so that "when Gabriel blows his trumpet in the eastern sunrise, the dead could rise up and walk toward the east without having to turn around."[70] At the gravesite, pots were broken, symbolizing the loss and freeing of a person's spirit to leave possessions and find unity. Other African connections include staying with the coffin until it is buried under the dirt and cemented over, family members sprinkling dirt on the grave, placing flowers on the freshly cemented grave, and allowing children to march around the casket of their deceased father, and/or be passed over the casket. Often, persons placed cooked food on tables and cemetery graves on the eve of All Saints Day to prevent roaming of "hungry" spirits.[71] One further performative aspect of funerals that needs mentioning is the expected "uproar":

> A negro funeral without an uproar, without shouts and groans, without fainting women and shouting men, without pictures of triumphant deathbeds and judgment day, and without the gates of heaven wide open and the subjects of the funeral dressed in white and rejoicing around the throne of the Lamb, was no funeral at all.[72]

Marriage

In 2020, most Black peoples and many persons of varied ethnic designations are familiar with the practice of "jumping the broom," which usually occurs at the conclusion of marriage ceremonies. Enslaved *AfricansinAmerica* often requested the addition of a broomstick ritual to the regular ceremony, believing it authenticated the proceedings.[73] Countless wedding ceremonies have included this practice, and awareness of it has been transmitted through several contemporary movies, including one aptly named, *Jumping the Broom*. In the movie, the groom's family matriarch, portrayed by Loretta Devine, upset that her son and his fiancée have decided not to include the practice in their wedding, shares its significance: "Jason, enough is enough! You've got to jump the broom! The slaves were not allowed to marry; jumping the broom was the only way to show their union. . . . It *is* a cultural necessity."[74] Jumping the broom, however, was not the only African aspect of Black antebellum marriage ceremonies. Indeed, it was only a visible representation of the meaning underlying an African conception of marriage. As John Mbiti notes:

---

[70]Costen, *African American Christian Worship*, 59.
[71]Costen, *African American Christian Worship*, 56.
[72]Sobel, *Trabelin' On*, 199–200.
[73]Costen, *African American Christian Worship*, 55.
[74]Arlene Gibbs and Elizabeth Hunter, *Jumping the Broom*, Sony Pictures Releasing, 2011.

> For African peoples, marriage is the focus of existence. It is the point where all the members of a given community meet: the departed, the living and those yet to be born. All the dimensions of time meet here, and the whole drama of history is repeated, renewed and revitalized. Marriage is a drama in which everyone becomes an actor or actress and not just a spectator. Therefore, marriage is a duty, a requirement from the corporate society, and a rhythm of life in which everyone must participate. . . . Failure to get married under normal circumstances means that the person concerned has rejected society and society rejects him in return.[75]

Sobel notes that though African marriage practices varied widely across countries and tribes, "West African peoples had rigid and traditional sexual and marital patterns," and "virtually all patterns involved contractual relationships between kin groups."[76] During the antebellum period, marriage between enslaved persons was extremely precarious. If they were allowed to wed at all, their marriages generally were not sanctioned or recognized legally. *AfricansinAmerica* were painfully aware, as well, that either partner could be killed or sold to another slaveholder at any time. Furthermore, monogamy as a practice was virtually nonexistent within enslavement. Black women and men were used to breed and bear generations of children, some the products of rape or other forced unions, regardless of marital status. However, because of African retentions surrounding the concept of marriage, enslaved women and men were determined to observe and honor the practices of their ancestors, some participating in secret covenantal marriage ceremonies, sneaking between plantations afterward to visit one another. Some couples, particularly those who joined Baptist or Methodist churches, asked a visiting preacher to sanction the marriage, and following Emancipation, many visited courthouses to have marriages legalized.

The Impact of Eurocentric Theologies

What theologies undergirded the development and/or evolution of these rituals and worship practices and how were they taught to and espoused by *AfricansinAmerica*? Furthermore, how did they impact and influence the development of liturgies in independent Black congregations during and following Emancipation? To answer these questions, we must look at the denominations and underlying theological doctrines that were prevalent

---

[75]John S. Mbiti, *African Religions and Philosophy*, 2nd ed. (Portsmouth, NH: Heinemann, 1990), 130.

[76]Sobel, *Trabelin' On*, 175.

in British North America during the antebellum period. The two dominant theological movements during this time were Calvinism and Anglicanism. The established Calvinist churches—Presbyterian and Congregationalist—followed a Puritan theological tradition, and the Episcopalian churches followed an Anglican tradition. These traditions had direct implications on *AfricansinAmerica.*

We have discussed, briefly, the reluctance of many slaveholders to introduce Christianity to enslaved persons. In New England, this was due primarily to English law, which freed Christianized slaves. Some colonies, especially those that had been impacted by slave insurrections, enacted laws that prohibited the freeing of enslaved persons that had been converted and baptized. However, many proponents of slavery decided to use Christianity to uphold the practice and institution of enslavement. No one was more adept at this hypocrisy than Cotton Mather.

Puritanism

Cotton Mather, a New England Puritan cleric, was among the first colonists to advocate for the catechization of enslaved *AfricansinAmerica.* He believed that Africans had been sent to America through the providence of God for the purpose of being converted to Christianity. His catechesis involved teaching scriptural and doctrinal beliefs, though he doubted they had the intellectual capacity to learn and retain the information, and posited that the civilization and salvation of Africans depended on their becoming Christianized. Puritan theological tradition, however, was based on highly problematic doctrines and prevailing beliefs. Several of these had extensive, debilitating impacts on the Black persona and psyche, which then became evident in the development and performance of worship acts and liturgies in Black independent congregations.

Anti-Blackness

One of the leaders regarding anti-Blackness in the Puritan tradition is Joseph Washington Jr., who defines anti-Blackness as "an ancient, historical, primordial . . . culturally determined, frame of reference, which, (in some cultures more than others) develops out of a curious association with selected strangers of differing hue, as either sheer fascination (attraction), or, morbid repugnance (repulsion)."[77] He also connected this concept with Puritanism:

> New England Puritans leave no reasonable doubt, and Cotton Mather confirms it: slavery and anti-Blackness were potentially inherent in

[77]Joseph Washington, *Anti-Blackness in English Religion, 1500–1800* (New York: Edwin Mellen Press, 1985), xiii.

> English Puritanism. Anti-Blackness (the negative thrust of the positive lust for purity) was in Englishmen, thus anti-Blackness was in American Evangelical theology before the law or English slavery. Slavery was adapted and anti-Blackness adapted later when laws were created in New England. These laws were the result of the affirmation of slavery by learned theologians who sought holiness through anti-Blackness (or to be pure and free of blackness, that is, sin and evil). Their theologies allowed slavery, and anti-Blackness.[78]

New England Puritans believed that whites were called by God to be masters, and Blacks, to be slaves. They believed that whites who were Puritans possessed saved souls and Blacks possessed damned souls. Washington remarked that "Puritans had the truth and were the light, and in Africans, they virtually saw only blackness."[79] This correlation of Blackness with evil grew out of the Puritan notion of the Devil, whose color was always described as "black." Mather instructed enslaved Africans to refrain from evil insisting that evil would cause them to become blacker and further insisted that their souls would be washed clean in the white blood of Jesus. He warned enslaved Africans in his preaching against Blackness, exhorting them to refrain from making themselves "infinitely Blacker than you already are."[80] Because of their disdain of Blackness, Puritans—and most other whites during this period—perceived themselves as racially superior. Puritans did not create this idea of racial superiority, however; they had brought it across the waters with them. Ibram X. Kendi writes:

> Richard Mather and John Cotton inherited from the English thinkers of their generation the old racist ideas that African slavery was natural and normal and holy. These racist ideas were nearly two centuries old when Puritans used them in the 1630s to legalize and codify New England slavery—and Virginians had done the same in the 1620s.[81]

Historian Jean Devisse asserts that even before Europeans encountered Black peoples, "Blackness as a hermeneutic was able to grow and thrive in Western Europe"[82]—evolving from a theological, even biblical association of dark and black with sinfulness, and white with purity.

Beginning with the 1453 publication of Gomes Eanes de Zurara's *The*

---

[78]Washington, *Anti-Blackness*, 195

[79]Washington, *Anti-Blackness*, 200.

[80]Cotton Mather, *A Good Master Well-Served: A Brief Discourse on the Necessary Properties and Practices of a Good Servant* (Boston: B. Green and J. Allen, 1696).

[81]Ibram X. Kendi, *Stamped from the Beginning: The Definitive History of Racist Ideas in America* (New York: Bold Type Books, 2017), 22.

[82]Jean Devisse, *The Image of the Black in Western Art: From the Early Christian Era to the "Age of Discovery,"* vol. 2 (Cambridge, MA: Harvard University Press, 1990), 58–62.

Chronicle of the Discovery and Conquest of Guinea, a biography of Prince Henry of Portugal and defense of his African slave trading, several theories regarding racial inferiority of Africans came forth. Zurara's claims that Africans "lived like beasts, without any custom of reasonable beings," and Prince Henry's rationale for enslaving them was justified by the cause of salvation of their souls.[83] This theory came to be known as the "beast theory." Other theories that supported the racial inferiority of Africans included the heat theory of Jean Bodin—that Africa's heat caused Africans' hypersexuality; the climate theory of Montesquieu—that cold climates produce high-functioning intellectual characteristics while hotter climes weaken human mental capacity, thereby ensuring the intellectual superiority of persons in cold climates; and the curse theory of George Best—that because of Ham's moral depravity and/or evil hypersexuality, "God wills that Ham's descendants shall be 'so blacke and loathsome that it might remain a spectacle of disobedience to all the world.' "[84] Many white preachers expounded upon this theory, asserting that, according to scripture, Blacks, as Ham's descendants, would be destined to serve their brothers for all eternity.[85] In conclusion, I must agree with Geraldine Heng who notes that "within Christianity the color black accrued a slate of negative significations that yoked the 'abstraction' of blackness to sin, ignorance, shame, error, and the state of unredemption."[86]

Visible Sainthood

One reason anti-Blackness was so prevalent among Puritans was their belief in visible sainthood, as a result of being converted. Visible saints were "people whose faith suggested that they were also among the invisible saints of the elect, known only to God."[87] Because of their Blackness, *AfricansinAmerica*, slave or free, could not be part of the visible sainthood. They could, according to Mather, be converted to Christianity, and were under Satan's power until Christian conversion. To be converted and viewed as part of the elect, however, their souls had to become white. Mather believed that the Puritans' "errand in the wilderness" was to serve God by saving the white souls of enslaved Africans who suffered from inherent inferiority.[88] He proclaims:

---

[83]Kendi, *Stamped from the Beginning*, 22–34.

[84]Washington, *Anti-Blackness*, 114.

[85]That Canaan, not Ham, is the one cursed, and that neither race nor skin color are mentioned in Genesis 9 seems irrelevant to those who espouse(d) this theory.

[86]Geraldine Heng, *The Invention of Race in the Middle Ages* (New York: Cambridge University Press, 2018), 186.

[87]Peter J. Thuesen, *Predestination: The American Career of a Contentious Doctrine* (New York: Oxford University Press, 2009), 71.

[88]Washington, *Anti-Blackness*, 183.

> On this Pretense it is, that poor Negro's especially are Strangers to the way of life: they are kept only as Horses or Oxen to do our Drudgery; but their Souls; which are as white and good as other nations, their Souls are not look'd after, but are Destroyed for lack of knowledge. This is a desperate Wickedness. But are they dull? Then instruct them the rather; That is the way to sharpen them.[89]

In his work *A Good Master Well Served: A Brief Discourse on the Necessary Properties & Practices of a Good Servant*, Mather submits that Blacks may attain salvation by washing in the white blood of Jesus:

> So, though your Skins are of the colour of the Night, yet your Souls will be washed White in the Blood of the Lamb, and be Entitled unto an Inheritance in Light. Though you are in Slavery to men, yet you shall be the Free-men of the Lord, the Children of God. Though you are Fed among the Dogs, with the Orts [offal; scraps] of our Tables, yet you shall at length Lie down unto a Feast with Abraham himself in the Heaven of the Blessed. Been't you Discouraged; it will be but a Little, a Little, a Little While, and all your pains will End in Everlasting Joys.[90]

Divine Superiority

Not only did Puritans perceive themselves racially superior, they also believed they enjoyed divine superiority. They viewed themselves as part of a covenanted community of visible saints, beneficiaries of God's divine covenant with the Israelites. They believed they were the descendants of Jacob, the new Israel, a "city on a hill," and, as such, they were God's elect. Richard Bailey argues that enslavement of Africans and Native Americans functioned as one of the foundational aspects for the promotion and building of the "city on a hill." He notes:

> Combined with their assumptions about the will of God and the place that God had established for them in society, white New Englanders viewed the forced labor of Africans and Indians as a way to promote the founding of a "city upon a hill," as well as an opportunity to carry out their errand into the wilderness, civilizing the heathens and savages within their society.[91]

---

[89]Cotton Mather, *Small Offers towards the Tabernacle in the Wilderness* (Boston, 1689; Ann Arbor: Text Creation Partnership, 2011), Sect XV, p. 58, https://quod.lib.umich.edu/e/eebo/A50162.0001.001/1:4.15?rgn=div2;view=fulltext.

[90]Cotton Mather, *A Good Master Well Served: A Brief Discourse on the Necessary Properties & Practices of a Good Servant* (Boston: B. Green and J. Allen, 1696).

[91]Richard A. Bailey, *Race and Redemption in Puritan New England* (New York: Oxford

Consequently, New England Puritans used theological constructs to justify their active participation in the institution of slavery as slaveholders. Based on Calvinist notions of providence, predestination, and divine superiority, they rationalized their place in society as that which God had ordained for the "city on a hill." The institution of slavery, ironically, was crucial in the work of God's redemption. Though they believed that productivity and hard work were signs of divine election, ironically, this divine election did not extend to enslaved Africans, regardless of how hard they worked.

Anglicanism

The Church of England was established in the American colonies with the arrival of English settlers in Jamestown, Virginia, in 1607. Over time, many colonists became dissatisfied with the church, particularly as a source of guidance and ecclesiastical authority. By the mid-1700s, many leading families wanted a church they could control without having to endure institutional demands. As a result, the church as an institution was rendered too weak to effect any real change regarding enslavement. According to researcher Denzil Clifton, the Anglican Church "did not sponsor any cause or lead any effort on behalf of the manumission of the Negro."[92] Clifton reports:

> There is no evidence to indicate that any colonial Anglican minister or congregation in the period spoke out against the institution of slavery. The clergy did not condemn the master class for owning human slaves. In fact, they owned them themselves. In short, the Anglican Church remained indifferent to the abolition of slavery during the colonial era. Therefore, whatever the church was to do for slaves it was to do within the system, always demonstrating its respect for property and social order. Although discouragingly passive then in its acceptance of slavery as a way of life for the unfortunate African, the church was, nevertheless, concerned about his conversion.[93]

What some Anglican religious leaders did criticize was the church's inability to instruct and convert the enslaved. Two Anglican clerics who would be foundational in the effort to catechize *AfricansinAmerica* were Thomas Bray and William Meade.

University Press, 2011), 36.

[92]Denzil Clifton, "Anglicanism and Negro Slavery in Colonial America," *Source: Historical Magazine of the Protestant Episcopal Church* 39, no. 1 (1970): 29–70, https://www.jstor.org/stable/42973244, 52.

[93]Clifton, "Anglicanism and Negro Slavery in Colonial America," 52.

In 1701, Welsh-born and Oxford-educated, Thomas Bray established the Society for the Propagation of Christian Knowledge (SPCK) and the Society for the Propagation of the Gospel (SPG) to educate and proselytize enslaved persons. Clifton notes:

> The policy of the SPG in its ministry to the Negro slaves was to combine humanitarianism with expediency. The strategy of the SPG campaign was to win the support of the slave holders. It was evident that the best way to convert the slave was by enlisting their masters to countenance and promote their conversion. The SPG insisted therefore that Christianity would not undermine slavery but rather the Christian slave would be both more diligent and docile than the heathen African.[94]

William Meade, bishop of the Protestant Episcopal Church in Virginia during the early nineteenth century, was one of the leading champions of Christianizing *AfricansinAmerica*. A slaveholder himself, Meade believed Africans much more suited to evangelization than Native Americans, but still identified them as savages. Like Cotton Mather and other white religious leaders, Meade maintained that whites were superior to those of brown and black hue and, therefore, had the right to subjugate lesser humans for economic benefit. Moreover, English colonists believed that they inherited Christianity through their bloodlines, further undergirding their contention of racial superiority. This fueled a theological premise known as hereditary heathenism.

Hereditary Heathenism

Rebecca Goetz developed the idea of hereditary heathenism while studying Anglo-Virginians' integration of superiority and universality in the seventeenth and eighteenth centuries. Goetz defined hereditary heathenism as "the notion that Indians and Africans could never become Christian," and argued that Anglo-Virginians invented race in colonial Virginia using Christianity.[95] Creating a dichotomy between Christianity and heathenism, English colonists produced an ideology of superiority based not only on religion, but on race, where Christianity equals whiteness, and heathenism equals brownness or Blackness. There is no doubt that the notion of hereditary heathenism and the subsequent ideology of white/Protestant superiority/supremacy either

[94]Clifton, "Anglicanism and Negro Slavery in Colonial America," 55.

[95]Rebecca Anne Goetz, *The Baptism of Virginia: How Christianity Created Race* (Baltimore: Johns Hopkins University Press, 2012), 3.

emerged from or found additional support in the aforementioned Enlightenment theories regarding racial categorization.

Paternalism

White paternalism was an effort by slaveholders to civilize enslaved *AfricansinAmerica* through Christianization. According to Eugene Genovese, the paternalism of white colonial America mirrored the feudal world of medieval Europe, "in which lords and serfs (not slaves) faced each other with reciprocal demands and expectations."[96] However, as Genovese remarks, the paternalism of the old South was unique; while "it did encourage kindness and affection, it simultaneously encouraged cruelty and hatred. The racial distinction between master and slave heightened the tension inherent in an unjust social order."[97] The point and power of proslavery paternalism was to justify and perpetuate enslavement in a manner sufficiently acceptable to the enslaved, in order to keep the system working. Genovese notes: "For the slaveholders paternalism represented an attempt to overcome the fundamental contradiction in slavery: the impossibility of the slaves' ever becoming the things they were supposed to be. Paternalism defined the involuntary labor of slaves as a legitimate return to their masters for protection and direction."[98]

These issues, like the mind-sets and theories that created them, were not unrelated, as proslavery paternalism reflected the ideology of anti-Blackness. The establishment of white supremacy as a religion in the Anglican Church emerged directly from the Puritanical theology of white superiority. According to Eric Weed, the correlation of white superiority and Black inferiority, based on the dichotomy of Christian and heathen, was evident in an ontology of white supremacy.[99] He asserts, "The very bedrock of white supremacy is constructed out of the symbols and traditions of Protestant Christianity as they developed over the past five centuries."[100]

AfricansinAmerica living during these historical periods and the resulting political and theological developments were saddled with navigating this treacherous terrain while attempting to construct their own faith systems and traditions, both within and without the existing religio-political structures.

The effects of anti-Blackness, hereditary heathenism, and proslavery paternalism, which emerged from centuries-old global theories of Black racial

---

[96]Eugene D. Genovese, *Roll, Jordan, Roll: The World the Slaves Made* (New York: Vintage Books, 1976), 5.

[97]Genovese, *Roll, Jordan, Roll*, 4

[98]Genovese, *Roll, Jordan, Roll*, 5.

[99]Eric A. Weed, *The Religion of White Supremacy in the United States* (Lanham, MD: Lexington Books, 2017), 3.

[100]Weed, *The Religion of White Supremacy in the United States*, xix.

inferiority, directly impacted worship practices and liturgical traditions of Black congregations, even independent ones. Some religious leaders of Black congregations superficially replicated acts and orders of worship from Eurocentric services with which they were familiar. Others fully adopted theological and doctrinal tenets of Calvinist (Puritan) and/or Anglican/Anglican-descended denominations and ordered worship services accordingly. The fallout of these decisions included losses and even negation of African heritage and Afro-centrism. Not only were performances of Africanisms/African retentions strongly discouraged or forbidden in many Black churches, African cosmological understandings of Creator, Spirit, and community were often abandoned in favor of Eurocentric ideologies, especially the adoption of much more individualistic, private, and economic understandings of Christianity. Wrestling with these perceived dichotomies and coupled with the internalization of anti-Blackness theories, led to the development of a double-consciousness regarding self, community, and worship.

6

Double-Consciousness and Evangelical Theology

It is a peculiar sensation, this double-consciousness, this sense of always looking at one's self through the eyes of others, of measuring one's soul by the tape of a world that looks on in amused contempt and pity. One ever feels his two-ness—an American, a Negro; two souls, two thoughts, two unreconciled strivings; two warring ideals in one dark body, whose dogged strength alone keeps it from being torn asunder.

—William Edward Burghardt Du Bois, *The Souls of Black Folk*

Since the 1903 publication of *The Souls of Black Folk*, Du Bois's concept of "dialectical double-consciousness" has been used in examining the historical development of *AfricansinAmerica*. The concept is also useful in exploring the impact of white supremacy on the development of Black worship and liturgical practice. Ibram Kendi regards Du Bois's concept as both antiracist and assimilationist.[1]

While Du Bois recognized and heralded the beauty and strength of the Negro people and fought vigorously for the dismantling of ideas and systems built on white racial superiority, his witness was weakened by his own classist ideas and politics of respectability. The notion of the "Talented Tenth" uplifting the race by "filtering culture downward to the masses through talent and character"[2] spoke of Du Bois's own struggle with his perceptions of Black inferiority. Du Bois expected Blacks to bear the responsibility for changing "racist White minds," through Black behavior, and justified some of the consequences of those racist minds, which placed an unfair burden on their Black victims. However, decades of forward movement by Black independent congregations would witness this very strategy of "uplift suasion" as a way of "becoming equal" to whites in worship.

[1]Ibram X. Kendi, *Stamped from the Beginning: The Definitive History of Racist Ideas in America* (New York: Bold Type Books, 2017), 288–294.

[2]Kendi, *Stamped from the Beginning*, 293.

During the antebellum period, *AfricansinAmerica* had little choice but to live within the dialectic of this double-consciousness. Surviving enslavement meant making oneself as palatable as possible to the white gaze and mind. It is perhaps here that the "dogged strength" mentioned in the opening quotation was most needed, for none but the most tenacious in heart and mind could withstand the ceaseless stress of deciphering how to please and satisfy the capricious whims of slaveholders. To navigate entirely different languages, commands, and instructions for work, all while being forced to endure backbreaking labor, and attempt to elude punishment for even imperceptible or imagined infractions had to be exhausting and mind-numbing. Furthermore, reconciling in one's mind that one has no human or civil rights, because one's humanity is no longer recognized or honored, had to cause some inner destruction, simply because of the ridiculousness of it all. From chiefs, queens, and kings of reigndoms, respected and revered medicine women and men, shamans and griots, warriors and hunters, cooks and herbalists, to despised and disparaged chattel, on auction blocks and whipping posts, how could one be free one day and a slave the next? Surely, in order to survive, a duality had to be created in one's mind—one place of temporal acquiescence and another of eternal significance; one to feign gracious compliance and another to imagine, and perhaps plan, active resistance. As ethicist Riggins Earl asserts:

> This means that the slave had to live between the creative tension that was derived from the dialectical awareness of "having a body" and "being body." The notion of "having a body" suggested that one's body was the master's property. It was recognizing the body's ability to make use of instruments and utensils as it inhabits the world. The slave came to accept his or her body as "myself in my lived concreteness." His or her body becomes a recognizable incarnate feeling, willing, and thinking project. The slave as the living embodiment of his or her experience is able to say "I can" as well as "I feel."[3]

This incarnate feeling, willing, and thinking process would be expressed in the experiences and development of Black worship and liturgical practices from the invisible institution to the present. Unfortunately, the negative impact of double-consciousness would make its presence known and felt as well.

As stated earlier, worship in the invisible institution emerged from the mental, emotional, and psychological needs and states of enslaved *AfricansinAmerica*. As they began to navigate the terrain of the New World, literally and figuratively, they created space to remember and honor the gods of their

[3]Riggins R. Earl, *Dark Symbols, Obscure Signs: God, Self, and Community in the Slave Mind* (Knoxville: University of Tennessee Press, 2003), 174–175.

ancestors. As they were introduced, either intentionally or by happenstance, to the slaveholders' god and religion, they syncretized some beliefs and practices during their secret worship services. Prayers that might have been uttered in native tongues to native spirits and ancestors melded into and meshed with prayers to the Christian deity—to Jesus and to the Holy Spirit. Chants and melodies from African shores infused lyrics about biblical heroes and personal testimonies and became spirituals. Exhortations took on the character of sermons that extolled the power and righteousness of God, the sweet majesty of King Jesus, and paralleled the trials and victories of the Israelites with those present in the brush arbor. Conjuring the Spirit and subsequent possession experiences were recast as conversion experiences that required being indwelt by the Spirit of God.

In some ways, this worship, in and of itself, was representative of double-consciousness. The syncretization of African worship with white theological beliefs and practices surely rang differently in the ears of those who remembered the Motherland. Even many born on these shores surely sensed an entirely different cosmological foundation for worship, particularly in slaveholder churches. However, as *AfricansinAmerica* were catechized and taught various doctrines and practices, the insidious presence of white supremacy permeated their experiences and tainted the development of worship and liturgical practices in their own independent congregations. I have already discussed theologies and doctrines that undergirded prevailing denominational bodies in colonial society and white supremacist notions that emerged from these. Let us now examine how these notions impacted the worship and liturgical patterns of *AfricansinAmerica* from the antebellum period through Reconstruction.

Anti-Blackness, Visible Sainthood, and Double Self-Negation

Historian Kristopher Norris notes three examples of dualism that constitute early thought on materiality.[4] The first was the adoption into Christianity of Platonic dualisms of spiritual and material, soul and body, privileging the spiritual/soul while demonizing the material/body. The second was Docetism, a theological strand that denied Christ's embodiment and characterized the body as sinful. A third example of duality was the use of color labels in early Christian texts. Norris writes, "Blackness, within the biblical and social

[4]Kristopher Norris, *Witnessing Whiteness: Confronting White Supremacy in the American Church* (New York: Oxford University Press, 2020), 44–45.

imagination of the early church, and later of European Christians, symbolized sin and evil."[5] The dichotomy of spirit versus flesh, as well as anti-Blackness prejudice imbued Protestant theologies and, where enslavement was concerned, caused those responsible for catechizing *AfricansinAmerica* to ask: "Can we teach slaves to think of themselves as being absolutely worthless before God without being guilty of thinking of ourselves more highly than we ought before God?"[6] According to Earl, this theological issue "constituted a hermeneutical circle of double negativity."[7] At the core of this enterprise was the wicked assignment to teach the enslaved that they were "black of body" and "blacker of soul," meaning that they "only had negative value, both before masters and God."[8] One of the prayers taught to enslaved persons evinces this double negation of body and soul, "O Thou great God, the Maker of all creatures, I, a poor black sinner, black in body and still blacker in sin."[9] Further evidence of this concept of anti-Blackness is present in testimonies of the conversion experiences of enslaved Blacks. Those who saw themselves on the brink of hell testified to seeing the devil, "a great monster," "his face as black as it could be and his eyes are red as fire."[10] The guide who is sent to lead the person from hell to heaven is generally reported to be a "little white man" who takes them to Jesus or God, both of whom are described most often as white. As Sobel describes it, heaven is also characterized by whiteness, its walls, white, angelic robes, white, and a white Holy Mother.[11] In becoming converted, enslaved persons also became "white." Clifton Johnson records such testimonies, "The next morning everything was white. My hands were like snow. They just shined. They looked like the sun was on them," and "in a world of light, peace, and harmony . . . I didn't see anything but myself and other white images like me."[12]

Perhaps the most devastating theological concept regarding anti-Blackness and visible sainthood was the idea that being converted and/or baptized could make one "white as snow," or wash one "white as snow." To need to become "white as snow" in conversion would have originated in the idea that being created Black was the result of being accursed by God or created originally by the devil. Earl recounts one such creation story found in African American

[5]Norris, *Witnessing Whiteness*, 45.

[6]Earl, *Dark Symbols, Obscure Signs*, 22.

[7]Earl, *Dark Symbols, Obscure Signs*, 22.

[8]Earl, *Dark Symbols, Obscure Signs*, 22.

[9]Henry Pattillo, *The plain planter's family assistant: containing an address to husbands and wives, children and servants . . .* (Wilmington, DE: Printed by James Adams, 1787), 51–52.

[10]Sobel, *Trabelin' On: The Slave Journey to an Afro-Baptist Faith* (Princeton, NJ: Princeton University Press, 1988), 112.

[11]Sobel, *Trabelin On*, 112–113.

[12]Clifton H. Johnson, ed., *God Struck Me Dead: Religious Conversion Experiences and Autobiographies of Ex-slaves* (Philadelphia: Pilgrim Press, 1969), 64–173.

folklore.[13] According to the story, God created the white race, and out of rebellion for being thrown out of heaven, Satan created the Black race. This creature initially had no life or soul, as the devil could only make the human shape of a man, but because God felt sorry for the creature, God decided to give it both the same breath and soul of whites. While God is viewed here as being the only entity powerful enough to bestow true being/life on the creature (evidence of an enslaved theological concept of the devil as ultimately powerless against God), it is still telling that Blacks would be willing at all to believe and repeat this negative portrayal of their creation. Being washed or made "white as snow" was the only way that Blacks could hope to achieve salvation. As mentioned previously, the Protestant catechetical process that many enslaved persons underwent assured them that the white blood of Jesus would save them from their Blackness. This white supremacist theological and ontological perspective would continue to inform and permeate Black worship and liturgy through the present day.

The Impact of Double Self-Negation

Living with and attempting to overcome one's Blackness in worship had long-lasting deleterious effects on Black worshippers. During the colonial and early republic periods, it caused enslaved persons to experience an even deeper estrangement from their African heritages. If being Black in color was the thing that caused their dreadful circumstances, then one way to overcome this was to be "not Black." For those who internalized this idea, they worked and strove to rid themselves of the "stain" of Blackness, which meant taking on as many of the characteristics of whiteness as propriety would allow. Aligning oneself with the slaveholder or overseer, being overly accommodating and pleasant to curry favor, using any product available to whiten or lighten one's skin, and imitating any of the ways that whiteness behaved with the intent of "appearing" white were some ways *AfricansinAmerica* attempted to overcome the burden of Blackness.

AfricansinAmerica who wanted to overcome the association of Blackness with evil or sin fought this stigma religiously. They sought catechesis and conversion as a way of becoming, not only "not black," but white. White was considered holy, pure, and righteous, and the only way for Blacks to achieve this same spiritual, not bodily, status was to be converted. This was the basis of Cotton Mather's and others' calls for Blacks to be converted—they would be able to achieve whiteness for their souls. Blacks who followed this line of reasoning sought to be excellent students, and

[13]Earl, *Dark Symbols, Obscure Signs*, 51.

many became excellent exemplars—of white Christianity. Doing so meant renouncing, negating, or neglecting any worship or liturgical practice that may have appeared African in origin. This meant praying prayers to the Christian deity only, in a manner that would have been deemed respectful and orderly, singing hymns in the appropriate tune and rhythm set by the song leader, listening quietly and reverently to sermons, without uttering any response, and restraining any emotional outburst that might have occurred in response to a particular act of worship. Moreover, enslaved persons would be expected to affirm their belief in and allegiance to the system of enslavement and their place in it.

The anti-Africanness of antebellum white Christianity would germinate and continue to grow and spread as independent Black congregations arose in the American North and South. One of the first signs of this anti-Africanness was the continuation of many independent Black churches to remain within, adopt, or adapt the names of the denominations out of which they arose. If Black worshippers had experienced the sting and slander of white supremacist oppression in white Baptist, Methodist, and Presbyterian churches, why would they continue to carry the names of these denominations when they became independent? This practice was particularly interesting in the development of African Methodism. When Richard Allen and Absalom Jones left St. George's Methodist Episcopal Church, they formed the Free African Society. Wilmore notes that the Free African Society "represented the first bid for independence among blacks in the North" and was "a fellowship of black citizens who craved independence and social progress without reference to the creeds and confessions used in most of the mainline white churches."[14] However, when Allen decided to form a church, he kept the word, "African," but added the name of the very group that had oppressed him and other Blacks. One might argue that Black churches kept these names because they had been catechized within them and felt that the faith tradition in and of itself held no oppressive will and exacted no oppressive behavior toward them. However, what faith traditions were they following, exactly? If they were the faith traditions of colonized, English/white Christianity that enslaved persons had been taught and converted within, did that not make these traditions bastardized versions of Christianity? Did those who learned and quoted slave catechisms realize that they were underscoring their own devaluation as they recited them? Did enslaved and free *Africans-inAmerica* who had experienced conversion and baptism realize that the double negation characteristic of and present in "official" conversions and baptisms in white churches compromised and corrupted the presentations

[14]Gayraud S. Wilmore, *Black Religion and Black Radicalism: An Interpretation of the Religious History of African Americans* (Maryknoll, NY: Orbis Books, 1998), 108.

and representations of these faith traditions? To be sure, many did, which is why some Blacks wanted nothing to do with Christianity, before or after Emancipation. Others fought for the recognition and valuation of Black personhood in all aspects within traditional denominational structures, "eating the fish and spitting out the bones," as it were. Still others became members of denominations that recognized, from inception, the worth of all humanity, regardless of race or color.

A second sign of anti-Africanness in these independent Black congregations was also related to denominationalism. Not only did many of these congregations keep the names of the white denominations that preceded them, they also retained theological doctrines of these denominations. As noted, many of these theological tenets were based on English/white ideologies of white superiority and related oppressive beliefs, particularly as they were lived out on American soil. Calvinist doctrines of providence, total depravity, and divine election became, in the sermons and catechisms of English settlers, weapons of racist exclusion and support for the practice of enslavement. Anglican ideologies of Christian superiority based on race resulted in hereditary heathenism and white paternalism. These theologies and ideologies would not be identified as anti-African and rooted out, but would become embodied in many Black congregations, as the oppressed became the oppressor, practicing in some ways their own brand of separation from other Blacks they considered heathen, uneducated, too dark, or too emotive in worship.

Independent Black congregations exhibited a third sign of anti-Africanness—the retention of worship and liturgical practices experienced in white congregations, coupled with the denigration and extraction of African and African-related rituals and worship practices. Black Baptist and Methodist bodies generally retained the orders of worship and related acts in their congregational services, even though many of the acts and orders did not necessarily meet their needs. This became a source of conflict as some church leaders witnessed the display of Africanisms that were part of the invisible institution. Some churches sang the old spirituals and lined hymns and participated in the shout after the official worship service ended. They allowed emotion to permeate the worship space, made room for extemporaneous prayers, songs, testimonies, and exhortations, and gave themselves over to the move of the Holy Ghost, as they shouted, danced, and were slain in the Spirit. Black Methodist bishops Richard Allen and Daniel Payne were two of the more insistent leaders encouraging a dismissal of the old ways and assimilation to the English/white ways of worshipping. Bishop Allen, the first to compile hymns into a book specifically for Black worship, composed several himself, most written in the tradition of English/white hymnody and song, and they even sometimes included admonitions against emotionalism:

> Such groaning and shouting, it sets me to doubting,
> I fear such religion is only a dream;
> The preachers are stamping, the people were jumping,
> And screaming so loud that I neither could hear,
> Either praying or preaching, such horrible screeching
> 'Twas truly offensive to all that were there.[15]

Bishop Payne was even more forceful in his determination to stop the display of African retentions in Black Methodist worship. He castigates a group who sang the "music of the folk" through a story he tells of his experience with church members participating in a ring shout:

> I have mentioned the "Praying and Singing Bands" elsewhere. . . . I attended a "bush meeting," where I went to please the pastor whose circuit I was visiting. After the sermon they formed a ring, and with coats off sung, clapped their hands, and stamped their feet in a most ridiculous and heathenish way. I requested the pastor to go and stop their dancing. At his request, they stopped their dancing and clapping of hands, but remained singing and rocking their bodies to and fro. . . . I then went, and taking their leader by the arm requested him to desist and to sit down and sing in a rational manner. I told him also that it was a heathenish way to worship and disgraceful to themselves, the race, and the Christian name.[16]

Lest we think this reaction was only true of Black Methodist leaders and churches, scholar Walter Pitts describes how, after the excitement and fervor of the Great Awakening camp meetings died down, there was among Baptists and Methodists in the South an "enticement of respectability within reach."[17] He recounts how the enthusiastic singing of the camp meeting was gone, although Ira Sankey and Dwight Moody attempted to recapture it with a collection of camp meeting spirituals, *Sacred Songs and Solos with Standard Hymns*. Pitts notes, however, that the effort was found lacking, as these songs were more solemn than original camp meeting songs. Also, these new songs called for piano and organ accompaniment, for many churches a sign of upward mobility and respect. Pitts writes:

---

[15]Wendell P. Whalum, "Black Hymnody," in *Readings in African American Church Music* (Chicago: GIA Publications, 2001), 170.

[16]Whalum, "Black Hymnody," 171.

[17]Walter F. Pitts Jr., *Old Ship of Zion: The Afro-Baptist Ritual in the African Diaspora* (New York: Oxford University Press, 1993), 82.

> Just as many freed men and women changed their old slave names and former gloomy styles of dress, and took up new social activities, so black Baptists adopted these white-inspired songs as a symbol of their new free status. The antebellum Negro spiritual, while still sung in the Afro-Baptist ritual, was pushed aside as a stigma reminding blacks of their recent condition of servitude.[18]

Many former enslaved persons and those born into freedom shared these attitudes. Robert Russa Moton, who would succeed Booker T. Washington as the second principal of Tuskegee Institute, matriculated through Hampton Institute in the years from 1872 to 1875. While there, he heard the choir singing Negro spirituals in chapel services and was dispirited, stating:

> I was disappointed to hear these songs sung by educated people and in an educational institution. I had expected to hear regular church music such as would be sung by white people mostly, and such as was written as I supposed by white people also. I had come to school to learn to do things differently; to sing, to speak, and to use the language, and of course, the music, not of coloured people but of white people.[19]

Moton's visit home after having been at Hampton for a while is also telling:

> While I very much enjoyed the two weeks at home visiting old scenes and old friends, there was nevertheless an element of sadness in it all. The dwellings, barns, and fences were unkempt; there was an air of disorder and confusion about most things and most people also; our church and the choir, as well as the sermon of our pastor, seemed so different and disappointing and so unsatisfactory that I was rather relieved to get away from it. Before leaving I discussed this with my mother; but she felt that things were not so very different, that many things were actually better, that the difference was with me. I had changed.[20]

Furthermore, Moton objected to "exhibiting the religious and emotional side of our people to white folks; for I supposed the latter listened to these songs simply for entertainment and perhaps amusement."[21]

Lawrence Levine notes that this attitude "typified that of many first- and

---

[18]Pitts, *Old Ship of Zion*, 82–83.

[19]Robert Russa Moton, *Finding a Way Out: An Autobiography* (Garden City, NY: Doubleday, Page, 1921), 8.

[20]Moton, *Finding a Way Out*, 15.

[21]Moton, *Finding a Way Out*, 8.

second-generation freedmen who were determined to divest themselves of the behavioral patterns of a slave past."[22] Other former enslaved persons, however, decried the loss of what they considered authentic Black worship and liturgical expressions. One retorted, "Dese young heads ain't wuth killin', fur dey don't keer bout de Bible nor de ole hymns . . . de big organ and de eddication has done took all de Holy Spirit out en 'em till dey ain't no better wid der dances and cuttin' up dan de white folks."[23] Others noted, "Deze last few y'ars day hab got ter stylish ter shout." "They have college preachers now. They don't have religion like they used to."[24] One can ascertain from these divergent points of view another impact of double self-negation on the development of Black worship and liturgical practice. It was a double-edged sword. On the one hand, it caused those who had an understandable desire to better themselves and their circumstances through education to feel ashamed of the Blackness of their culture. On the other hand, it caused those who believed the "old-time ways" of Black religious culture significant and transformative to disparage newer ways of worship and, perhaps most detrimental, to disparage formal education.

The Impact of Evangelical Movements[25]

The Great Awakenings

According to Whelchel, the First Great Awakening "laid the foundation and provided opportunities for the religious and intellectual development of Africans."[26] Hundreds, if not thousands, of *AfricansinAmerica*, enslaved and free, learned to read because of the evangelistic efforts and publications of preachers such as George Whitefield, Jonathan Edwards, Samuel Davies, and John Wesley, and the educational outreach of the Society for the Propagation of the Gospel. During the revivals, Black worshippers experienced music, preaching, and the frenzy of spirit possession akin to what they experienced

---

[22]Lawrence Levine, *Black Culture and Black Consciousness: Afro-American Folk Thought from Slavery to Freedom*, 30th anniv. ed. (New York: Oxford University Press, 2007), 162.

[23]Jeannette Robinson Murphy, "The Survival of African Music in America," *Popular Science Monthly* 55 (1899): 662, 664.

[24]WPA manuscripts, interview with Lillie Knox, South Carolina File, Archive of Folk Song. B. Fisk University, Unwritten History, 46–47.

[25]Here I am using Charles Irons's definition of "evangelicals," who are "those Protestants who set themselves apart from Catholics, Anglicans, Congregationalists, and other Christians by their emphasis on a personal, saving experience of faith and their sense of mission." Charles Irons, *The Origins of Proslavery Christianity* (Chapel Hill: University of North Carolina Press, 2008), 3.

[26]Love Henry Whelchel, *Hell without Fire: Conversion in Slave Religion* (Nashville, TN: Abingdon Press, 2002), 55.

in the invisible institution. Michael Battle notes that "the importance of the felt presence of the Holy Spirit through shouting and spirit possession relates to a similar importance placed on an Africanism of spirit possession that goes back to West African spiritual practices."[27] Additionally, *AfricansinAmerica* were much more attuned and open to the immediacy of the revival conversion experience than the catechetical enterprise of Puritanism and Anglicanism. Battle further expounds on the theological ethos that permeated the First Great Awakening:

> In addition to some natural harmony with African sensibilities, the Great Awakening's theological ethos appealed to Africans because of its reliance on a "priesthood of all believers" mentality. Anyone who was saved and felt a calling to preach could do so. Because preaching the gospel was not limited to those with formal training, this allowed enslaved Africans to assume a role seldom held before this period. . . . In areas without restrictions concerning black preachers, those of African descent could proclaim the gospel as authoritatively as white preachers.[28]

Though a new theological viewpoint was being preached at this time, with some evangelists proclaiming that Blacks, as well as whites, had souls and could be converted just as efficaciously, white supremacy would continue to make its presence felt. Many in the white religious establishment did not approve of Blacks preaching and teaching the gospel. John Barnett, an Anglican minister in Brunswick, North Carolina, expressed his displeasure in 1766: "The illiterate among them are their Teachers [and] even Negroes speak in their meetings."[29] Furthermore, most evangelists who preached the equality of Negro souls did not preach an abolitionist message. Jonathan Edwards, for example, criticized the slave trade, but not domestic slavery. George Whitefield endorsed the institution of slavery, whether out of his concern for slave insurrections or his own popularity among slaveholders.

After the Revolutionary War, America began to expand west. Evangelists set out to proselytize settlers in these new territories, inciting a Second Great Awakening. Frances Fitzgerald notes the desire of frontier revivalists to "reach their audience by creating a simplified form of evangelicalism: a folk religion characterized by disdain for authority and tradition."[30] American frontier

---

[27]Michael Battle, *The Black Church in America: African American Christian Spirituality* (Malden, MA: Blackwell, 2006), 61.

[28]Battle, *The Black Church in America*, 61.

[29]Jeffrey J. Crow, *The Black Experience in Revolutionary North Carolina* (Raleigh, NC: Department of Cultural Resources, 1977), 47.

[30]Frances Fitzgerald, *The Evangelicals: The Struggle to Shape America* (New York: Simon and Schuster, 2017), 26.

worship was characterized by a hostility toward liturgical worship which was evident in spontaneous and extemporaneous prayers, exuberant singing, a primacy of preaching, informal enthusiasm, and experiences of emotional ecstasy. There were no set forms or orders of worship, leaving worship open to a spirit of immediacy.[31] The influence of revivalism on frontier worship "reduced all prayer and praise and reading of the Scriptures to 'preliminary exercises' sacrificing other elements for the experience or shared ecstasy of conversion."[32]

Because this iteration of the crusade happened in isolated frontier towns, Blacks and whites of every Protestant denomination, and even some Native Americans, were involved and caught up in the fervor and frenzy of revivalism. The first camp meeting recorded was led by Rev. James McGready, a Presbyterian minister, and occurred in Logan County, Kentucky, in July 1800, drawing thousands of attendees.[33]

Later camp meetings were dominated by Methodist ministers and would be held in numerous locations including West Virginia, Delaware, the Carolinas, Tennessee, and further south. Under the influence of preachers such as Charles Grandison Finney, Dwight L. Moody, and Billy Sunday, evangelical Christianity spread rapidly through camp meeting revivals. Occasionally, Black ministers would preach at the camp meetings, having served as circuit riders, itinerant preachers in the Methodist tradition. Black churches began to hold their own camp meetings, common in the Philadelphia-Baltimore-New York circuit of the AME church, and drew thousands of worshippers, Black and white. Raboteau describes the religious mutuality shared in the camp-meeting experience: "In the fervor of religious worship, master and slave, white and Black, could be found sharing a common event, professing a common faith and experiencing a common ecstasy."[34] The two denominations that most benefited from these revivals were the Baptist and the Methodist, noting phenomenal membership growth during this time. Baptist churches grew from 40,000 members to almost 300,000, and the ranks of the Methodist Episcopal Church South, which had separated from the Anglican Church in the 1780s, swelled from 40,000 in 1790 to over a million members by 1865, reaching 5 million members, Black and white, by 1890. Although both the First and Second Great Awakenings presented opportunities for *AfricansinAmerica* to participate in worship that was perhaps more akin to

[31]Kenneth Phifer, *A Protestant Case for Liturgical Renewal* (Philadelphia: Westminster Press, 1965), 103.

[32]James Hastings Nichols, "The Rediscovery of Puritan Worship," *Christian Century* (April 25, 1951).

[33]Eileen Southern, *The Music of Black Americans: A History*, 2nd ed. (New York: W. W. Norton, 1983), 82.

[34]Albert Raboteau, *Slave Religion: The Invisible Institution in the Antebellum South* (New York: Oxford University Press, 2004), 314.

African customs or sensibilities, the experiences were still characterized by white supremacist beliefs and customs.

Black Independent Movements and Religious Sects

The Great Migration also had serious effects on Black religious bodies. Wilmore cites three factors impacting Black churches. First, he notes that many Black churches turned inward from the world as they "tried to fend off the encroaching gloom and pathology of the ghetto."[35] Most were not overly concerned with social issues, because of either otherworldly or apathetic perspectives about Black life in America. Second, the overwhelming number of churches and rivalries between them diluted the power of potential economic and political influence Black churches might have exacted. This led to the everyday "man on the street" becoming disillusioned with the church, leveling criticisms such as "church is a racket," "churches are a waste of time and money," "ministers don't practice what they preach," and the "church places too much emphasis on money."[36] Third, mainstream churches were facing competition from secular organizations that provided suitable, even preferred, outlets for community socializing and organizing.[37]

While many mainline Black denominations and their churches were seeking "respectability" according to white definitions, imitating their theologies and worship practices, others had "no great admiration for their oppressors, nor any desire to 'be like white folks.' "[38] During this period, cities in the North would see a rise in Black independent movements like Marcus Garvey's United Negro Improvement Association (UNIA), Noble Drew Ali's Moorish Science Temple of America, the Black Jews, and W. D. Fard's Nation of Islam. These movements highlighted Black consciousness, liberation, and self-sufficiency while rejecting Christianity and Black assimilation into dominant culture. Judith Weisenfeld notes:

> The black "cities within cities" of the early twentieth century offer many compelling stories . . . of migrants from the South and immigrants from the Caribbean encountering preachers and teachers who insisted that black people had been laboring under the false belief that they were Negroes. These preachers proclaimed that this misconception had caused social, economic, psychological, physical, and spiritual damage, and they taught that the only way to restore complete health for individuals

---

[35] Wilmore, *Black Religion and Black Radicalism*, 191.
[36] Wilmore, *Black Religion and Black Radicalism*, 191–192.
[37] Wilmore, *Black Religion and Black Radicalism*, 191–193.
[38] Wilmore, *Black Religion and Black Radicalism*, 171.

and black people as a whole was to embrace one's true identity. They found many eager listeners, hungry for meaning in an urban world of simultaneous promise and hardship and in an era of continued struggle for civil rights.[39]

Another response to the decline of popularity in mainline Black churches was the rise of Black Pentecostal sects such as the Mt. Sinai Holy Church of America, Inc., pastored by Bishop Ida Robinson, Father Divine's Peace Mission, and the United House of Prayer for All People led by Bishop Marcelino Manuel de Graça, better known as "Daddy Grace." These churches followed a separatist, puritanical moral ethic and engaged in ecstatic, charismatic worship popular with Blacks who desired what they considered a more authentic worship experience than that of the mainline Black congregations.

A New Era in Evangelical Christianity

Following the end of the Second World War, churches saw a rapid increase in membership, from seventy to a hundred million people during the decade from 1945 to 1955. The outcome of the Scopes trial had been a major blow for fundamentalism while heralding the modernist cause for liberal progressivism. The reputation of fundamentalism as a theological and ecclesiological system primarily inhabited by rural, uneducated "Bible-thumpers" caused many churches identified with fundamentalism to become separatists, abstaining from popular culture and taboo recreational activities, and spending as much time in church during the week as possible. As a result, many fundamentalist churches and groups felt a sense of isolation and second-class American status in a country that seemed literally hell-bent on progressivism. In response, fundamentalists regrouped and attempted to build a multidenominational coalition known as the National Association of Evangelicals (NAE). They hoped to garner enough social and political clout to engender a national revival, "a new era in evangelical Christianity."[40] This new era would be popularized by evangelists across the nation, through radio broadcasts such as Charles Fuller's *The Old Fashioned Revival Hour* and Percy Crawford's *Young People's Church of the Air*, and in-person "Youth for Christ" rallies that formed a generation of revivalists and televangelists determined to win back America for Christ.[41]

[39]Judith Weisenfeld, *New World A-Coming: Black Religion and Racial Identity during the Great Migration* (New York: New York University Press, 2016), 23–24.

[40]Joel A. Carpenter, *Revive Us Again: The Reawakening of American Fundamentalism* (New York: Oxford University Press, 1997), 146–149.

[41]Fitzgerald, *The Evangelicals*, 143–167.

The most well known revivalist of the twentieth century was Billy Graham. Born William Franklin Graham in 1918, Graham grew up on a farm in Charlotte, North Carolina. Though he grew up as a Presbyterian, he was "born again" at a tent revival when he was sixteen. He attended Florida Bible Institute, a school designed to train evangelists, and began preaching publicly after experiencing a "serious spiritual crisis" while in school. Following the lead of one of the school deans, Graham was re-baptized, ordained a Southern Baptist, and left Florida for Wheaton College. He led revivals around the country, preaching against Communism, paganism, and the immorality of modern America. He met with a modicum of success until he was credited with saving Stuart Hamblen, a popular radio show host, and given front-page newspaper space by William Randolph Hearst. Graham was catapulted into national stardom and preached around the globe a fundamentalist, evangelical, Christian doctrine painted in apocalyptic imagery in hopes of inspiring "a spiritual ecumenical movement of all born-again believers."[42] Graham had the ear of and gave counsel to several U.S. presidents, and partly because of his preaching and influence, American patriotism became America's civil religion.

As this infusion of evangelicalism into American politics was occurring, Pentecostalism was experiencing a major upsurge. Privileging ecstatic experiences over doctrine and particular orders of worship, Pentecostals sought worship where the Holy Spirit was welcome to manifest at any time, especially through prophetic utterances and miraculous healings.[43] One of the first to claim the ability to perform these miracles and to broadcast them publicly on television was Asa Alonso Allen. He was also one of the first to claim financial success based on faith principles and divine reciprocity. This would become significant in his ministry, as competition from other prominent faith healers grew stiffer. Allen would emphasize a prosperity gospel and his use of "the word of faith"—or the power to speak things into existence. Another element of Allen's ministry that became a standard of televangelist broadcasts was the inclusion of inspirational sacred music performed by professional singers or groups.

Ironically, Allen's divine healing ministry was inspired after attending a tent revival held by Oral Roberts. Roberts's revivals differed from Graham's in that he would elicit sponsorship from a group of pastors or the regional Pentecostal fellowship in a particular city before conducting the revival. Furthermore, Roberts built a broadcasting conglomerate to disseminate his meetings in the U.S. and Canada. Considered a faith healer, Roberts sent "deliverance cloths" across the country and suggested appropriate donations

[42]William G. McLoughlin Jr., *Billy Graham: Revivalist in a Secular Age* (New York: Ronald Press, 1960), 483.

[43]Fitzgerald, *The Evangelicals*, 212.

according to the cloths' healing powers. Roberts, like Allen, amended the focus of his ministry from healing to prosperity and called those who contributed to saving souls his "faith partners," promising to share with them "spiritual, physical, and financial" blessings.[44] Roberts's studio broadcasts followed the televangelistic pattern of the time, with short sermons, inspirational singers, and occasional celebrity guest-star interviews.

Other early televangelists who followed Allen's and Roberts's examples include Jerry Falwell, Jim and Tammy Faye Bakker, Pat Robertson, Jimmy Swaggart, Kenneth Copeland, and Benny Hinn. Several important insights that Fitzgerald makes about televised Pentecostalism include:

> Other traditions depended on liturgy and/or the exegesis of biblical texts, but Pentecostals could dispense with these drags on the airwaves. Further, they didn't need a church setting, for the move of the Holy Spirit could happen anywhere, including on a glitzy set with singers crooning in the background. Celebrity guests could recount "miracles" of being saved from dreadful accidents, or they could break down weeping as the spirit moved in the studio. Hosts could announce revelations from God, or they could relay the news that someone in their audience was just being healed of arthritis or a back injury. The shows were exciting, and all about immediate experience—as opposed to rational linear exposition.[45]

Falwell's broadcast, *The Old Time Gospel Hour*, Robertson's *700 Club*, the Bakkers' *PTL Club*, and *The Jimmy Swaggart Telecast*—four of the more visible and financially successful television ministries—all followed similar programming formats and gained (and lost) millions of viewers since their inceptions in the 1960s and 1970s. While not all necessarily preached an explicit prosperity gospel, all relied on television ratings and sponsors to continue broadcasting.

While a few of the evangelists mentioned enjoyed and curried political clout and favor, none used these to effect any significant changes for *Africansin-America*. Pentecostalism, generally, is more otherworldly focused. Nevertheless, Graham, Falwell, and Robertson all had multiple opportunities to use their significant national platforms to speak out against racial injustice. Graham openly criticized Martin Luther King's civil disobedience, while neither Falwell's Moral Majority nor Robertson's "Agenda for Public Action" addressed issues of social justice, choosing instead to prioritize issues of

---

[44]Fitzgerald, *The Evangelicals*, 215–217.
[45]Fitzgerald, *The Evangelicals*, 219–220.

abortion and same-gender sexuality. This stance, of course, was not limited to Pentecostals, nor televangelists. It was common among predominantly white theologically conservative denominations and ministries of the time. If any did address racial injustice, prevailing sentiments included calls for racial reconciliation rather than repentance and reparations, holding that racial injustice was a "sin" issue, not a justice issue, and thus had to be addressed by individuals rather than groups or the government.

Religious Race Records and Black Broadcasters

Right alongside the radio and television broadcasts of white evangelists were those of Black pastors and preachers. Before either of these, however, came religious race records. Preachers such as Rev. J. M. Gates, Rev. Calvin P. Dixon (known as the Black Billy Sunday), A. W. Nix, and Rev. Leora Ross allowed record companies, including Columbia, Victor, and Paramount, to capture their homiletical presentations for purchase.[46] However, companies did not record sermons only. They wanted to apprehend for their customers the essence of the Black worship experience, not because of its inherent importance, but because those records sold better. Early records allotted only three minutes for an opening hymn and sermon in total, and because companies wanted the full worship experience, singers would lift a hymn and often hum throughout the sermon, punctuating the preacher's cadence with encouraging responses.[47] This gave listeners the feeling of being in an actual worship service. The subject matter of these sermons most often centered on avoiding the pitfalls of sinful lifestyles, and preachers warned of fire and brimstone punishments for those not living a life of Christian piety. Records that featured sermons about societal ills like racism and poverty among Black communities were few and far between, for two main reasons: (1) it was difficult to preach about those topics within three minutes, and (2) those topics did not sell well to the average consumer.

Black religious radio programs brought the Black worship experience, particularly preaching, to an even larger American audience. Jonathan L. Walton mentions three broadcasters of note: Elder Solomon Lightfoot Michaux, Mother Rosa Horn, and Rev. C. L. Franklin. Elder Michaux produced his *Radio Church of God* program in Alexandria, Virginia, on WJSV, a small station which became the major broadcasting outlet on the eastern seaboard after CBS purchased it. An evangelical entrepreneur, Michaux owned several

---

[46]Lerone Martin, *Preaching on Wax: The Phonograph and the Shaping of Modern African American Religion (*New York: New York University Press, 2014).

[47]Jonathan L. Walton, *Watch This! The Ethics and Aesthetics of Black Televangelism* (New York: New York University Press, 2009), 33–37.

profitable businesses while positioning himself as a "radio prophet to the nation."[48] Mother Rosa Artimus Horn left Georgia for Indiana, settling in Brooklyn in 1926. She started the Pentecostal Faith Church in Harlem and her radio broadcast, *Radio Church of God of the Air* on station WHN. Known as the "Pray for me Priestess," Mother Horn enjoyed immense popularity, and her church boasted thousands of members, including James Baldwin during his teenage years.

The most prominent Black radio broadcaster during this time was the Rev. Clarence LaVaughn Franklin, who pastored the Salem Baptist Church in Detroit. He broadcast his church's Sunday night services at 10:00 p.m. on WJLB, one of Detroit's leading Black radio stations. Rev. Franklin's preaching produced two very notable legacies in Black homiletical development. The first was his preaching style, featuring a chanted cadence that came to be known as "hooping," which has been widely mimicked by men and women who witnessed Franklin's success, both as a pastor of a large Black congregation, and as a broadcasting legend, in radio and on wax.[49] The second was Franklin's demonstrated commitment to the Civil Rights Movement. Walton notes that Franklin "was an unabashed political progressive who advocated for civil rights legislation, sided with the working class, and promoted equitable socio-economic conditions for all American citizens."[50]

The Rise of Televangelism

As radio broadcasts gave way to the unmistakable influence of video, television became the preferred purveyor of religious broadcasting. Following in the tradition of revivalists Asa Alonso Allen and Oral Roberts, Frederick J. Eikerenkoetter II, better known as Rev. Ike, established his church, the Miracle Temple, in Boston. He began his ministry as a faith healer, but, with the relocation to Washington Heights and renovation of the former Loew's Theater, Rev. Ike changed his theological and philosophical ideology to "the Science of Living."[51] Influenced by southern rural Black evangelicalism, New

[48]While Michaux did speak on political issues, Walton notes that his comments most often reflected the popular political positions of the time, and therefore did not create significant undue conflict or trouble for Michaux.

[49]Franklin's sermons are still highly popular and available in CD and mp3 formats for the twenty-first-century listener. One of his sons in the ministry, Rev. Jasper Williams Jr., senior pastor of the Salem Bible Church in Atlanta, Georgia, has even taught a class on Franklin's preaching style, titled, *Hoopology 101*.

[50]Walton, *Watch This!*, 44.

[51]Eikerenkoetter describes "the Science of Living" as "self-image psychology. The ultimate goal is to teach the individual to be master of his own mind and affairs by changing his own self-image." Rev. Ike, "Rev. Ike Speaks On," in United Christian Evangelistic Association Publicity

Thought ideology, and Pentecostal worship styles, Rev. Ike's services drew thousands of attendees, and his radio and television broadcasts (from the church's own production studio) were heard and viewed by millions of people across the United States, Mexico, Canada, and the Caribbean.

Another significant influence of Roberts on Rev. Ike (and many others) was his method of securing financial resources for ministry. Roberts developed the "Blessing Pact," a financial partnership program based on an agrarian concept of planting and reaping, refashioned as a spiritual principle of sowing and harvesting. Members would sow a financial seed into Roberts's ministry, and in turn, he would pray that they would receive a tenfold return on their offerings. Roberts claimed that this principle followed the natural order of God's law: "Believers would reap materially in tenfold proportion to what they had sown materially by faith."[52] Undergirding Roberts's ideology of financial blessing was the scriptural verse, "I wish above all things that thou mayest prosper and be in health, even as thy soul prospereth" (3 John 2; KJV). This verse was foundational to Roberts's ministry and fund-raising efforts and would serve as the theological basis for his and many other ministries, particularly those in the Word of Faith movement.

Early religious broadcasting companies including Pat Robertson's CBN and Paul and Jan Crouch's Trinity Broadcasting Network (TBN) soon discovered the draw of Black preaching and worship. Realizing their audiences contained significant numbers of Black Americans, they began to include Black singers, preachers, and show hosts whose theological and political beliefs were in line with theirs, at least on the surface.[53] Rev. Fred K. Price, Bishop Carlton Pearson, Rev. E. V. Hill, BeBe and CeCe Winans, Rev. Andrae Crouch, Larnelle Harris, and Babbie Mason are just a few of the Black evangelists and singers who graced the stages of burgeoning programming on these networks. Later networks followed this trend, some catering primarily to Black audiences, including The Word Network, Black Entertainment Television (BET), and TVOne.[54] Bishop T. D. Jakes, the late Rev. Eddie Long, Dr. Juanita Bynum, and Pastor Creflo Dollar are four of the more well known and recognized figures whose religious broadcasts have been streamed around the globe, garnering millions of followers and dollars.

Part of the appeal of contemporary televised services are the aesthetics. Most of the sanctuaries are nontraditional, with large stages, rather than

Packet, United Christian Evangelistic Association, Boston, n.d. (received in 2005).

[52]Oral Roberts, "Do You Want God to Return Your Money Seven Times?" *America's Healing Magazine*, April 1954, 10.

[53]Walton, *Watch This!*, 85.

[54]BET and TVOne do not broadcast exclusively religious content, but each has dedicated religious programming times and shows.

pulpits and lecterns, enhanced with professional lighting and video screens. Instead of pews, attendees sit in amphitheaters or rows of cushioned chairs. If there is a choir, it is immense and populated by dozens, if not hundreds of singers. Generally, the music is provided by professional musicians, and most of the singing is performed or led by a praise team composed of professional singers. Very seldom is any religious iconography present, although the church's logo or a contemporary artistic rendering of a cross may be seen. The worship itself feels extemporaneous, though it may be planned down to the second. Musical selections are programmed to set the atmosphere and tone for worship, and for broadcast purposes, often are upbeat and lively, to give the appearance that everyone is inspired, joyful, and full of the Holy Spirit. If there is a slower music selection, it is often performed by a soloist, and is designed to elicit emotional responses that prepare the audience to receive the preacher's message. Preaching can range from charismatic, extemporaneous exhortations, to less emotive, yet still intense, teachings on some spiritual and/or biblical principle. While audiences are allowed, and perhaps encouraged, to respond in spiritually ecstatic fashion in worship, televised services are not stopped or altered to respond to these outbursts; ushers or other personnel simply attend to the people involved, and the service continues. For this reason, some pastors will simply televise certain portions of their services rather than the service in its entirety.

Most of these ministries fall into one of Walton's three categories of African American religious broadcasting: Neo-Pentecostal, Charismatic mainline churches, or Word of Faith.[55] "Neo-Pentecostal ministries," Walton observes, "originated from one of the recognized classical Pentecostal movements" and "integrate traditional Pentecostal beliefs with the cultural characteristics of the contemporary moment."[56] They are not separatists, in the traditional way of Pentecostalism; rather, they aim to convert the prevailing culture to Christ. These ministries are not characterized by austere or ascetic lifestyles but offer a variety of activities, ministerial and recreational, considered appealing by today's society. Accruing wealth is not taboo but is considered a sign of divine blessing. Further, neo-Pentecostals privilege scriptural texts regarding healing and deliverance over those concerned with hellfire and brimstone. Walton is careful to note, however, that neo-Pentecostals do not view the acquisition of wealth or material blessings to be a guaranteed right of all Christians; therefore, it is not a pure prosperity gospel.

Charismatic mainlines are ministries that emerge individually from one of the traditional Black mainline denominations. These ministries "integrate a

---

[55]Walton, *Watch This!*, 78.
[56]Walton, *Watch This!*, 79.

Pentecostal-like experiential encounter with the divine in worship."[57] While Charismatic mainline churches are more traditional in aesthetic presentation, in sanctuaries and clergy vestments, this is not to say they are outmoded or unfashionable. Worship in these churches is much more fluid and ecstatic in expression than mainline traditional churches, and members are encouraged to seek "levels of spiritual encounter and expression" and experiences that show "evidence of experiential encounters" with the Divine.

Word of Faith ministries are "an emerging, loosely organized fellowship of churches that belong to the larger neo-Charismatic movement."[58] While pastors of neo-Pentecostal and Charismatic mainline churches may apply tenets of the prosperity gospel in preaching and teaching, Word of Faith churches teach prosperity as a life principle and one of three core beliefs and practices.[59] Following "professed spiritual laws of scripture," Word of Faith adherents believe biblical texts are a contract between God and believers, and if believers honor this covenant relationship, they will receive all of God's promises, walk in spiritual authority and divine favor. A second core belief, positive confession ("naming it and claiming it"), is an indication of one's faith; conversely, speaking negatively over one's life indicates a lack of faith. Positive confession, coupled with knowing who one is in Christ, unlocks prosperity, which is available to everyone who follows these spiritual principles. True believers (those who keep their end of the contract) have the capacity to become millionaires, never become ill, and transcend "isms" of the world's systems by living a "higher life."[60] Worship in Word of Faith churches is dominated by the pastor's message. Choirs and musicians may perform during the worship service, but the focus is on hearing the Word as brought forth in the preaching moment.

Black liturgy has developed alongside and under the pervasive influences of double-consciousness, double self-negation, and evangelical theology. Original sins emerging from the theological tenets based on anti-Blackness, visible sainthood, colorism, and classism negatively impacted the development of liturgy and worship practices in Black congregations, denominations, and fellowships, leading some to break away from established churches and start independent movements and sects. The emergence of a new era in evangelical Christianity gave rise to radio and television broadcast revivalism, and bestowed celebrity status on preachers who became most publicly associated

[57]Walton, *Watch This!*, 86.

[58]Walton, *Watch This!*, 93.

[59]Milmon Harrison, *Righteous Riches: The Word of Faith Movement in Contemporary African American Religion* (New York: Oxford University Press, 2005), 10.

[60]Creflo A. Dollar, *The Color of Love: Understanding God's Answer to Racism, Separation, and Division* (Tulsa, OK: Harrison House, 1997), 187–190.

with the genre. While theological foundations of these movements may differ, there are many similarities in worship styles and sermon presentations. Though some early Black televangelists preached and affirmed the relationship between liturgy and justice, more often than not, most pastors of churches espousing evangelical theologies have not presented this link as a significant or essential connection. In the next chapter I will consider the development of the link between liturgy and justice in Black faith communities during Black freedom movements in America to ascertain why this connection has been crucial for the "sur-thrival" of *AfricansinAmerica*.

7

Liturgical Practice and Justice

Significant in the development of liturgical practice in the Black church is the link between worship and justice. As noted, throughout the antebellum period Black worshippers engaged in acts of prophetic resistance as they prayed, sang, exhorted, preached, and danced. In the invisible institution, they developed a liturgical process that, while extemporaneously performed, held meaning and was ordered to achieve maximum transformational impact. This process continued to evolve through praise/pray's house worship and the development of independent congregations and denominations. Through each stage of development, worship continued to be tied to the immediacy of Black life. Whatever was happening to Black people would be addressed in some way in Black worship. It may have been through prayers uttered for safety from white supremacist persecution or songs that lamented Black communal oppression, while affirming God's sovereignty and justice, or through preaching that directly addressed connections between the biblical text, Black suffering, and eschatological hope for deliverance.

The link between liturgical practices and justice was not a new phenomenon on American shores, but a retention of African cosmological worldviews centered on divine relationality and kinship. Despite efforts by human traffickers and slaveholders to divide and conquer African humanity, *AfricansinAmerica* devised methods of communication, and, as they learned ways of surviving in the New World, began to re-create the bonds of community as best they could. Worship became important, if not integral, to the formation of communal identity once enslaved persons were able to gather in their own spaces. This is not to suggest that every enslaved or free Black person attended worship in any space. However, once slaveholders began to catechize *AfricansinAmerica*, many were drawn to Christianity as a way of becoming free, literally or metaphorically. Even some who were not manumitted because of baptism and conversion reported feeling different afterwards, the experience having given them a new perspective, and they focused from that moment forward on otherworldly freedom and reward, awaiting the

Day of Judgment, when God would right every wrong. Others believed their newfound deliverance undergirded their rights to be free physically as well as spiritually, and propelled them to participate in righteous opposition to the practice of enslavement. While these two perspectives were conflicting, both were grounded in the view that the God of justice and righteousness was the Creator of all; therefore, African-descended persons were God's children, too, and deserved a right to live as free people.

These calls for freedom and deliverance found expression in historical movements that happened as *AfricansinAmerica* took initiative to change racial and economic status quos and reacted to the ongoing domestic terrorism of white supremacy. Here, I examine Emancipation and Reconstruction, the Harlem Renaissance, the Great Migration, and the Civil Rights Movement of the 1950s and 1960s. Germane to my discussion will be the development of worship and liturgical practices in Black independent congregations during and as a result of these movements.

Emancipation and Reconstruction

The American nation was built upon the institution of enslavement of Africans and their descendants. Just as there were always proponents of slavery, there were always opponents to it. According to James Dormon and Robert Jones: "Antislavery attitudes existed in America from the very beginning of chattel servitude. Most blacks, slave and free, opposed the existence of racial slavery. However, . . . antislavery feelings were not limited to blacks. White Quakers and many white Methodists opposed the institution from the outset."[1] Certainly, antislavery feelings on the parts of sympathetic whites did not mean they desired a society where Black persons were fully integrated and equal; it simply meant they doubted or disagreed with the notion of enslavement, "in a Christian nation professing to believe in the promise of the Declaration of Independence."[2]

Many enslaved and free Blacks, however, did desire such a society, and would engage in all manner of resistance to enslavement, becoming known as abolitionists, and calling for an immediate end to the practice. Several scholars note the impact of antislavery publications on the American landscape, including the first Black abolitionist newspaper, *Freedom's Journal*, David Walker's *Walker's Appeal, in Four Articles*, William Lloyd Garrison's *The Liberator*, and Frederick Douglass's *North Star*. These and other writ-

[1]James H. Dormon and Robert R. Jones, *The Afro-American Experience: A Cultural History through Emancipation* (New York: John Wiley and Sons, 1974), 228.

[2]Dormon and Jones, *The Afro-American Experience*, 229.

ings pressed diligently the case for immediate cessation of involuntary and immoral servitude. Samuel E. Cornish, one of the men responsible for *Freedom's Journal*, was a Black Presbyterian minister who organized the first Black Presbyterian congregation in New York. Ministry was one of the few professions that Blacks could inhabit as leaders and use to foment change for their communities. As independent congregations and denominations arose, Black ministers within them often used their platforms to preach and teach antislavery sentiments and uplift for the race. To understand the link between liturgy and justice, we will explore the impact of this abolitionist work on denominational development.

African Methodist Resistance

Richard Allen began the Free African Society as a response to the maltreatment of Black people in a Christian context. It was founded, not only as a place of worship, but also to meet the needs for social welfare and community uplift in Black communities in Philadelphia. Gayraud Wilmore asserts:

> The interests of the Free African societies were both religious and secular, and never became exclusively one or the other. They created, therefore, the classic pattern for the black church in the United States—a pattern of religious commitment that has a double focus: free and autonomous worship in the African American tradition, and the solidarity and social welfare of the black community.[3]

Wilmore notes how the marriage of worship with communal uplift became a sort of prophetic resistance that spread throughout African Methodism, causing a "rebelliousness" that led to several Black groups withdrawing from white Methodist churches to join either Allen's group or form their own.[4] Joseph Washington Jr. recounts how, after resistance to Black leadership, Black members withdrew from the John Street Methodist Church in New York City to form the African Methodist Episcopal Zion Church. From its founding, the AME Zion Church played a significant role in the abolitionist movement, with several of its churches serving as way stations on the Underground Railroad. And it was hailed by Frederick Douglass as instrumental in forming and shaping his gifts as a public speaker and freedom fighter.[5]

Dormon, Jones, and Wilmore note the influence of Black churches and other social organizations on the Negro Convention Movement, which began

---

[3]Gayraud S. Wilmore, *Black Religion and Black Radicalism: An Interpretation of the Religious History of African Americans* (Maryknoll, NY: Orbis Books, 1998), 108.

[4]Wilmore, *Black Religion and Black Radicalism*, 109.

[5]Wilmore, *Black Religion and Black Radicalism*, 115.

in 1830. These national meetings brought together representatives to discuss and formulate what, today, might be called a "national Black agenda." Black clergy sent delegates from their congregations to participate in conversations that resulted in specific demands regarding discrimination, economic advancement, and abolition. The use of conventions as a way of identifying goals and objectives for Black empowerment and advancement set a tone and pattern for Black Baptists who would employ this model after the Civil War for their own national meetings.

Black Baptist Resistance

James Melvin Washington attests that disdain for the continued discrimination experienced at the hands of white Baptists and a desire for self-determination are what spurred Black Baptists to form their own convention.[6] Following the Civil War, there was a very brief period where it seemed that Black people, especially in the South, could effect significant change in the ways their world had previously operated. During the Reconstruction era, there seemed, finally, to be an opportunity for Black people to enjoy a modicum of freedom and even exert political power, with the passage of the Thirteenth, Fourteenth, and Fifteenth Amendments to the Constitution and election of over a thousand Black men to political office. However, Reconstruction would last a scant fourteen years, and the backlash was that any gains—personal and political—made by Blacks would be brutally erased. The rise of the Ku Klux Klan, Black codes, Jim Crow laws, and other white supremacist disenfranchisements ensured that Black people and communities would not experience justice or equality in any great manner for almost another hundred years. It was during this "nadir"[7] that "the nationalist consciousness of the black Baptist church came of age," according to Evelyn Brooks Higginbotham,[8] She asserts:

> Race consciousness reached its apogee with the creation of the National Baptist Convention, U.S.A. in 1895. Determined to create a forum through which black people could voice their spiritual, economic, political, and social concerns, the convention's leaders equated racial self-determination with black denominational hegemony. . . . By the late

[6]James Melvin Washington, *Frustrated Fellowship: The Black Baptist Quest for Social Power* (Macon, GA: Mercer University Press, 1991), 38–45.

[7]Rayford W. Logan refers to the period between 1877 and 1901 when more than 2,500 Blacks were lynched as the "nadir," meaning the lowest point of fortune for an individual or organization. See Rayford W. Logan's *The Negro in American Life and Thought: The Nadir, 1877–1901* (New York: Dial Press, 1954).

[8]Evelyn Brooks Higginbotham, *Righteous Discontent: The Women's Movement in the Black Baptist Church, 1880–1920* (Cambridge, MA: Harvard University Press, 1994), 4.

> nineteenth and early twentieth centuries all the black denominations had established community institutions and advanced the philosophy of racial self-help. But it was in the black Baptist church where this philosophy found its largest following.[9]

As with independent Black denominations in the North, Black Baptists in the South played a significant role in publicizing the national crises of white supremacist terrorism and the continued struggle of Blacks to gain personal and collective freedom. "In 1900, Black Baptists at the local and state levels published forty-three newspapers, the great majority of which were located in the South."[10] Two that were national in scope and instrumental in helping develop a "Black civic vision" were *The Free Speech and Headlight* of Memphis, which employed Ida B. Wells-Barnett, and *The National Baptist Magazine*, a publication of the National Baptist Convention, which felt its literature must be "capable of keeping the identity and increasing race pride of the rising generation or they must be entirely overshadowed by the dominant race of this country."[11]

Black Pentecostal, Holiness, and Sanctified Church Resistance

William Seymour, a Black man born five years after the end of the Civil War, is credited with starting the Azusa Street Revival and the Pentecostal movement that swept the nation in the nascent days of the twentieth century. Born to former enslaved parents, Seymour grew up witnessing African worship practices of the invisible institution syncretized with Creole religion. Rejecting his Baptist heritage as an adult, Seymour joined the Holiness Church and met Charles Parham in 1905, in a church pastored by Lucy Farrow, a Black woman. Seymour studied under Parham, enduring segregated seating and Parham's racist ideologies in the classroom. He moved to Los Angeles to pastor a Nazarene church, where he was expelled for his preaching and insistence on glossolalia. After conducting prayer meetings with fellow Holiness refugees, Seymour experienced an explosive outpouring of the Spirit on Azusa Street that lasted three years. During this three-year revival, some white Pentecostals, including Parham, attempted to segregate and/or denounce its interracial composition. As a result of these conflicts, Seymour revised the doctrines, discipline, and constitution of the Pacific Apostolic Faith movement to recognize himself as "bishop" and guarantee that each successor would always be "a man of color."[12]

---

[9]Higginbotham, *Righteous Discontent*, 6.

[10]Higginbotham, *Righteous Discontent*, 11.

[11]William Edward Burghardt Du Bois, ed., *The Negro Church* (Atlanta: Atlanta University Press, 1903), 115.

[12]H. Vinson Synan, "William Joseph Seymour," in *Dictionary of Pentecostal and Charismatic*

Cheryl Sanders notes two stages of denominational racism in the Sanctified Church movement: "First, Blacks came out of Baptist and Methodist churches because of racism; then, they came out of Black Baptist and Methodist denominations because of a commitment to holiness."[13] For some, there was a third stage—reuniting with whites in denominational fellowships after whites had come out of other Protestant denominations. For whites, there was also a fourth stage—"coming out" of interracial denominations as a result of pressure from those committed to upholding segregation. Within the Sanctified Church movement, Sanders identifies five types of denominational churches. The first type she describes as a Black Holiness denomination that retains its Black Holiness identity after the Pentecostal revival, one such example being the Church of Christ Holiness, U.S.A., which was founded in 1894 by Charles Price Jones and Charles Harrison Mason, two ordained Baptist ministers who were "disfellowshipped" by the Baptists in Mississippi because of doctrinal differences. After Mason participated in the Azusa Street Revival and adopted Pentecostal teachings and practices, particularly speaking in tongues, he and Jones parted ways. This led to the establishment of the Church of God in Christ (COGIC), a second type of denomination—a Black Holiness denomination becoming a Black Pentecostal denomination.[14]

Ironically, the COGIC Church, the first Southern holiness denomination to be legally chartered, became interracial after white ministers flocked there to receive ordination. This was not to protest white supremacy, but to receive benefits as a legally bonded clergyperson, including performing marriages and claiming clergy rates on railroads. The other three types of denominations Sanders mentions all have interracial beginnings. When these groups were forming, racial lines were not distinct, and Black members were just as likely to hold leadership positions as whites. But as the various movements formed into denominations, and, particularly in the South where racial segregation was the norm, interracial Pentecostal groups found themselves conforming to societal pressure to follow this pattern. The two major Southern white Pentecostal denominations, the Church of God and the Pentecostal Holiness Church, began as interracial communions, having both Blacks and whites as ministers and members.[15] Again, because of racial tensions and attitudes in the South, and because of a demand from Black churches to self-govern, the Church of

Movements, ed. Stanley M. Burgess, Gary B. McGee, and Patrick H. Alexander (Grand Rapids, MI: Zondervan, 1988), 781.

[13]Cheryl J. Sanders, *Saints in Exile: The Holiness-Pentecostal Experience in African American Religion and Culture* (New York: Oxford University Press, 1996), 497–498.

[14]Sanders, *Saints in Exile*, 329–333.

[15]Vinson Synan, *The Holiness-Pentecostal Tradition: Charismatic Movements in the Twentieth Century*, 2nd ed. (Grand Rapids, MI: William B. Eerdmans, 1997), 175.

God allowed Black churches to separate, requiring, however that the General Overseer always be a white man. This policy continued from 1926 to 1966.[16]

The Harlem Renaissance

Between the Civil War and the Civil Rights Movement occurred an era that, at first glance, had little to do with the church or religion. But, looking closer, one can see parallels between the evolution of Black theological development and social commentary located in the artistry of the Harlem Renaissance. As Blacks fled the ubiquitous racism and economic oppression of the South for what they had heard or presumed were greener Northern pastures, many settled in Harlem, a northern, or uptown, section of Manhattan. In addition to Southern Blacks, Harlem became a popular destination for Black immigrants from the Caribbean, including Jamaica and Haiti. The wealth of cultural diversity produced an artistic and aesthetic legacy heretofore unknown. It was as Black as it was beautiful, creating entire art forms and genres that appealed to the proletariat as well as the intelligentsia. Its effects would be felt around the world and across America, in museums, dance halls, jazz and social clubs, literary societies, and in the church.

William Edward Burghardt Du Bois

An intellectual forerunner of the Harlem Renaissance was William Edward Burghardt Du Bois. Du Bois moved to New York City in 1910, having written a seminal masterwork on the sociological and cultural history of Black Americans. As Du Bois described it:

> I have sought here to sketch, in vague, uncertain outline, the spiritual world in which ten thousand Americans live and strive. . . . Leaving, then, the world of the white man, I have stepped within the Veil, raising it that you may view faintly its deeper recesses—the meaning of its religion, the passion of its human sorrow, and the struggle of its greater souls.[17]

Du Bois had come to New York as director of publicity for the NAACP and editor of *The Crisis*, its monthly publication. Because of his reputation as a brilliant political analyst, Du Bois was continually sought after for his opinion on politics, particularly as it impacted Black communities. He became aware of a new artistic movement occurring in New York and sought to find a way

[16]Synan, *The Holiness-Pentecostal Tradition*, 175.

[17]W. E. B. Du Bois, *The Souls of Black Folk* (New York: Vintage Books, 1990), 3.

to influence its development. As one scholar notes, "Long before the likes of Alain Locke and James Weldon Johnson, it was Du Bois who recognized that artistic and literary creation, far more than a crude acceptance of industrial education and discrimination, would prove black legitimacy in a world of white creation."[18] In *The Souls of Black Folk*, Du Bois makes three compelling assertions that, together, guide the conversation around the role of justice in the Black church: (1) "The Music of Negro religion . . . still remains the most original and beautiful expression of human life and longing yet born on American soil"; (2) "The Negro church of today is the social centre of Negro life in the United States, and the most characteristic expression of African character"; and (3) "For fifty years Negro religion thus transformed itself and identified itself with the dream of Abolition, until that which was a radical fad in the white North and an anarchistic plot in the white South had become a religion to the black world."[19] In the Harlem Renaissance, the work and words of Alain Locke, James Weldon Johnson, and Adam Clayton Powell Sr. bear out the foresight of Du Bois's claims.

Alain Locke

Ironically, one of the most well known artists of the Harlem Renaissance was neither artist, musician, nor Harlem resident. Alain Locke was, however, a philosopher, cultural critic, journalist, and academician, having been the first Black to be named a Rhodes Scholar. Like Du Bois, Locke had studied in Germany and returned to teach at a historically Black institution. Unlike Du Bois, Locke had been prevented from discussing race in his position as philosophy instructor at Howard University. He more than compensated for those lost opportunities with his 1925 publication, *The New Negro: Voices of the Harlem Renaissance*. Locke had been selected for this task by Paul Kellogg, editor-in-chief of *Survey* magazine, on the recommendation of Charles S. Johnson, editor of *Opportunity* magazine. The significance of this text to the visibility and justification of Black life and art cannot be overstated. At the time, it was a targeted response to white supremacist literature, which consistently and continually vilified Blacks as racially and culturally inferior, and threats to white purity and virtue. Moreover, *The New Negro* was not merely a text about Blacks, it was a text by Blacks about themselves. Contributions ranged from the most intellectual prose to poems and stories in the dialect and vernacular of "the folk." Locke asserts:

[18]Charles River Editors, *The Harlem Renaissance: The History and Legacy of Early 20th Century America's Most Influential Cultural Movement*. Charles River Editors. Kindle.

[19]Du Bois, *The Souls of Black Folk*, 138, 139, 145.

> In these pages, without ignoring either the fact that there are important interactions between the national and the race life, or that the attitude of America toward the Negro is as important a factor as the attitude of the Negro toward America, we have nevertheless concentrated upon self-expression and the forces and motives of self-determination. So far as he is culturally articulate, we shall let the Negro speak for himself.[20]

James Weldon Johnson

Perhaps most well-remembered as the lyricist of what has come to be known as the Negro National Anthem, "Lift Every Voice and Sing," James Weldon Johnson contributed a wealth of artistic material during the years surrounding the Harlem Renaissance. A native of Jacksonville, Florida, Johnson moved to New York City at the turn of the twentieth century after almost being lynched in a park. At the time, he was serving as principal of Stanton School, which he expanded into the first public high school for Blacks in the state of Florida. After moving to New York, Johnson joined the NAACP and worked with Du Bois to protest lynching and riots. While serving in this capacity, Johnson published several important works across literary genres, including *Fifty Years and Other Poems*, *The Book of American Negro Poetry*, *The First* and *Second Books of American Negro Spirituals* (both coauthored with his brother, J. Rosamond Johnson), *God's Trombones*, and *Black Manhattan.*

Though he considered himself an agnostic, Johnson grew up in the Methodist faith, and through his works, one sees an earnest respect for Black Christian religious traditions. In writing *God's Trombones*, Johnson stated that he wanted to "take the primitive stuff of the old-time Negro sermons and, through art-governed expression, make it into poetry."[21] Johnson's "aim was to interpret what was in the mind, to express, if possible, the dream to which, despite limitations, he strove to give utterance."[22] He was inspired to write "The Creation," the first of seven poems in the work, after hearing a black preacher's sermon delivery and performance in Kansas City. Johnson exclaimed that this "unnamed black preacher 'excited my envy,' and stirred 'something primordial in me.' "[23] Of his volumes of Negro spirituals, Johnson remarked, "I was in touch with the deepest revelation of the Negro's soul that has yet been made, and I felt myself attuned to it."[24]

---

[20]Alain Locke, Foreword to *The New Negro: Voices of the Harlem Renaissance*, ed. Alain Locke (New York: Touchstone, 1997), xxv.

[21]Rudolph P. Byrd, ed., *The Essential Writings of James Weldon Johnson* (New York: Random House, 2008), 143.

[22]Byrd, ed., *The Essential Writings of James Weldon Johnson*, 144.

[23]Byrd, ed., *The Essential Writings of James Weldon Johnson*, 143.

[24]Byrd, ed., *The Essential Writings of James Weldon Johnson*, 144.

Johnson articulates the effects of the Harlem Renaissance on prevailing American culture, claiming its impact on helping to dismantle racism:

> At any rate, it is the individual Negro artist that is now doing most to effect a crumbling of the inner walls of race prejudice; there are outer and inner walls. The emergence of the individual artist is the result of the same phenomenon that brought about the new evaluation and appreciation of the folk-art creations. But it should be borne in mind that the conscious Aframerican artist is not an entirely new thing. What is new about him is chiefly the evaluation and public recognition of his work.[25]

Johnson was careful to note that Blacks were not doing new work in the Harlem Renaissance, in the sense of creating or performing something with which they had no relation or familiarity. Rather, they were generating artistic endeavors from the same historic literary and musical legacies as their own African and African-descended heritage. The debilitating despair and bitterness many Blacks felt during this period in history was represented in the works of many Renaissance artists, and this New Negro movement gave them opportunities to address publicly, albeit behind an artistic veil, the disparities that continued to encumber Black communities. The world would serve as the Negro's audience and would acknowledge the authenticity of a Black aesthetic. Johnson remarks, "Doubtless it is also true that the new knowledge and opinions about the Negro in Africa—that he was not just a howling savage, that he had a culture, that he had produced a vital art—had directly affected opinion about the Negro in America."[26]

Adam Clayton Powell Sr. and the Abyssinian Baptist Church

Reggie Williams provides an excellent synopsis of this Black counternarrative of the Harlem Renaissance:

> The New Negro movement radically redefined the public and private characterization of black people. . . . The New Negro, as Locke and his authors appropriated the term, described the embrace of a contradictory, assertive black self-image in Harlem to deflect the negative, dehumanizing historical depictions of black people. The New Negro made demands, not concessions: "demands for a new social order, demands that blacks fight back against terror and violence, demands that blacks

[25]James Weldon Johnson, "Race Prejudice and the Negro Artist," in *The Essential Writings of James Weldon Johnson*, Rudolph P. Byrd, ed., 211–212.

[26]Johnson, "Race Prejudice and the Negro Artist," 215.

reconsider new notions of beauty, demands that Africa be freed from the bonds of imperialism."[27]

Williams explores not only the cultural impact of the Harlem Renaissance, but he also examines it through a theological lens. Focusing on Dietrich Bonhoeffer's experience with the Abyssinian Baptist Church in Harlem, Williams posits that Bonhoeffer was introduced to and steeped in a Black liberative theology of Christian social ethics. Central to the church's identity with education and mission regarding this theology was the church's pastor, the Reverend Adam Clayton Powell Sr. Powell taught and preached a communal gospel at Abyssinia, and argued that the church as the body of Christ was the center of community. Its inner functioning (priestly/otherworldly) and its social and political activity (prophetic/this-worldly) is ministry described as attention given to human suffering in the name of Christ. Powell called it "applied Christianity."[28]

Not only was the gospel that Powell preached based on a communal ethic, but it was infused with what would come to be known as Black liberation theology. A most jarring aspect of this theology would be the rejection of the white Christ, who Black Renaissance artists and intellectuals viewed as "complicit in race terror as an opiate Jesus who sedated black people, convincing them to accept racism and sub-humanity as divinely ordained by God."[29] The art, aesthetic, and theology of the Harlem Renaissance "rebuked" the violence and oppression of the white Christ as a way of "disrupting" white supremacy.[30]

As Powell struggled to help his congregation repudiate an accommodationist, otherworldly eschatology in favor of a more immediate and communal ethic of protest, he pushed for a church that demonstrated "their creeds by their deeds." Powell preached a theology of Black resistance against oppression, coupled with an ecclesiology of social and political action on behalf of the marginalized, and backed it up with his own personal financial offerings as well as those of his church. Because of Powell's message and the witness of Abyssinian Baptist Church, Bonhoeffer, Harlem, and the world were introduced to "a black tradition of Jesus that connected faithfulness to God, the recognition of suffering, and the presence of Christ as cosufferer."[31]

---

[27]Reggie L. Williams, *Bonhoeffer's Black Jesus: Harlem Renaissance Theology and an Ethic of Resistance* (Waco, TX: Baylor University Press, 2014), 31.

[28]Adam Clayton Powell, "The Church in Social Work," address delivered at the National Urban League Conference, Pittsburgh, PA., Friday, October 20, 1922, Abyssinian Baptist Church Archives.

[29]Williams, *Bonhoeffer's Black Jesus*, 54.

[30]Williams, *Bonhoeffer's Black Jesus*, 57.

[31]Williams, *Bonhoeffer's Black Jesus*, 109.

The Great Migration

Between 1916 and 1970, over six million Blacks moved from Southern towns to Northern cities. The first iteration, from 1916 to 1940, brought over one million Blacks to industrialized cities such as Chicago, Philadelphia, Detroit, and New York City; from 1940 to 1970, Blacks moved both to northern and western areas of the country. According to Love Henry Whelchel:

> The Great Migration was one of the defining events of the twentieth century. The Great Migration became the Exodus of the African-American experience, though unlike the Hebrews of the Old Testament, their release from their oppressors did not occur immediately after their release from slavery.[32]

Nicholas Lemann notes that "in sheer numbers, it outranks the migration of any other ethnic group—Italians, Irish, Jews, or Poles—to the United States. For blacks, the migration meant leaving what had always been their economic and social base in America and finding a new one."[33] Research conducted by W. T. B. Williams, the only Black member of a government-sponsored team sent to Florida to survey residents regarding the causes for the migration, uncovered deeper reasons for leaving than economic ones. According to some interviews, Black people were leaving because they were tired of second-class treatment. Milton Sernett writes that this insight, "suggests that the Great Migration was more than a response to the pull of industrial opportunity in the North. It was most fundamentally a mass movement in rebellion against conditions in the South, a revolution against oppression, which many participants and observers saw as a divinely inspired 'Second Emancipation.' "[34]

The effects of the Great Migration on Black churches were twofold: first, churches in the South experienced major declines in membership and clergy; and second, there was a rise in the number of new, smaller churches, called storefront churches, in the North, as a result of the negative reception many Black migrants experienced in the larger, more urban congregations, because of their more rural attire and ecstatic expressions in worship. Whelchel recounts the declamation of one Northern congregant, "No wonder white people laugh at colored people and their peculiar way of worshipping. I don't believe in

[32]Love Henry Whelchel, *The History and Heritage of African American Churches: A Way Out of No Way* (St. Paul, MN: Paragon House, 2011), loc. 2984–2993 of 7042, Kindle.

[33]Nicholas Lemann, *The Promised Land: The Great Black Migration and How It Changed America* (New York: Alfred A. Knopf, 1991), 6.

[34]Milton Sernett, *Bound for The Promised Land: African American Religion and The Great Migration* (Durham, NC: Duke University Press, 1997), 55.

shouting. I like a church that is quiet. I just can't appreciate clowning in any church."[35] Storefront churches offered a more welcoming atmosphere and a freer worship experience than the larger, wealthier, and often more class- and color-conscious Black church.

Another impact of the migration on northern Black churches was the collaboration between white factory owners looking for cheap, "safe" labor and Black pastors who were willing to curry white favor by engaging in exploitative practices to fill factories while they filled their church treasuries and personal pockets. As a result, "the traditional 'prophetic voice' of the Black churches was often silenced, and the stage was set for widespread corruption and abuse of the prestige and influence of churches."[36]

Scholars note that by the end of the 1930s, northern Black communities were saturated with churches. Though some were the institutional mainline denominational churches that had been present since the late 1700s, others were independent, storefront Sanctified, Pentecostal, Holiness, and "quasi-Baptist" congregations. Wilmore argues:

> The extreme proliferation of churches weakened the total impact of black religion in the urban community by reducing the economic and political viability of individual congregations and shattering the institutional solidity of the historic denominations. Rivalry between denominations and congregations, and among elite ministers vying for the most desirable pulpits and preferments—such as powerful national offices and bishoprics—diverted energies and money from self-help and community welfare concerns to ecclesiastical gamesmanship and institutional housekeeping.[37]

Weisenfeld notes that "Black religious and political leaders as well as black academics examining these developments worried that the theologies, practices, political attitudes, and social organization of the religio-racial movements undermined the case for African American fitness for full citizenship."[38] The Great Depression of 1929 was still raging at this time and, as its devastating effects wore on, many pastors and congregations who had participated in Black self-improvement or political movements focused on racial equality turned inward. Wilmore characterizes this period as the "deradicalization of the Black church."[39] Eric Lincoln and Lawrence Mamiya note the character-

[35]Whelchel, *History and Heritage of African-American Churches*, loc. 3064–3072, Kindle.

[36]James H. Cone, *Black Theology and Black Power* (New York: Seabury Press, 1969), 113–115.

[37]Wilmore, *Black Religion and Black Radicalism*, 191.

[38]Judith Weisenfeld, *New World A-Coming: Black Religion and Racial Identity during the Great Migration* (New York: New York University Press, 2016), 9–10.

[39]Wilmore, *Black Religion and Black Radicalism*, Chapter 7.

istics of this deradicalization, including "a strong conservative strain among black clergy and churches, a withdrawal from political and social involvement in their communities, and a pronounced tendency toward assimilation into mainstream white culture, accompanied by a denial of black heritage and black nationalism."[40]

In some sense, the link between liturgy and justice would begin to be severed during this period. As Black Christian denominations began to lose or renounce moral and political power, social organizations and other religious traditions began to rise, in response to communal needs for fellowship, worship, and uplift. According to Weisenfeld, "No longer bound by the traditions of small community life and often feeling that Protestant churches had failed to address their material needs and spiritual longings, many migrants set aside long-standing ways of thinking about black identity, claiming different histories and imagining new futures."[41] Critique and outright criticism of pastors, churches, and religion, as a whole, would begin to surface publicly, calling into question the influence and impact of the Black church as an institution.

The Civil Rights Movement

In examining the growth and evolution of the American Black Christian church from the invisible institution through the mid-twentieth century, it is clear that an ethic of justice was present in some shape or form. Coupled with a love for God has been a communal self-love that, in the white supremacist dominant culture, has also made an ethic of resistance necessary. The Civil Rights Movement was certainly no different, and, in some ways, was the pinnacle of the link between liturgy and justice in Black worship. Aldon Morris argues that "the larger significance of black protest lies in the fact that it is forever present in some form. This persistent struggle has given rise to a protest tradition, which includes hundreds of slave revolts, the underground railroad, numerous protest organization, the Garvey movement, and A. Philip Randolph's March on Washington Movement (MOWM)."[42]

Blacks in Northern and Southern cities had many of the same issues—poverty, inadequate housing, unemployment and underemployment; however, in the South, these issues were compounded by legislation that all but ensured the perpetuation of racist practices as a way of life—and violence when that

---

[40]C. Eric Lincoln and Lawrence Mamiya, *The Black Church in the African American Experience* (Durham, NC: Duke University Press, 1990), 209.

[41]Weisenfeld, *New World A-Coming*, 8.

[42]Aldon D. Morris, *The Origins of the Civil Rights Movement: Black Communities Organizing for Change* (New York: Free Press, 1984), x.

way of life was challenged. However, as Morris notes, segregation in the South did have some positive consequences, including the development of Black institutions and the building of close-knit communities due to limited housing and social options for recreation.[43] He asserts:

> It was the church more than any other institution that provided an escape from the harsh realities associated with domination. Inside its walls blacks were temporarily free to forget oppression while singing, listening, praying, and shouting. The church also provided an institutional setting where oppression could be openly discussed and resources could be developed to organize collective resistance.[44]

The role of the Black church during the Civil Rights Movement was of paramount importance; indeed, without the Black church, there may have been no significant movement, for it was that very entity that supplied the movement with ministers, money, and motivation to continue the struggle for liberation. Even the National Association for the Advancement of Colored People (NAACP) could not effect mass movements as well as the church because its decisions were mired in bureaucracy and protocol. Churches, however, were minister-led, meaning that, if the minister supported the cause, the church did, as well. Furthermore, churches provided sanctuaries for mass meetings several nights of the week and took up collections to fund the movement. Just as significant, Black churches were institutions free from the white gaze and white control and many of their ministers were paid well enough to be economically independent, meaning that they could preach justice and lead movements without fear of economic reprisals. For these reasons, most of the protest organizations that developed during the Civil Rights Movement emerged from, or had deep ties to, the Black church. The Baton Rouge Movement, Montgomery Improvement Association (MIA), Inter-Civic Council, Alabama Christian Movement for Human Rights, Southern Christian Leadership Conference (SCLC), and the Student Nonviolent Coordinating Committee were all church-related protest organizations, with either ministers or church members at their helms.

Reverend Wyatt Tee Walker, who, in 1960, was pastoring the Gillfield Baptist Church in Petersburg, Virginia, was one such minister. Walker was selected that year as the executive director of the SCLC because he had led successful protests in Petersburg, and because he was a minister. He became Martin Luther King's chief of staff, brought a more organized structure to SCLC, and increased its yearly revenues. However, Walker was clear about

---

[43]Morris, *The Origins of the Civil Rights Movement*, 3.
[44]Morris, *The Origins of the Civil Rights Movement*, 4.

the role of the Black church in Black communities and their protest movements. He stated:

> The Negro church, more than any other institution, has dominated every facet of life of the Southern Negro. Its role as it relates to the Negro Community is perhaps a unique sociological phenomenon. The Civil Rights struggle of the Negro community has directly paralleled the activity and development of the Negro church. The Negro church is his only forum, owned, operated and controlled by him; it affords him the broadest opportunity for social intercourse; it is generally the headquarters of the Negro's struggle for full citizenship.[45]

Walker outlined the following seven reasons why church and clergy had to be involved in the struggle for civil rights:

1. Churches are located in practically every community.
2. The church membership meets regularly, usually each Sunday, and often several members meet during the week.
3. Churches are committed to the idea of serving or meeting the basic needs of people and having genuine concern for their problems.
4. Church membership cuts across all age, economic, educational, class, and geographic lines in a community.
5. Churches have the resources and techniques for motivating people to voluntary and altruistic service.
6. The schedules of pastors can be adjusted more naturally and easily than those of persons in most other professions
7. Churches remain free from narrow partisan and divisive handicaps more easily than other types of organizations.[46]

In Montgomery, the Montgomery Improvement Association (MIA) was organized initially to address racist practices on city buses. Composed of a coalition of ministers from the Baptist and Interdenominational Ministerial Alliances, the MIA used weekly mass meetings as its primary vehicle of communication and motivation. These meetings were not run in a typical business manner, with a printed agenda, reports from committees, and comments from attendees. Rather, they were conducted very similarly to worship services, because the leaders, most of whom were pastors of the people present, knew the importance of music and preaching as a way of organizing and bolster-

[45]SCLC, "Southwide Voter Registration Prospectus," prepared by M. L. King Jr., and Wyatt Walker during 1961, Martin Luther King Jr. Papers, 1954–1968, Boston University, Boston, MA.

[46]SCLC, "Southwide Voter Registration Prospectus."

ing the courage of protesters. The liturgies of these meetings followed very closely the liturgies used on Sunday mornings, not because leaders were unable to envision other ways to conduct the meetings, but because they knew replicating this pattern would ensure attendance and participation. Morris notes that "mass participation at meetings was usually guaranteed because scripture, reading, prayer, and hymns were built directly into the program."[47] E. D. Nixon, who had organized the Black Brotherhood of Sleeping Car Porters Union in Montgomery and was the head of the Progressive Democrats and the MIA's first treasurer, remarked, "A whole lot of people came to the MIA meetings for no other reason than just to hear the music, some came to hear the folks who spoke."[48]

During the Birmingham movement, the SCLC held mass meetings on sixty-five consecutive nights, and each night the liturgy of scripture reading, prayer, and song was observed. The Birmingham Movement Choir, part of the Alabama Christian Movement for Human Rights (ACMHR), used music as an organizing and crowd participation tool. One of the leading songs in this effort was "Ninety-nine and a Half Won't Do," during which the tempo and volume increased to a final exhortation—"A hundred percent will do." Music, especially, had a way of inspiring and motivating protesters. Dr. King remarked on music's role in mass meetings:

> An important part of the mass meetings was the freedom songs. In a sense the freedom songs are the soul of the movement. . . . I have stood in a meeting with hundreds of youngsters and joined in while they sang, "Ain't Gonna Let Nobody Turn Me Round." It is not just a song; it is a resolve. A few minutes later, I have seen those same youngsters refuse to turn around before a pugnacious Bull Connor in command of men armed with power hoses. These songs bind us together, give us courage together, help us to march together.[49]

At a 1959 protest in Richmond, Virginia, Reverend Wyatt Tee Walker marched in the snow with more than 1,500 persons, and recounts:

> Two blocks from the Mosque it happened all over again. When I looked back across a small park that adjoins the Mosque I saw a number behind me that "no man could number." We began singing, at this point, the great hymns of the church and Negro spirituals. It was in these moments that I felt keenest the solidarity of our struggle in the south.[50]

---

[47]Morris, *The Origins of the Civil Rights Movement*, 47.

[48]Morris, *The Origins of the Civil Rights Movement*, 47.

[49]Morris, *The Origins of the Civil Rights Movement*, 257.

[50]Wyatt Walker, "Letter to M. L. King Jr.," January 16, 1959, Martin Luther King Jr. Papers, 1954–1968, Boston University, Boston, MA.

This music sung in marches and mass meetings was not a gimmick meant to temporarily attract crowds; neither were the prayers or sermons. They were, instead, direct descendants of a worship tradition forged in the crucible of oppression.

Just as these acts embodied the meanings of what it meant to be God's Black children in the invisible institution, they became codified as liturgical acts and expressions of faith and belief in Black independent congregations and organizations, and inspired generations of believers to resist dehumanization. The same "view of religion that guided the slave revolts of Nat Turner and Denmark Vesey, the work of Frederick Douglass and Harriet Tubman as they fought the slave regime, guided the leaders of the Civil Rights Movement, and became institutionalized through songs, sermons, and the literature of the church."[51] Morris contends it was a new message of "refocused religion" that seeped into the "revival" of mass meetings, a message that "a religion true to its nature must also be concerned about man's social conditions."[52] Perhaps after the deradicalization of many Black churches during the Great Migration, this "social gospel" message and ethic of prophetic resistance was being recovered and used to spur an entire country to live out the true meaning of its creeds. Maybe what had become familiar and comfortable about religion (and its liturgical practices) was recast in the mass meetings of the Civil Rights Movement as militant and even apocalyptic.

The messages of justice and righteousness and the ethic of prophetic resistance had always been present in the worship of *AfricansinAmerica*. The difference was that now these liturgical practices were used systematically to inspire revolution. The next chapter explores the prophetic nature of the biblical link between liturgy and justice and its relationship to the formation and sustainability of the Black church.

---

[51]Morris, 97.

[52]Martin Luther King Jr., *Stride toward Freedom* (New York: Harper and Row, 1958), 36.

8

The Unbroken Circle

In light of the impacts of Eurocentric theologies, double-consciousness, and evangelicalism on Black religion, worship, and liturgical practices across centuries, what, now, can the Black church say to the question, "Does the Black church still equate liturgy with justice?" Even if we argue, "The Black church is not monolithic," is there a preponderance of Black churches whose worship services connect liturgy with justice? Why is a connection between liturgy and justice significant? There are three main reasons: first, the biblical mandate that connects liturgy with justice; second, this connection is foundational to the formation of the Black church; and finally, the link between liturgy and justice is paramount to the sustainability of the Black church as an institution.

The Biblical Mandate

Regardless of theological doctrines or tenets, Black Christian churches generally accept the full canon of Christian scripture as sacred. Whether considered conservative or liberal in interpretation, most Black Christian churches preach and teach using both the Hebrew Scriptures and Greek New Testament. The biblical mandate connecting liturgy with justice runs through both sections, particularly in prophetic and gospel texts. Several well-known and often preached Hebrew passages include Micah 6:6–8, Amos 5:21–24, and Isaiah 58.

As a prophet, Micah was concerned with social justice. As someone from a small village outside the capital city of Judah, Micah probably saw many of the poor bear more than their share of oppression. He felt that the leaders were to blame for much of the people's suffering. They had not "done justice." To do justice meant to do what was right concerning all people—the poor as well as the wealthy. When God calls the people to judgment, they ask Micah how they shall come before the Lord. Their offerings grow increasingly larger and more excessive, ending in an offer of the firstborn. This pushes the point of acceptance to the extreme: Is there any way that one can be acceptable to God? Micah responds by changing the focus of the question to help the Israelites understand that though there is nothing they can do to make themselves acceptable before the Lord, God does expect a response for God's faithfulness:

> He has told you, O mortal, what is good;
> and what does the Lord require of you
> but to do justice, and to love kindness,
> and to walk humbly with your God? (Micah 6:8)

The people were focused on what they could do outwardly to show God that they were God's people. However, Micah's response indicates that God is not concerned with outside show. God is particularly not pleased with worship rituals or ceremonies performed by those who have not kept covenant with God and neighbor. Offering, a part of worship performed in response to God's faithfulness, though ritually appropriate, is not acceptable if not brought by a people who have lived righteously in God's sight.

> Take away from me the noise of your songs;
> I will not listen to the melody of your harps.
> But let justice roll down like waters,
> and righteousness like an ever-flowing stream. (Amos 5:23–24)

Worship is a gift; the ability and opportunity to exalt God, through various acts of singing, playing instruments, speaking verses, proclaiming the Good News, are all gifts made possible by the Creator. Offerings of these acts are gifts back to God. But here, God is refusing the gifts of God's people. Not only is God refusing the gifts, but God is emphatically stating that God hates these offerings being made, and they are to be taken away from God's presence. The language here is clear: God does not want the people's gift of worship. Why wouldn't God accept the people's worship? There is no indication in the text that the people have performed the rituals incorrectly. They are holding feasts and solemn assemblies in accordance with Israelite worshipping traditions. They are bringing the usually accepted sacrifices of grain and livestock, which are then being prepared for presentation in religious observances. But God refuses to accept them.

Verse 24 offers a glimmer of insight into God's refusal: "but let justice roll down like waters and righteousness like an ever-flowing stream." Justice and righteousness—words Amos has mentioned earlier—are here being offered seemingly as an alternative to the rites and rituals the people have been practicing in vain attempts to appease God. Biblical understandings of justice and righteousness are calls to live in right relationship with all people, treating everyone with equity, making sure that the orphan, the widow, and the stranger are taken care of, not abandoned or mistreated, and that the burdens of the oppressed are lifted from their shoulders. And the words here, "let justice roll down like waters . . . an ever-flowing stream," are the call to God's people that this is to be a daily practice, not a special event.

The people of Israel were observing the rituals of ceremonial worship, but living in ways that were antithetical to God's calls for justice and righteousness. They knew all the right words to say, all the right creeds and responses to affirm; but they weren't living out the meaning of these creeds and responses once they left the sanctuary of the Lord to go back out into the community. They were not being communally just; and for that, God refused to receive their sacrifices, knowing they did not come from contrite hearts. God refused to hear their melodious music, knowing that the songs of love and mercy would not extend to those they saw as beneath them. Their offerings were empty, void of the humility God sought in their hearts, and as a result, God would destroy them.

> Look, you serve your own interest on your fast day,
> and oppress all your workers.
> Look, you fast only to quarrel and to fight
> and to strike with a wicked fist.
> Such fasting as you do today
> will not make your voice heard on high . . .
> If you remove the yoke from among you,
> the pointing of the finger, the speaking of evil,
> if you offer your food to the hungry
> and satisfy the needs of the afflicted,
> then your light shall rise in the darkness
> and your gloom be like the noonday . . .
> Your ancient ruins shall be rebuilt;
> you shall raise up the foundations of many generations;
> you shall be called the repairer of the breach,
> the restorer of streets to live in. (Isaiah 58:3–4; 9–12)

In this passage, the prophet Isaiah is called to announce to the Israelites their sins against God. God notes how they seek God in an effort to know God's ways, as if they were a nation practicing righteousness. However, it is clear in the language the writer uses that God is not pleased with Israel's efforts. Once again, the people come before God with ritually appropriate actions but unclean hearts. They participate in ritual fasts, anointing themselves with ashes and dressing in sackcloth, participating in ceremonies that, on the surface, acknowledge human frailty and sinfulness. But God rejects their fasts as insincere and unacceptable because they have been serving their own interests rather than God's. God's interests, as noted by the writer, are to feed the hungry, clothe the naked, to let the oppressed go free, and to break the yoke of oppression. The Israelites' worship must be bound with justice and righteousness if it is to be deemed acceptable in God's sight. Once the Israelites link liturgy with justice, as a way of everyday life, treating their neighbors, orphans, widows, and strangers as God has instructed them, then their offerings and rituals will be accepted and they will be restored as a nation.

In the Gospels, Jesus speaks several times regarding particular acts of worship, including fellowship, prayer, offering, and the ritual of Eucharist. Jesus also has an in-depth conversation with a Samaritan woman during which he expounds on the meaning and practice of true worship. In each of his discourses regarding acts of worship and worship itself Jesus focuses on the authenticity of the experience, rather than the ritual. Regarding fellowship, Jesus promises his presence wherever two or three are gathered in his name (cf. Matt 18:20). Jesus prayed often, stressed the importance of prayer, and taught his disciples how to pray (cf. Matt 6:5–8 and Matt 6:9–13):

> "And whenever you pray, do not be like the hypocrites; for they love to stand and pray in the synagogues and at the street corners, so that they may be seen by others. Truly I tell you, they have received their reward. But whenever you pray, go into your room and shut the door and pray to your Father who is in secret; and your Father who sees in secret will reward you." (Matt 6:5–7)

Jesus is critiquing those who engage in the ritual act of prayer as a public display of piety and righteousness, calling them "hypocrites." He further criticizes the Gentiles for their verbosity while praying, instructing his disciples not to imitate or pattern their prayers in this manner. Jesus's use of the word "hypocrites" tells the reader that Jesus is not impressed by their prayers because their motivation is not authentic. This is an important distinction, for Jesus is not telling his disciples not to pray corporately but, rather, to make sure their prayer comes from a sincere desire to communicate with the Divine; not in an attempt to impress anyone with feigned humility or holiness, speaking ability, or excessive vocabulary.

What is significant about the Lord's Prayer (cf. Matt 6:9–13) is its communal nature. Jesus does not teach them a prayer using singular pronouns; he does not teach them to say, "My Father," or "Give me this day my daily bread." Rather, he uses plural pronouns to indicate communal, collective supplications. This indicates that the prayer should be spoken by the gathered group. Moreover, Jesus's phrases regarding daily sustenance, the forgiveness of debts, and rescue from trial indicates that the group not only avers a collective belief in God and God's power to effect God's will, but that what affects the individual also affects the community. If one professes to be part of a community, it is not enough to say, "God, send me enough for today." One is called to join with others in the community to ask for sufficient sustenance for everyone involved. Likewise, debts are not viewed as individual responsibilities, which indicates that the debts to which Jesus is referring are not necessarily financial, but a reference to any sin that would cause a person to be out of right relationship with another. The second half of the phrase regarding debts, "as we forgive our debtors," is an example of reciprocity, a further indication of the communal nature of Jesus's prayer. To be forgiven, one must be willing to forgive. Finally, the appeal to be rescued from the time of trial may indicate Jesus's prescient knowledge that his followers will be persecuted, and thus will need to stand together as a collective unit against oppression.

Jesus teaches his disciples to be just as restrained in their public giving of offerings as they are in public prayer. He tells them:

> "So whenever you give alms, do not sound a trumpet before you, as the hypocrites do in the synagogues and in the streets, so that they may be praised by others. Truly I tell you, they have received their reward. But when you give alms, do not let your left hand know what your right hand is doing, so that your alms may be done in secret; and your Father who sees in secret will reward you." (Matt 6:2–4)

Again, this does not seem to be a proscription against public giving, for Jesus says, "when you give alms." Rather, it is a caveat against giving alms as a way of looking "holy" in public. Indeed, Jesus begins the sixth chapter of Matthew warning his disciples against "practicing piety in public," as a show of one's righteousness, for the reward of public praise. Jesus, like the prophets in the Hebrew Scriptures, warns his audience of the dangers of empty worship, the temptation to participate in ritual out of habit or expectation, the lure of public praise, and most detrimental, observing communal worship rituals while forgoing communal responsibilities. Indeed, Jesus saves his harshest criticisms regarding inauthentic worship for the religious rulers and teachers of the Law:

> "Woe to you, scribes and Pharisees, hypocrites! For you clean the outside of the cup and of the plate, but inside they are full of greed and self-indulgence." (Matt 23:25)

For Jesus, there can be no authentic worship without justice; to engage in worship rituals without practicing justice in all areas of life is to make a mockery of worship.

Three passages conclude this section on the biblical mandate linking worship and justice. The first is Jesus's encounter with the Samaritan woman at the well, in John 4:

> The woman said to him, "Sir, I see that you are a prophet. Our ancestors worshiped on this mountain, but you say that the place where people must worship is in Jerusalem." Jesus said to her, "Woman, believe me, the hour is coming when you will worship the Father neither on this mountain nor in Jerusalem. You worship what you do not know; we worship what we know, for salvation is from the Jews. But the hour is coming, and is now here, when the true worshipers will worship the Father in spirit and truth, for the Father seeks such as these to worship him. God is spirit, and those who worship him must worship in spirit and truth." (John 4:19–24)

Jesus has come to a well in Samaria and is engaging in dialogue with a Samaritan woman, violating several cultural taboos, based on gender and ethnicity. During their dialogue, Jesus reveals knowledge about the woman that causes her to refer to him as a prophet. That leads her to ask him a question about appropriate worship. Jesus responds by turning her understanding of worship on its head. Where she is concerned with correct observances of ritual, Jesus, once again, reveals prophetic knowledge about true worship. Jesus's breaking of social and religious taboos is significant, as he communicates with a foreign enemy (a woman, no less!) as an equal conversation partner, engaging in theological and eschatological dialogue with her as one whose humanity is worthy of recognition. Moreover, Jesus does not exclude her or her kinspeople from being heir to this eschatological worship participation. While Jesus reminds her that salvation is "from the Jews," it is not only for the Jews. The ability to worship the true God is not an exclusive invitation to the privileged insider, but an open invitation to those who will abide by God's calls to justice and righteousness. This shifts the notion of "God's chosen people" to any who walk in God's way of communal love, responsibility, and accountability, regardless of ethnicity, race, gender, sexuality, class, or church affiliation.

The second passage is Jesus's institution of the Eucharist or Holy Communion that is recorded in all three Synoptic Gospels:

> While they were eating, Jesus took a loaf of bread, and after blessing it he broke it, gave it to the disciples, and said, "Take, eat; this is my

body." Then he took a cup, and after giving thanks he gave it to them, saying, "Drink from it, all of you; for this is my blood of the covenant, which is poured out for many for the forgiveness of sins. I tell you, I will never again drink of this fruit of the vine until that day when I drink it new with you in my Father's kingdom." (Matt 26:26–29)

Here, Jesus is sharing a meal with his disciples, what would come to be known as his last meal or supper with them before his arrest and subsequent crucifixion. While eating, Jesus takes the common elements of bread and wine and uses them to establish a communal ritual designed to create a sense of being one with him and one with each other. The covenant (some translations use the modifier "new") to which Jesus refers is the one he has instituted with his ministry and the offering of his body and blood. Again, this ritual is characterized by communal actions and the continued formation of communal identity. They are gathered for a communal meal, Jesus takes communal elements, distributes them communally, and establishes a communal covenant that offers communal forgiveness. The message is clear: as a follower of the way of Jesus, there is no individual identity, no individual consciousness, only a communal ontology, or way of being. That means that the individual's life is tied to community, the individual is responsible to community and the community helps meet the individual's needs.

The last passage is taken from Jesus's sermon in Luke 4. He opens the scroll and locates the following passage from Isaiah 61:1–2:

"The Spirit of the Lord is upon me,
because he has anointed me
to bring good news to the poor.
He has sent me to proclaim release to the captives
and recovery of sight to the blind,
to let the oppressed go free,
to proclaim the year of the Lord's favor." (Luke 4:18–19)

Writing to a post-exilic people, the prophet Isaiah was providing words of comfort and restoration to those who had been oppressed and who were in mourning, giving them a praise in place of their collective lament. Jesus chooses this text perhaps to accomplish similar objectives—to give a people who were under Roman oppression a reason to hope amid their despair. The prophet's message links communal liturgy with communal justice, preaching good news of liberation to the poor and imprisoned and restoration of sight to the blind, under the unction of the Holy Spirit. Jesus builds his ministry upon this text, proclaiming communal liberation and restoration for anyone willing to follow his example. To engage in these actions is to connect the worship of the Creator with the communal justice the Creator mandates.

Liturgy and Justice as Foundational to the Black Church

I have discussed the inception and formation of Black Christian religion, liturgy, and worship in the United States and how *AfricansinAmerica*—enslaved and free—perceived and responded to the hypocritical nature of white Christianity on American shores. In this section I merely reiterate the significance of this link in the formation of Black Christian religion and religious experience and that it continues to be foundational to the Black church and should still be considered a necessary part of the formation of Black Christian religious traditions and experiences. The invisible institution emerged from the need for *AfricansinAmerica* to engage in what they believed were authentic religious experiences.

Through each historical period in American history, there has been a corresponding period of development in Black Christian religious traditions and experiences. Each period of development, in some way, contained or reflected threads of the preceding period, whether the succeeding iterations perpetuated previous modes of religious thought and expression, expanded, refashioned, or reformulated them, or discarded them in favor of new concepts and ideas. Overall, however, within each period were responses from Black Christian movements and institutions that evince connections between liturgy and justice, in attempts to address God's call for communal righteousness among God's people. The necessity of having a liturgy infused with justice created the invisible institution, inspired slave revolts, served as the impetus for the creation of independent Black Christian congregations, catalyzed the Civil Rights Movement, spurred the development of Black liberation theology, and continues to stimulate intellectual and religious discourse across liberative theological frameworks. It is this very link, along with African retentions of rites, rituals, worship elements, and music that make Black American Christianity unique and significant.

The Sustainability of the Black Church

On May 25, 2020, George Floyd, a forty-six-year-old unarmed Black man, was killed while being arrested in Minneapolis, after a convenience store clerk called 911 to report the man allegedly using a counterfeit bill. Police officers restrained Mr. Floyd, and one knelt on his neck for eight minutes and 46 seconds, cutting off his breath until he died. This death once again reignited a firestorm of protests and riots across the country; a firestorm that had never completely died out after the death of Trayvon Martin, an unarmed seventeen-year-old Black boy who was shot and killed on his way home from a neighborhood convenience store by a neighborhood watch volunteer. In the seven years between Trayvon Martin's and George Floyd's murders, there have been numerous high-profile cases of unarmed Black people killed by police officers and vigilantes. With each report, protests rage, and while Black clergy and church members have participated, the Black church, as an institution, has not been centered in these efforts. Watson Jones III stated in a recent radio podcast:

> While you may have had many black pastors and clergy who may have shown up at events, and you may have had a lot of people from black churches who were at these marches and protests, from 2014 to the present, by and large, this has not been a theological movement. It hasn't been a movement that has started in the basements of churches, in prayer meetings, and altars that flooded out into the street.[1]

In a 2020 interview with Ferguson, Missouri, pastor and activist Brenda Salter McNeil, McNeil recounted how young Ferguson activists took the institutional church to task because of its failure to address systemic racial injustice in the United States. Furthermore, they railed against the church's culture of homophobia and misogyny. During this meeting, Pastor Salter McNeil and other clergy members asked the activists how the church could support them; they responded harshly: "They told us that they hated the church's misogyny and hypocrisy, and how we treated LGBTQ people. They said, 'It seems like you work harder to keep people out of the church than to let them in.' "[2]

The leading protest movement since 2013 has been the Black Lives Matter movement, "a global organization in the US, UK, and Canada, whose mission is to eradicate white supremacy and build local power to intervene in violence inflicted on Black communities by the state and vigilantes."[3] It was founded by three Black women, Alicia Garza, Patrisse Cullors, and Opal Tometi, in response to the acquittal of Trayvon Martin's killer. The link

---

[1]Morgan Lee, "Where the Black Church Is in the Black Lives Matter Movement," Quick to Listen Podcast, Episode 16, https://www.christianitytoday.com.

[2]Eliza Griswold, "How Black Lives Matter Is Changing the Church," *New Yorker*, August 30, 2020, accessed December 8, 2020, https://www.newyorker.com.

[3]"Black Lives Matter: ABOUT," accessed December 5, 2020, https://blacklivesmatter.com.

titled "HERSTORY" on the Black Lives Matter website tells the origin and purposes of the movement:

> Black Lives Matter is an ideological and political intervention in a world where Black lives are systematically and intentionally targeted for demise. . . . Black liberation movements in this country have created room, space, and leadership mostly for Black heterosexual, cisgender men—leaving women, queer and transgender people, and others either out of the movement or in the background to move the work forward with little or no recognition. . . . To maximize our movement muscle, and to be intentional about not replicating harmful practices that excluded so many in past movements for liberation, we made a commitment to placing those at the margins closer to the center.[4]

In this story of origin, there is a clear critique of institutions whose liberative activism performs and is performed in particular ways by particular people, in this case, Black heterosexual, cisgender men. The Black church historically has functioned in this manner, from the staunch refusal to ordain women that continues to this day in some Black denominations and independent churches, to the exclusion of same-gender loving persons from clergy ordination, marriage rites, leadership roles, or even membership. Though women may now be ordained in many Black denominations and churches,[5] they still are often subject to rampant sexism, including marginalization, exclusion from leadership roles, and sexual harassment. The Black church's failure to address the systemic ills of sexism, heteronormativity, and homophobia within its own ranks weakens its moral authority and claims of liberative activism. The link between liturgy and justice demands that the worship of a God of liberation requires that the liberative work done in the name of this God would be for all creation, in order that all might live into God's calling and purpose for their lives. Working to make the link between liturgy and justice for all creation evident and inherent in Black churches is essential if the Black church as an institution is to sustain itself.

If the Black church was formed in and through an ethic of resistance with obvious and critical links between its liturgy and the justice it sought for its people that caused it to become the leading institution in Black communities for over a century, why does it find itself now decentered in Black justice movements? Moreover, why is it now suffering from decline and serious critiques from those within and without its walls? Certainly, all mainline

[4]"Black Lives Matter: HERSTORY," accessed December 5, 2020, https://blacklivesmatter.com.

[5]To date, there are no historically Black denominations whose doctrine affirms the ordination of same-gender loving persons.

denominations have suffered declines in membership and attendance for the past twenty years, but in national polls, Black people still constitute one of the most religious demographics in this country. Though, according to statistics, Black Americans are more likely than the general public to be Protestant Christians,[6] there has been a downward trend in church affiliations and attendance in the last two decades. Furthermore, there has been a rise in Blacks who identify as "nones," meaning having no religious affiliation, particularly among millennials (ages 24–39) and Generation Y (ages 8–23).[7] Why are Black churches experiencing this downward trend, particularly in certain generations? In one especially telling article, Meagan Jordan tells her story of growing up in the Black church, participating fully in activities through her high school years. After a Sunday service during which the female pastor began to preach against same-gender loving sexuality (Jordan believes in response to the entrance of a rumored lesbian), Jordan began questioning her church membership. She recounts:

> The preacher returned to her seat thinking she'd spoken the word of God, but in actuality unknowingly led two people (that I know of) away from the church that day. The woman never returned again and although forced to go to church under the roof and rules of my parents, I began to mentally and spiritually check-out.[8]

Jordan wrote this article in response to an article by *Washington Post* columnist Christine Emba that critiqued millennials who had stopped attending church, stating that they were too busy gaming, indulging in other recreational activities, or focused on career goals to attend church regularly.[9] Jordan rebuts:

> Black millennials aren't leaving the church because we are too driven in our respective careers, we're leaving because our faith is broadening. And we're resonating with the traditional spiritual beliefs of our ancestors. . . . In the past, Christian spaces left millennials without refuge to worship and thrive spiritually. The argument that we are leaving the church because we want to clink mimosa glasses around is irresponsible and deserves further discussion. We are leaving in search of a practice[s]

---

[6]David Masci, Besheer Mohamed, and Gregory A. Smith, "Black Americans Are More Likely Than Overall Public to Be Christian, Protestant," Fact Tank, April 23, 2018, accessed December 2, 2020, https://www.pewresearch.org.

[7]"Blacks Who Are Unaffiliated (Religious 'Nones')," Pew Research Center, accessed December 2, 2020, https://www.pewforum.org.

[8]Meagan Jordan, "Millennials Aren't Skipping Church, the Black Church Is Skipping Us," *Black Youth Project* Online Magazine, December 31, 2019, http://blackyouthproject.com.

[9]Christine Emba, "Why Millennials Are Skipping Church and Not Going Back," *Washington Post*, October 27, 2019, https://www.washingtonpost.com.

that is overtly inclusive of our sexuality, ancestral practices, and race—both in who we see or interact with in the congregation, as well as the pictorial representation in worship spaces.[10]

Why has the Black church, an institution birthed out of a response to injustice, struggled so much with offering inclusion to and seeking justice for all creation? Scholars posit that it is because the Black church struggles with several types of crises, three of which include identity, theological, and psychological.

Current Crises in the Black Church

Identity

In 1982, scholar Cornel West addressed the struggle of African Americans "fighting to enter modernity on [their] own terms."[11] He offered four theoretical constructs that help define and delineate "Afro-American historical traditions of thought and action."[12] A brief overview of these constructs will guide my discussion of the identity crises currently experienced by the Black church.

The Exceptionalist Tradition

This construct extols African American superiority, either ontologically (Afro-Americans are exceptional because of genetic or innate characteristics, or because of divine preferential selection) or sociologically (Afro-Americans are exceptional because of their values, behavior, or gifts acquired by enduring marginalization, oppression, and exploitation).[13] From this construct come such issues as classism, colorism, respectability politics, and quietism. As noted, Black churches, particularly those with historically "upper-" and "upper-middle-class" sensibilities, North and South, practiced and perpetuated classist ideas of caste, taking into account a person's "pedigree" and often one's skin color, before welcoming him or her into the church. Once one became a member of a church, she or he was expected to behave in accordance with the prevailing notions of what was acceptable behavior for someone of the church's status and position in the community. If the church did participate in justice-seeking activities, it was done in a socially acceptable manner, and sometimes the only institutional response to racial injustice was an appeal to the Creator for "just

[10]Jordan, "Millennials Aren't Skipping Church."

[11]Cornel West, *Prophesy Deliverance! An Afro-American Revolutionary Christianity* (Louisville, KY: Westminster John Knox Press, 2002), 69–70.

[12]West, *Prophesy Deliverance!*, 70.

[13]West, *Prophesy Deliverance!*, 70.

enough grace to make it one more day, for it will all be over, afterwhile." In these churches, women and men carried themselves with dignity and pride, often making sure to separate themselves from those in churches deemed "lower-class," and especially the unchurched who did not meet their requirements for membership. Men were expected to be leaders in their communities and uphold accepted standards regarding family order. Women were expected to be demure, but industrious, never idling away time. Sexuality was a private, taboo subject, even for married couples. There were rarely conversations or messages officially communicated in the church other than conservative, accepted "biblical" standards of morality, purity, and chastity.

The exceptionalist tradition continued to infuse Black congregations through the twentieth century, even as the Black Power and Women's Rights movements swept through the nation. In many cities and towns, churches of varying denominations were categorized by social designations, for example, "That's the 'bourgeoisie' Black Baptist/CME/AME/AMEZ church," or "That's the church where all the Black professionals in town belong." Often, the types of worship services held in these churches were part of the exceptionalist tradition, characterized by the singing of classically arranged spirituals and anthems directed by musicians who had been classically trained and educated in music, sermons preached by pastors who were seminary-trained, and members who dressed a certain way and exercised a certain decorum in worship. While these churches may, and often do, participate in justice-seeking ministries, it is generally within socially accepted means and through coalitions with other equally exceptionalist organizations. Even the impacts of the sexual revolution and Women's Rights movements have not caused a significant change to Black church mores or public attitudes regarding sexuality in exceptionalist churches. While there may be silent acceptance of unmarried sexual activity, as well as a "don't ask, don't tell" policy regarding same-gender-loving people, there is still public denouncement and denigration among Black churches regarding unmarried sex and same-gender sexuality.

Many Black churches in the twenty-first century carry on the exceptionalist tradition, particularly as Black liberation theology and other pro-Black ideologies and organizations have made their marks and become accepted, even institutionalized segments of society. However, the classist (and even colorist) ideals remain, as well as the legacy of respectability politics. This identity, as noted in Meagan Jordan's article, has driven and kept away persons who would become part of these congregations.

The Assimilationist Tradition

According to West, this construct "considers Afro-American culture and personality to be pathological, rejecting any idea of an independent, self-supportive Afro-American culture."[14] This tradition is also categorized by ontological and sociological types and is an exact inverse of the exceptionalist tradition. Whereas the exceptionalist tradition claims that Afro-Americans stand above other racial groups, the ontological assimilationist claims they stand below, also because of genetic and innate characteristics, deemed deficient by this tradition. The sociological assimilationist believes they stand below other racial groups because of values, behaviors, and defects brought about because of oppression and exploitation.

Black assimilationist churches also contribute to the identity crises within the institution because everything Black is deemed inferior. In these churches, there is no pride or dignity in being Black, but Blackness is a defect to be overcome through becoming white. While it may seem no Black church on earth would still fall into this category, many do, if not in every way, in subtle, insidious ways. The legacies of anti-Blackness, visible sainthood, hereditary heathenism, and white paternalism have deep roots that have yet to be excised from many Black churches.

Historically, these churches carried the theological and ideological ideas, as well as worship and liturgical practices, of white parent or exemplary congregations. Blacks who sought to assimilate into white society and culture determined that Black ideas, thoughts, and ways of worshipping were not suitable or adequate. Therefore, every aspect of the church, from theological doctrines, administration, education, politics, worship, and outreach had to be modeled after white churches. Educational curricula for Sunday school and Bible studies written and/or published by Black authors and publishing houses were rejected in favor or those that came from white authors and publishers. Worship carried an overtly European/white flavor; spirituals, Black hymnody, and gospels were eschewed in favor of hymns and songs by white composers. Preaching in assimilationist churches was characterized by political and social conservatism and/or quietism. Discipleship carried with it the promise of being "washed white as snow."

Even during the Great Migration, Black Church Freedom Movement, and Civil Rights Movement, the assimilationist tradition permeated the institutional Black church in myriad ways. Some churches refused to participate in freedom movements and activist causes. Whelchel recounts how almost half of the Black churches in Birmingham refused to participate in the Civil Rights Movement of the 1960s, being satisfied with the "sublime serenity of mindless passivity."[15] As the Evangelical movement of the 1970s and 1980s

---

[14]West, *Prophesy Deliverance*, 70.

[15]Love Henry Whelchel, *The History and Heritage of African American Churches: A Way Out of No Way* (St. Paul, MN: Paragon House, 2011), loc. 3922–3938 of 7042, Kindle.

moved through America, countless Black churches cast their lots with white churches and denominations, hoping to curry favor and economic enfranchisement by association. The same is true of the twenty-first-century Black church, especially in light of those who espouse prosperity theologies. If a race-related message is preached on Sundays, it is usually advocating reconciliation and tolerance. Worship elements are decidedly European or Anglo in nature; music overwhelmingly is chosen from the contemporary Christian genre, and scriptures and sermons focus on a message of individual salvation and a personal relationship with Christ. Churches in the assimilationist tradition do not engage in Black political activism, communicating the well-worn notion that politics do not belong in the pulpit or church.

The Marginalist Tradition

The marginalist tradition is interesting in that it involves both a rejection of Afro-American culture and American society. Blacks who fall within this category cannot find sufficient meaning either in their own racial background and history or in the white world, resulting in a negative view of self and environment.[16] This view helped to create a need for Black independent churches that separated themselves from the world and focused primarily on an otherworldly destiny. Fearing the results of interacting with the contemporary evils of society, these churches turned, and continue to turn, inward, seeking the favor of a God who punishes even the slightest human missteps, trusting that a devotion to holiness and piety will be pleasing enough to make it to heaven, which is the fervent goal. Churches within this tradition did not and do not participate in political activism or justice-seeking movements, and because they consider themselves set apart, worldly issues are not addressed, except to point out the futility of engaging in worldly matters. Worship in these churches follows an extremely pietistic, theologically conservative model. Music, prayers, scriptures, and sermons focus on heavenly reward, living holy lives, rebuking evil, maintaining a personal relationship with God, and seeking strength to live piously in an evil, reprobate world.

The Humanist Tradition

The humanist tradition claims neither Afro-American superiority nor inferiority, genetically or culturally, according to West, but views Afro-American culture as "the expression of an oppressed human community imposing its distinctive form of order on an existential chaos, explaining its political predicament, preserving its self-respect, and projecting its own special hopes for the future."[17] While most Black Christian churches, particularly at their

---

[16]West, *Prophesy Deliverance!*, 80–85.
[17]West, *Prophesy Deliverance!*, 85.

inception, would not identify as humanist, in any sense of the word, there were members of churches, and perhaps even pastors, who identified with the self-image of the humanist tradition. That is, they would agree that the Afro-American is neither a hero nor a pitiable character; instead, the Afro-American is fully human, with strengths and weaknesses, triumphs, and failures, like any other human. It would be difficult, however, for a church to claim a humanist tradition, first because the potential for moving forward is centered on the individual's self-determination, not on God, or the community. Second, this self-determination is not touted as promising eventual victory, for the individual or the community. Third, in the humanist tradition, the meaning of life is to be found in the struggle, in every aspect of a person's being, not an attractive concept for prospective members.

Today, most Black congregations, particularly those in mainline denominations, would not aver a humanist tradition, primarily because these churches espouse faith in the sovereignty of God and trust in God's omnipotence, omniscience, and omnipresence. While many might agree with the importance of introspection and self-determination in an individual's development, Black churches generally do not espouse an "it-is-what-it-is" existential reality, but use scripture, prayer, sermons, and exhortations to be more hopeful and optimistic in life. Interestingly, the critique of many millennials and Gen Y-ers regarding the Black church as an institution involves the church's unwillingness to have honest, introspective dialogues about life and its vicissitudes. Many feel the Black church does not respond realistically to the struggles they (and everyone) face, but instead offers platitudes and clichés that are irrelevant and trite.

Theological Contradictions and Incongruities

Another issue that confronts the Black church and has led to its decline is the paradox of theological doctrines that govern most Black churches. As noted earlier, most mainline Protestant denominations, including Black independent ones, follow Calvinist or Anglican theologies and doctrines. Though many Black churches proudly assert their independent historic roots, most did not revisit theological constructs and subsequent doctrines before adopting them from white denominations and churches. This is not to suggest from a twenty-first-century place of privilege that Blacks in the eighteenth and nineteenth centuries would have or should have been able to revisit decisions made at Nicaea or Chalcedon, but to say that these institutional bodies would have benefited from placing their theological beliefs and doctrinal standards in context and conversation with their Blackness. The effects of enslavement and marginalization are clear in that independent Black denominations and churches did not substantively critique the anti-Black, classist, and exclusivist mores and values of Puritan morality and Anglican privilege. Instead, many of them adopted the same interpretations of scriptural texts and subsequent doctrinal standards as European/Euro-descended bodies.

The Great Awakenings were also problematic for *AfricansinAmerica*, theologically. Both movements focused on evangelism, individual salvation, and personal piety, none of which had ties to African cosmology. Though the Second Great Awakening would foster more antislavery preaching and embrace more racially integrated and ecstatically spirited camp meetings than the First, the overall tenor of each was permeated by white paternalism and Black assimilationism. Theological language that promoted one's personal relationship with Jesus as savior, equated whiteness with purity of soul and spirit, taught individual piety as holiness, and threatened hellfire and brimstone for nonbelievers found its way into songs, prayers, exhortations, and sermons and remains there to this day in many Black churches.

Black liberation theology, which arose in response to the deaths of civil rights leaders, the rise of the Black Power movement, provocative treatises such as *The Black Manifesto*, Vincent Harding's "Black Power and the American Christ," and Albert Cleage's *The Black Messiah*, came to the fore as both rejection and correction of European/white theologies and doctrinal statements. However, some Blacks found Black liberation theology to be too radical, caustic, and costly to their livelihoods to support. Furthermore, Black liberation theology had its own internal conflicts and faults, addressing neither the dual issues of sexism and misogyny faced by Black women, nor the issues of homophobia and heteronormativity faced by what is now termed the LGBTQIA community. While many mainline Black churches would affirm that they are liberative spaces, liturgically, seldom would many affirm a Black God (or even a Black Christ) and most have not significantly changed theological or doctrinal statements to reflect Black liberation theology's critique of European/Anglo theologies, church doctrines, and liturgical practices. Moreover, those that follow a prosperity gospel theology would strongly disagree that God identifies with the poor and marginalized.

Womanism and Black feminism are two responses to cis-gendered Black male-centered liberation theology. *Womanism*, a term coined by writer Alice Walker, is a theological framework that centers Black women and their experiences, affirms their love of themselves and one another, and their mutual interdependence with men and all of creation. Black feminism, either subsumed under womanism, or a shoot from the same plant, depending on the scholar, also centers Black women, focusing not only on Black women's issues in the United States, but as bell hooks asserts, "by addressing our concern with the welfare of the human community globally."[18] Because womanism and Black

[18]bell hooks, *Talking Back: Thinking Feminist, Thinking Black* (Cambridge, MA: South End Press, 1989), 180.

feminism center the concerns of Black women and critique the misogynoir of the Black church, they are seldom used as primary frameworks, methodologies, or hermeneutic lenses for liturgical practices in most Black churches.

Psychological Trauma

Twenty years ago, the singing duo, Mary Mary, released a song titled "Shackles (Praise You)." The lyrics describe mental, emotional, and spiritual psychological trauma endured by the person represented in the song, and include supplications for God to remove the load or shackles so the singer is free to praise God in the midst of trial. "Shackles" became a number one hit in several countries and was a crossover success, ranking high on R&B and pop charts. While part of its appeal is its syncopated, funky beat, many people gravitated to the lyrics. It spoke directly to what they were going through in their lives, but instead of causing them to feel depressed, the joyful, hopeful message of God breaking chains uplifted the listener.

Reginald Davis speaks to the need for a psychological conversion in the Black church. He recalls the oppression endured by Black people throughout history and asserts that "the psychological transformation of the oppressed is the most challenging."[19] Issues of double-consciousness, economic distress, coupled with the various "isms" of the world, and subsequent marginalization of Black people due to these factors has, for many, led to a nihilistic outlook on life.

Although these are not new problems, the responses of Black people to these problems has shifted over decades. The church used to be the place Black people went to pray and hear a Word from the Lord regarding their problems. They would seek counseling from pastors and other members whom they trusted to give wise advice, based on scripture. Even if they did not receive sufficient answers to their problems, being in the service lifted their spirits and made them feel better. Today, though many Black people still attend church services and may feel better after being in worship, often they do not look to the church to provide long-term psychological comfort and relief. Because the stigma of seeking professional therapy is not what it once was, more Black people are seeking out psychiatrists and psychologists to deal with their issues, often at the encouragement of pastors who are not clinically licensed to address ongoing psychological trauma.

Furthermore, Davis critiques the Black church's response to psychological trauma, noting that "we get nowhere by resigning this world to oppressors and then begging God to meet our needs. . . . Martin Luther King Jr. and other freedom fighters realized that no other agent would come to do for them

---

[19]Reginald Davis, *The Black Church: Relevant or Irrelevant in the Twenty-First Century?* (Macon, GA: Smyth and Helwys, 2010), 54.

what they could do for themselves. . . . Black people need a consciousness that counters their oppression, not one that cooperates with it."[20]

In the lyrics of the song "Shackles," one can understand Davis's critique. The singer asks God to remove the shackles, not to be free from oppression, or even find ways to address the oppression, but to praise God in the midst of the oppression. To be sure, the lyrics request that the "load be lifted," but the agency to achieve that is left to God; the singer just wants to praise "in my circumstance." Of course, this song is just one of hundreds, perhaps thousands, that defer the power and ability to change one's circumstances to a benevolent, but seemingly arbitrary God, who chooses at will either to help or not. The song, and others like it, are reflective of theological beliefs that are often counterproductive to efforts to achieve Black liberation and communal transformation. This is not to suggest theologically that God is not interested or involved in liberation, but that humanity is called to participate as co-laborers with God in liberating activity. Theologians Edward and Anne Wimberly offer a helpful model:

> Because God's liberating activity is present and continues in the faith community through Jesus Christ and the Holy Spirit, our task is to be committed to and to cooperate with God's liberating activity within our faith community. The first step in commitment and cooperation is to be aware of what God is doing. The second step is to be open to what God is doing, and the third step is to organize the faith community's whole life around the central values and work of God, the liberator. To organize itself around the central liberating activity of God means that the worship, caring, nurturing, and witnessing life of the community must participate in and reflect the liberating work of God.[21]

Davis shares a similar sentiment regarding the Black church's responsibility to assist its members in achieving wholeness. He asserts:

> The black church must consistently address and demonstrate black people's inherent worth by constantly lifting up their history and struggling against unjust social structures that create psychological problems for them. . . . When the black church addresses and counsels the psychological as well as the spiritual needs of black people, then it is a relevant church.[22]

---

[20]Davis, *The Black Church*, 56.

[21]Edward P. Wimberly and Anne Streaty Wimberly, *Liberation and Human Wholeness: The Conversion Experiences of Black People in Slavery and Freedom* (Nashville, TN: Abingdon Press, 1986), 119.

[22]Davis, *The Black Church*, 54.

The link between liturgy and justice is significant in the Black church because of the biblical mandates that require this symbiotic relationship and because the link is foundational to its historic formation and future sustainability. Crises of identity, theological contradictions, and the impact of centuries of psychological trauma have taken their toll on Black faith communities and caused schisms that threaten to render the Black church irreparably broken.

Liberative theologies and subsequent liturgical practices that reflect and affirm Black humanity as worthy of love and healthful abundance and empower Black humanity to take agency as co-laborers with the Divine can be helpful in alleviating individual and collective psychological trauma and achieving mental, emotional, and spiritual freedom and wholeness. In the next chapter, I explore womanism as a liberative theological framework for dismantling death-dealing religious beliefs and practices, while developing a life-giving liturgical paradigm that will help reconstruct Black churches as healthy, whole, and free.

Part Three

A NEW PARADIGM

9

Foundations of a Womanist Liturgical Theology

What, then, shall we say to these things? If Black worship and liturgy have been beset by so many negative influences, if the sustainability of that which we call the Black church is questionable, if most Black Christian denominations and fellowships are facing rapid decline, why bother with any attempt to reform and/or revitalize worship and liturgy in these spaces? Conversely, if one has the mind-set that all is well with the Black church, there is still no need to bother with reform. However, statistics and empty churches (even before COVID-19) present a different story. More important, if one has the mind-set that there is no hope for the future of the Black church, that view, as well, precludes a need for reform. Regardless, we must not accept such a nihilistic stance, for not only is there hope for the future of Black denominations, fellowships, and churches, but the future of Black communities and the people in them rests in part on these entities thriving.

What is needed to accomplish this is a rediscovery and reclamation of what has been termed a "hidden wholeness."[1] If Black liturgy has become largely divested from justice, then our worship is incomplete at best, and inauthentic, at worst. If our understandings of the gospel of Jesus Christ are centered on personal salvation and an individual relationship with God that excludes communal justice and righteousness, we have missed Jesus's message and ministry. Moreover, if we believe our personal relationships with God and/or Jesus should manifest in material abundance as a result of formulaic prosperity theology, we have polluted the very gospel of Jesus.

What is the gospel? Jesus proclaims that the prophet Isaiah's words (Isa 61:1–2) had been fulfilled in the hearing of all gathered in the synagogue

[1]Michael I. N. Dash, Jonathan Jackson, and Stephen C. Rasor, *Hidden Wholeness: An African American Spirituality for Individuals and Communities* (Cleveland, OH: United Church Press, 1997).

that day (cf. Luke 4:21). The fulfillment that Jesus is proclaiming is that good news will be preached to the poor, prisoners will be freed, the blind will receive their sight, and the oppressed will be released. Furthermore, the Year of Jubilee, when all debts are canceled, land is returned to its original owners, and all is set aright, is part of Isaiah's proclamation and Jesus's fulfillment of it. Nowhere in this outline of Jesus's ministry is a reference to going to heaven, a personal relationship with God, or with him, as a benefit or goal of following him. Nowhere does he specify that he has come to lay down his life so his followers might be rich in material goods. In fact, Jesus angers the crowd gathered there by telling them they have no special claim on him or his miraculous abilities simply because they are "church folks," people of the Covenant. All will have the opportunity to share in this liberative good news, including the poor and oppressed.

When Jesus speaks of heaven, he is most often recorded as referring to it eschatologically as a kingdom, existing in both the now and the not yet. As Jesus describes it, it is not a place of pearly gates and streets encrusted with gold, but a reality in which God's communal justice and righteousness abide for all. Jesus does tell his disciples toward the conclusion of his earthly ministry that he goes to prepare a place for them, that in his Father's house there are many dwelling places. But interestingly, when Jesus shares a parable in Matthew's Gospel about the Day of Judgment (cf. Matt 25:31–46), the ones who are allowed into the kingdom are granted access, once again, not because they are God's special chosen ones, but because they brought good news to the poor and proclaimed the year of God's favor by feeding the hungry, clothing the naked, visiting the sick and imprisoned, and welcoming the stranger.

The "hidden wholeness" that many seek—and, unfortunately, may not find in their churches—is tied to this understanding of Jubilee Year, particularly in human relationships. As many persons, particularly those between the ages of eighteen and thirty-five have noted, it is not God or Jesus they are necessarily rejecting; it is the fragmented, broken models of "church" they have experienced or encountered. They, and indeed, most of us who seek God, desire to be made whole. But how can we be made whole with worship and liturgical encounters that are built on broken, fractured histories, that refuse to welcome and include everyone in their full personhood, and that rest on problematic, death-dealing biblical exegeses and theological tenets? This is the primary impetus for constructing a paradigm of worship and liturgical theology for the Black Christian church actively working to dismantle anti-Africanness, anti-Blackness, sexism and misogyny, homophobia and heteronormativity, problematic biblical exegesis, hermeneutics, and resultant theologies. A mammoth task, to be sure. Impossible, some might say, but necessary if Black churches and the communities in which they reside seek to be made whole.

Liturgical Theology

What is liturgical theology? If theology is simply "God-talk" or talk *about* God, then liturgical theology is talk about how what we believe, think, and say about God informs, shapes, and is present in our liturgy.

Primary and Secondary Liturgical Theology

Gordon Lathrop and Simon Chan both refer to two ways of understanding liturgical theology—primary and secondary. "Primary liturgical theology," Lathrop states, "is the communal meaning of the liturgy exercised by the gathering itself," and secondary liturgical theology "is written and spoken discourse that attempts to find words for the experience of the liturgy and to illuminate its structures, intending to enable a more profound participation in those structures by the members of the assembly."[2] Chan asserts that doing primary theology is the understanding that "in the very act of worship we are participating in the God who is truth."[3] He maintains that "the primary liturgical theology is a tacit form of knowledge that is fully expressed only in the act of worship." Secondary liturgical theology, according to Chan, "seeks to explain as fully as possible this primary experience of the church in its encounter with God which is expressed in its public act of worship."[4]

Everyone who participates in worship does primary liturgical theology, regardless of cognitive awareness or comprehension. Whether we engage from intuitive, aesthetic, emotional, and/or intellectual levels, we engage this tacit knowledge, even if it is beyond explanation or full comprehension. Where Lathrop is helpful, particularly for this discussion, is in his description of secondary liturgical theology. While many people engage in weekly worship, and may come away with feelings of having been in a communally meaningful experience, how often do they emerge with theological understandings of what they experienced? How often are worship experiences discussed from theological viewpoints? The sermon may be critiqued theologically, but how often do churches engage in theological exegesis of the other elements and acts of worship? Are worshippers even clear about the theological reasons for preaching? Do they know the theological meanings of the Apostles' Creed or the *Gloria Patri*? Do they understand the theological significance of the call to worship, The Lord's Prayer, or the offertory? Can they explain

[2]Gordon Lathrop, *Holy Things: A Liturgical Theology* (Minneapolis: Fortress Press, 1998), 5–6.

[3]Simon Chan, *Liturgical Theology: The Church as Worshiping Community* (Downers Grove, IL: InterVarsity Press, 2006), 48.

[4]Chan, *Liturgical Theology*, 50–51.

the meanings of baptism and Holy Communion? Would it be beneficial to worshippers to write or talk about worship experiences? Is it necessary to find words for the experience of the liturgy? If we want worshippers to gain a deeper comprehension of the experience, it is crucial for them to understand why the acts and elements of worship chosen from Sunday to Sunday are included, what they mean, and how the meaning impacts those present, both individually and corporately.

Liturgical theology helps ascertain the meaning of worship experiences by asking four guiding questions: (1) What does "this gathering" mean? (2) Why is it that people assemble, that biblical texts are read, that people are sometimes washed, that the fragment of a meal is held, and that these things are done side by side? (3) How do these patterns of words and actions, of ritual communication, carry that meaning? (4) How should one, whether coming new to such an assembly or long a participant, understand what the meeting is about?[5] In addition to these questions, we can add: What do these particular acts and elements of worship mean biblically, theologically, historically, and traditionally (to the Church Universal and the local congregation)? How do these acts inform and influence our communal engagement both inside and outside the church doors?

These questions are important for several reasons. First, an intelligent God has created us as intelligent creatures. God fully expects us to engage God with our minds, finite though they are. While we cannot apprehend the totality of God, we can attempt to understand that which is comprehensible, especially as it pertains to how we engage with God in relationship. If we are employing acts and elements of worship as a way of meeting, engaging, and knowing God, we should be able to understand and articulate why we are employing these particular acts and elements of worship, why and how they have meaning for us as the people of God. Second, these questions help us understand who we are as the *ekklesia*, the "called out," the Church, the body of Christ. Why are these acts essential for us as a community of believers? What do they do for us as Jesus's disciples? How do they shape, form, and inform us as followers of the Way? If we did not or were unable to practice these, would we still be the same community of believers, and if not, why not? How do they help us to be disciples of Jesus in the world? Third, these questions invite critical reflection on our theological doctrines and the worship that flows from them. They give us opportunities to wrestle with whether we believe what we profess (and confess) and what we practice in worship. This process helps us avoid the pitfall of traditionalism, which is the dead faith of the living, as opposed to tradition, which is the living faith of the dead. Often,

[5]Lathrop, *Holy Things*, 2–3.

it is not tradition that keeps us observing or participating in a particular act of worship, but traditionalism. Traditionalism causes us to hesitate or refuse to reform a practice that has little or no theological or ecclesial significance because "we've always done it that way."

Liturgical Theology in the Black Church

William McClain argues that "there is no more important day in the North American black community than Sunday. That is true of every Sunday—any Sunday—anywhere in black America."[6] Though statistics have shown a steady decline in worship attendance among Blacks in America, percentages of those who still avow regular worship attendance remain relatively high, particularly when compared with other racial and ethnic groups.

Liturgically, Sunday is a way of keeping time in the Black community. Those who are regular attendees can attest that each Sunday in most Black churches is distinctive, each Sunday having its own assigned choir, usher board, church officers, and perhaps preacher. Even if churches are not large enough for different personnel each Sunday, the attitude and atmosphere on each Sunday is unique.

Communion Sundays are viewed generally as most solemn and essential in attendance. Even if persons cannot or choose not to attend any other Sunday of the month, they will come to receive "*Circament*."[7] This speaks to the importance of communion as a communally binding ritual and tradition that has been communicated and passed down to church members generationally. Most Black churches will use a communion liturgy that has been approved by appropriate church authorities and seldom change it, especially if there is an approved denominational or fellowship-approved book of worship or discipline for its use. Orders of service are altered to include the communion liturgy or references to the observance of communion. Other distinctive liturgical elements on first Sundays include communion-themed service music, designated attire or vestments for those involved in preparing and serving elements of communion. The clergy most often wear white robes and/or

[6]William B. McClain, *Come Sunday: The Liturgy of Zion* (Nashville, TN: Abingdon Press, 1990), 27.

[7]"Circament" is an adaptive pronunciation of the word "sacrament" often used by elderly Black church members. It may be a conflation of the two words, "circuit" and "sacrament," fused together because itinerant circuit preachers celebrated the sacrament of Holy Communion when they periodically came to town. McClain posits it as "a black southern way of referring to Holy Communion, the Lord's Supper, the Eucharist." See "The African American Church and Sacraments: But Can We Still Get Our 'Circament?' " in *Companion to the Africana Worship Book*, ed. Valerie Bridgeman Davis and Safiyah Fosua (Nashville, TN: Discipleship Resources, 2007), 69.

stoles. There are special coverings for the altar. There are the chancel rails and pulpit furniture. These liturgical elements help distinguish Communion Sunday from other Sundays.

Other Sundays, as previously stated, have other distinctions, such as different lead liturgists, choirs, particular genres of music programming (e.g., traditional gospel, contemporary gospel, anthems, or spirituals), the inclusion of children, youth, and/or young adults in liturgical leadership, and performing groups such as dance or step teams. Orders of service may or may not be altered based on these variances, but the liturgical elements of worship generally remain the same. For example, if the order on a particular non-Communion Sunday includes the following elements on other non-Communion Sundays of the month, the order does not change significantly, but simply the performance of these acts by differing groups or persons.

Prelude
Processional
Call to Worship
Opening Hymn
Opening Prayer
Greeting/Passing of the Peace
Apostles' Creed/Church Covenant
Musical Selection
Scripture/Responsive Reading
Offertory
Musical Selection
Sermon
Invitation to Christian Discipleship/Altar Call
Announcements
Benediction and Sending Forth
Postlude

Although many Black churches may not follow the Christian liturgical calendar as outlined in the Revised Common Lectionary, the seasons of Advent, Christmas, Lent, Easter, and Pentecost are generally observed. Furthermore, in Black churches, there are special days that require observance during worship. These include Mothers' Day, Fathers' Day, Thanksgiving, Watch Night, Church Anniversary and/or Homecoming, Pastor's Anniversary or Appreciation, and days to celebrate the service of those on various boards and auxiliaries. Worship on these Sundays may follow the regular or typical order, with the exception of a dedicated time during the service to celebrate the particular focus of the day. Often, Church Anniversary and Homecoming are held at different times on Sundays than the typical church service, and, most often, have their own specially ordered liturgy for the service. Even so, most of the acts and elements of worship remain similar, if not identical, to Sunday morning worship. Thanksgiving occurs on Thursdays, and while Watch Night may occur on a Sunday, the time of the service usually occurs in the evening. These observances have unique foci, and their liturgies, like the others, flow from the meanings inherent in each.

Perhaps what is most significant about Sunday in the Black church is that it is the *Lord's Day*. According to McClain, for Black people, that means it is "the chief day of rest and worship, a day of celebration."[8] In this, he states, "they were soundly at one with the practice of the early church and the admonitions and spirit of the New Testament."[9] Therefore, whatever is happening in Black churches liturgically, the ground or foundation is—or should be—the acts of the Creator in and through history, particularly in the person of Jesus Christ, his life, death, and resurrection, and the experiential encounter with God and Jesus through the power of the Holy Spirit. Each Sunday, therefore, is a moment in time, not merely *chronos*, but, more importantly, *kairos*, where through liturgy, both primary and secondary, worshippers meet and are met by the full representation of God's identity.

Our ancestors may not have been able to articulate their experiences of primary liturgical theology, but that did not make the experience any less powerful or efficacious. Contemporary worship experiences, as primary liturgical theological engagement in Black worshipping contexts may be just as powerful and efficacious. However, this does not absolve the current Black worshipper from learning, understanding, and articulating what worship experiences mean theologically. The discipline or "doing" of secondary liturgical theology has the potential to strengthen our connections in and to the worship experience. To understand cognitively, intellectually, what we are doing in worship and why, gives us even more freedom and power to engage in these acts while helping us articulate and communicate the meanings of these acts with coming generations and prospective disciples.

What does the "doing of" liturgical theology look like in the Black church? While Black worshippers are engaging the acts and elements of worship, are they examining and evaluating why these acts and elements are meaningful and potentially transformational for those particular faith communities? Are there any discussions held before, during, or after worship that examine and evaluate how, from week to week, these acts, elements, and their place in the liturgy, hold theological import? Is there any research done to uncover

[8]McClain, *Come Sunday*, 33.
[9]McClain, *Come Sunday*, 33.

how these liturgies and the ways they are performed might be harmful to the body of believers? Have the liturgical histories been researched to determine whether theologies that undergird them are liberative and life-giving for Black bodies and Black faith communities? Unfortunately, the answer to each of these questions in most Black faith communities is overwhelmingly no. In fact, during the past sixteen years, of the approximately nine hundred Black students enrolled in my "Introduction to Worship" course, 95 percent or more responded that they had neither heard of liturgical theology nor engaged in it, as a practice, in their churches. If each student represents one church, then there are approximately nine hundred Black churches across the United States unfamiliar with the practice of doing secondary liturgical theology. Furthermore, if each student represents a Black denomination or fellowship, then it is entirely possible that neither of the eight mainline Protestant Black denominations[10] nor most Black Christian fellowships practice secondary liturgical theology in any organized or structured form. This is not to say that no Black church has ever practiced secondary liturgical theology or that no Black church, fellowship, or denomination has ever asked probing questions about its liturgy. However, it does indicate that there has not been, nor is there now, any structured or organized practice of examining and evaluating liturgies used in most Black churches and for the benefit of Black people and Black faith communities.

Now, there are many texts that do this work; most, if not all are written by persons of European/Anglo descent for worship in churches primarily based on Euro/Anglo-descended theologies, attended by persons of European/Anglo descent. That is not to say they do not offer theological explanations of liturgical acts and elements that are, in a general sense, applicable to worship in the Black church, but they do not capture the unique essence or aesthetics of Black liturgy, as a concept, nor Black worshipping experiences. Furthermore, if these theologies are beset by anti-Africanness, anti-Blackness, white paternalism, and evangelicalism, then the liturgies that flow from them will be as well. Additionally, even if there were no problems inherent in Euro/Anglo liturgies, they are not identical to Black liturgies. Black liturgy emerged from unique historical, cosmological, theological, and experiential origins. To understand, interpret, and articulate its multiple meanings necessitates a unique liturgical theology designed to address its unique identity. Developing a liturgical theology to examine, evaluate, and, hopefully, transform worship practices in the Black church requires a liberative, holistic ethic, framework, and methodology

[10]The eight mainline historically Black Protestant denominations are the African Methodist Episcopal Church, African Methodist Episcopal Zion Church, Christian Methodist Episcopal Church, National Baptist Convention of America, Inc., National Baptist Convention U.S.A., Inc., Progressive Baptist Convention, Full Gospel Baptist Church Fellowship International, and the Church of God in Christ.

committed to affirming the beauty of the Black worship experience while offering a corrective for practices that are antithetical to Black life.

A Womanist Liturgical Theology Framework

There is no more liberative, holistic ethic or methodological framework for this task than that imbued and infused by a womanist hermeneutic. Within the original definitions of the term, *womanist*, coined by writer Alice Walker in 1983, there are statements that evince the liberation and wholeness inherent in embodying womanism:

1. From womanish. (Opp. of "girlish," i.e., frivolous, irresponsible, not serious.) A black feminist or feminist of color. From the black folk expression of mothers to female children, "you acting womanish," that is, like a woman. Usually referring to outrageous, audacious, courageous or willful behavior. Wanting to know more and in greater depth than is considered "good" for one. Interested in grown-up doings. Acting grown up. Being grown up. Interchangeable with another black folk expression: "you trying to be grown." Responsible. In charge. Serious.
2. A woman who loves other women, sexually and/or nonsexually. Appreciates and prefers women's culture, women's emotional flexibility (values tears as a natural counterbalance of laughter), and women's strength. Sometimes loves individual men, sexually and/or nonsexually. Committed to survival and wholeness of entire people, male and female. Not a separatist, except periodically, for health. Traditional universalist, as in: "Mama, why are we brown, pink, and yellow, and our cousins are white, beige, and black?" Reply: "Well you know the colored race is just like a flower garden with every color flower represented." Traditionally capable, as in: "Mama, I'm walking to Canada and I'm taking you and a bunch of other slaves with me." Reply: "It wouldn't be the first time."
3. Loves music. Loves dance. Loves the moon. Loves the Spirit. Loves love and food and roundness. Loves struggle. Loves the Folk. Loves herself. Regardless.
4. Womanist is to feminist as purple to lavender.[11]

First, Walker is clear that to be womanist is to be Black, unequivocally and unapologetically. That, in itself, is liberative, for it makes no qualms about self-

[11]Alice Walker, *In Search of My Mother's Garden: Womanist Prose* (New York: Harcourt Brace Jovanovich, 1983), xi–xii.

identifying in one's truth of Blackness. Blackness is nothing to be ashamed of or whispered fearfully. To be womanist is to be Black, without compromise or accommodation. Furthermore, to be womanist is to be a Black feminist, which is to believe that "Black women are inherently valuable, that our liberation is a necessity not as an adjunct to somebody else's but because of our need as human persons for autonomy."[12] The words, *responsible* and *serious*, as well as the phrase, "in charge," are requirements for securing liberation for oneself as well as one's community. There can be no apprehension of freedom without one's commitment to being responsible, serious, and in charge of one's destiny.

Within the second part of the definition, Walker uses the exact phrase, "Committed to wholeness and survival of entire people, male and female." To be womanist means that one is dedicated to the entire well-being of one's people, including their existence. A womanist would not merely make comfortable someone ill until they died, without seeking every possible way to foster the person's healing. Moreover, a commitment to wholeness and survival means avoiding or fighting any threat to the community's well-being. Womanists exhibit flexibility, strength, and sexual liberation. To be womanist is to be also capable of bringing others to liberation.

Walker defines womanist as lover, and not just of easy things. While a womanist loves music, dance, and food (among other things), she also loves the Spirit and struggle. Most important, perhaps, she loves herself, *regardless*. This is as much a commitment to self-liberation and holistic empowerment as a communal embodiment of these principles.

What is womanism, as an ethical and theological construct? Reverend Dr. Katie Geneva Cannon, one of the first to use Walker's terms and definitions as a point of departure in the fields of ethics and theology, stated:

> Our objective is to use Walker's four-part definition as a critical, methodological framework for challenging inherited traditions for their collusion with androcentric patriarchy as well as a catalyst in overcoming oppressive situations through revolutionary acts of rebellion.[13]

Womanist ethicist Stacey Floyd-Thomas describes how the concept of womanism emerged:

> By various levels of inspiration, Black women could bear witness to the truth of their surroundings and situations. With changed names and changed minds, these Black women took hold of an emerging conscious-

[12] Keeanga-Yamahtta Taylor, ed., *How We Get Free: Black Feminism and the Combahee River Collective* (Chicago: Haymarket Books, 2017), 17.

[13] Katie Geneva Cannon, *Katie's Canon* (New York: Continuum, 2003), 23.

> ness that not only provided a new outlook on life but also ushered forth a new epistemology. An epistemology, or way of knowing, that took the experience of Black women as normative.[14]

Floyd-Thomas further clarifies womanist epistemology and theology:

> This self-avowed standpoint sought to do away with Black women forever feeling forced to be caretakers or surrogates to white men, white women, or Black men. Womanist theological reflection created frames of thinking and ways of being that took Black women being agents of their own destiny as the norm.[15]

A liturgical theology that addresses the unique composition of Black liturgy, with its varied worship acts and elements and seeks to ascribe meaning to it, needs to employ such a womanist ethic, hermeneutic, and epistemology.

To accomplish a womanist liturgical theology requires a centering of African and African-descended cosmological and theological worldviews and spirituality, an affirmation of embodiment in worship without qualification, employing womanist hermeneutics in all worship elements, as well as a womanist hermeneutic/spirituality of communal empowerment and agency. An absolute imperative for engaging these liberative, holistic, inclusive ways of worshipping and talking about worship is an unwavering commitment to applying womanist lenses to every aspect of these experiences. This involves reading, studying, and internalizing the four tenets of womanism—radical subjectivity, traditional communalism, redemptive self-love, and critical engagement—in order to engage this liturgical theological paradigm with integrity, not merely as a superficial response to worship critique.[16] It also means adhering to the use of intersectionality[17] as a method for evaluating the multiple meanings and implications of liturgy and worship, and the performance of each.

---

[14]Stacey Floyd-Thomas, "Writing for Our Lives: Womanism as an Epistemological Revolution," in *Deeper Shades of Purple: Womanism in Religion and Society*, ed. Stacey Floyd-Thomas (New York: New York University Press, 2006), 3.

[15]Floyd-Thomas, "Writing for Our Lives," 3.

[16]Floyd-Thomas, "Writing for Our Lives," 7.

[17]*Intersectionality* is a term coined by professor Kimberlé Crenshaw to describe how race, class, gender, and other individual characteristics "intersect" with one another and overlap. Womanist scholar Monica Coleman cites how womanists practice intersectionality, stating, "Womanist theology is known for its analysis of religion and society in light of the triple oppression of racism, sexism, and classism that characterizes the experience of many black women." Monica A. Coleman, *Making a Way Out of No Way: A Womanist Theology* (Minneapolis: Fortress Press, 2008), 7.

Centering African and African-Descended Cosmology and Theology in Black Liturgy and Worship

How do African and African-descended cosmologies and theologies, as discussed in Chapter 2, translate into a womanist liturgical theology? We first must be ready to question the God-talk that we are already doing. Womanist God-talk examines and critiques our theological and religious doctrines and beliefs, using its four tenets to construct alternate theologies that employ liberative womanist ethics. It would be impossible to include here all aspects of every womanist theology available, but there are core principles and beliefs that can provide a foundation for this liturgical theology.

God

Womanist theologian Karen Baker-Fletcher asserts that "from a womanist perspective, God, is Spirit":

> For womanists, "God is Spirit and those who worship God worship God in spirit and in truth" (Jn. 4:23). God as Spirit is the light, salvation, and strength of one's life. With such inner spiritual affirmation, sustenance, and empowerment, one need not fear the vicissitudes of life nor those who bear ill will against oneself, family, or community.[18]

Womanists describe God as "loving, creative activity," one who "makes a way out of no way," a God of survival and liberation, who is concerned with the well-being and survival of men and women. Simultaneously, womanist theologians wrestle with theological absolutes about God, particularly in light of biblical texts where God's role as liberator is questionable, even doubtful. This does not make the womanist an unbeliever; on the contrary, the womanist is the strongest kind of believer because she has allowed herself to question who God is in light of the biblical text, placed the question in conversation with who she has found God to be in her own text, and come away with a firm foundation on which she can build her theological position.

The understanding of God as Spirit is also found in African cosmology. As noted earlier, John Mbiti asserts that God is "outside and beyond [God's] creation . . . simultaneously transcendent and imminent."[19] Baker-Fletcher

[18]Karen Baker-Fletcher, "The Strength of My Life," in Emilie Townes, ed., *Embracing the Spirit: Womanist Perspectives on Hope, Salvation, and Transformation* (Maryknoll, NY: Orbis Books, 1997), 123.

[19]John S. Mbiti, *African Religions and Philosophy*, 2nd ed. (Portsmouth, NH: Heinemann, 1990), 29.

notes that "from an Igbo perspective, the nature of God most fundamentally is Spirit."[20] This way of thinking about God is particularly helpful for the building of a womanist liturgical theology, for it removes finite boxes in which we would place God, and which cause theological and ethical conundrums when God does not behave or respond according to the parameters we have set. It allows us to perceive the Creator as creative activity, "something greater than ourselves that surrounds us, embraces us, encompasses us, gives us life, and interconnects us within a web of creation and creative activity that is beyond our understanding. It precedes us and survives us."[21]

The concept of God as Spirit also underscores the inclusive nature of God. Alice Walker explores this understanding of God in her novel *The Color Purple*. The female protagonist, Celie, views God as "a silent God who bears our pain by allowing us to suffer our way through good works."[22] Delores Williams notes how Celie's view of God "resembles some of the theological views and ecclesiastical practices that have been alive in the Black community for years."[23] For Celie and many in Black churches, God is male, "divine authoritative, and mystical." Conversely, women are viewed just as "Mister" viewed Celie, "black, poor, ugly, a woman, nothing at all."[24] But as Emilie Townes argues:

> Walker's portrayal of a passive Celie and an all too human male God readies the way for a new understanding of God for black children, men, and women that is a pathway to a deepening spirituality and a liberating hope. . . . Shug teaches Celie to begin to believe in a God beyond gender, a God who is Spirit and intimately connected to the fabric of our existences. . . . This is a God of grace and grit that loves and angers, that expands our understanding of sexuality and loving, that is angered when we fail to see the beauty of creation, in ourselves and in one another.[25]

To be clear, neither Walker nor womanist theologians are advocating for a Black, gendered God. That view of God is just as problematic as a white, gendered God, and serve to uphold and perpetuate non-liberative perspectives of God. Townes notes that "our concepts of God either support the oppression of Black folk in gender-based, racist, classist construct, or they serve as

---

[20]Baker-Fletcher, "The Strength of My Life," 124.

[21]Baker-Fletcher, "The Strength of My Life," 124.

[22]Emilie M. Townes, *In a Blaze of Glory: Womanist Spirituality as Social Witness* (Nashville, TN: Abingdon Press, 1995), 70.

[23]Delores S. Williams, "*The Color Purple*: What Was Missed," *Christianity and Crisis* 46, no. 10, (1986).

[24]Townes, *In a Blaze of Glory*, 70.

[25]Townes, *In a Blaze of Glory*, 70–71.

companion and confederate to our struggle for liberation and faithfulness."[26]

Liturgically, then, this requires a divestment from the maleness of God, both in the biblical text and in our language about God in our liturgy and worship. Use of the male pronoun for God, as well as prayers and other liturgical acts that only or primarily espouse God as Father need to be changed to reflect the commitment to a more liberative, holistic view of the Creator. Some might argue this is not necessary, but the dismantling of androcentric patriarchy begins by de-gendering God.

Jesus

Who is Jesus, cosmologically and theologically, for womanists? Baker-Fletcher asserts that Jesus is the "human embodiment of Spirit."[27] Jacquelyn Grant notes that because they draw from both biblical texts and God's direct revelation in their lives for their understandings of God, Black women see Jesus as liberator, one who embraces the outcast and sufferer.[28] Often, in the Black church, it has been this identity of Jesus as "suffering servant" that many, especially Black women, have internalized. Grant argues that this is problematic because of the ways Black women have been servants, often falling victim to servitude, being unfairly compensated (if at all) for the work they do, being underemployed and treated as inferior.[29] In the Black church, however, Black women often embrace the term and role of servant, believing it to be a positive one, particularly when paired with the notion of redemptive suffering. Monica Coleman argues: "Black women have embraced the language of servanthood and inverted it to rebel against their oppression. Although black women have reinterpreted the language of servanthood, this interpretation is a survival strategy and cannot provide liberation."[30]

Grant offers a more liberative view of servant that is helpful for our liturgical paradigm, encouraging use of the term "discipleship" in place of "servant."[31] Although biblical texts identify Jesus's twelve disciples as male, biblical scholarship indicates that there were women in Jesus's ministry who were also his disciples. Grant advocates the concept of discipleship as a way of describing and internalizing being in relationship with Jesus. In relation to this, Coleman notes:

---

[26]Townes, *In a Blaze of Glory*, 71.

[27]Baker-Fletcher, "The Strength of My Life," 124.

[28]Jacquelyn Grant, *White Women's Christ and Black Women's Jesus: Feminist Christology and Womanist Response* (Atlanta, GA: Scholars Press, 1989), 212–218.

[29]Jacquelyn Grant, "The Sin of Servanthood and the Deliverance of Discipleship," in *A-Troubling in My Soul: Womanist Perspectives on Evil and Suffering*, ed. Emilie M. Townes (Maryknoll, NY: Orbis Books, 1993), 200–208.

[30]Monica A. Coleman, *Making a Way Out of No Way: A Womanist Theology* (Minneapolis: Fortress Press, 2008), 16.

[31]Grant, "The Sin of Servanthood and the Deliverance of Discipleship," 213–216.

> Discipleship language comes from both Jesus' inclusion of the outcast among his own disciples and the black church tradition of issuing a call for discipleship at the end of a worship service. At its best, discipleship is a call to be invited into power and participation in relationship to God and in the community of faith. . . . Grant's model of discipleship is empowering because it allows black women to undermine traditional exclusive understandings of discipleship that only include men and white people.[32]

In our liturgy and worship, then, a relationship with Jesus calls us to work as co-laborers with Jesus and community, as partners with him and each other in the work he has called us to do. This helps dismantle hierarchical language, as well as false piety regarding our roles in worship. Moreover, it helps us reject the notion of redemptive suffering. As Letty Russell states:

> God's power and glory are present in our human condition no matter what the dimension of our suffering, because in Christ's suffering God has chosen to stand with us. Yet when we look to see this power and glory in human life, it shines through most clearly in those whose lives are confronting the suffering by saying no to its dehumanizing power.[33]

Partnering with God, in and through the work of Jesus, grants agency to the community of worshippers, so that our liturgy and worship are not valued by how abased we can become, but by how we choose to respond in community to the proclamation of God's Word.

For Kelly Brown Douglas, a womanist understanding of Jesus begins with Jesus's ministry. "What Jesus did becomes the basis for what it means for him to be Christ. This makes Christ more accessible to ordinary Christians."[34] In other words, salvation comes to Black communities by imitating Jesus's prophetic role of inspiring communities to take agency to rid themselves of their own oppression. Salvation is not achieved through one's personal relationship with God or Jesus; salvation is founded upon the community's social, political, cultural, and religious well-being. In other words, as Coleman clarifies, "Salvation is not just the goal of that wholeness, but is found in *the struggle to attain* that wholeness."[35]

What do these liberative ways of seeing Jesus, and seeing ourselves as disciples, mean for the ways we consider becoming part of the kin-dom[36] of

---

[32]Coleman, *Making a Way Out of No Way*, 16–17.

[33]Letty M. Russell, *Becoming Human* (Philadelphia: Westminster Press, 1982), 57.

[34]Kelly Brown Douglas, *The Black Christ* (Maryknoll, NY: Orbis, 1994), 101.

[35]Coleman, *Making a Way Out of No Way*, 19.

[36]I prefer the term "kin-dom" over kingdom, as a way of dismantling hierarchical notions of eschatological community.

God? If Jesus is the human embodiment of God's Spirit, what does it mean to enter this kin-dom and become Jesus's disciple? How do our theologies of salvation change in reference to this paradigm shift? After summarizing several theories of atonement in which Jesus serves as surrogate figure for sinful humanity, Delores Williams refers to these theories as attempts by theologians to use the "language and sociopolitical thought of the time to render Christian ideas and principles understandable."[37] She argues:

> The womanist theologian uses the sociopolitical thought and action of the African American woman's world to show black women their salvation does not depend upon any form of surrogacy made sacred by traditional and orthodox understandings of Jesus' life and death. Rather their salvation is assured by Jesus' life of resistance and by the survival strategies he used to help people survive the death of identity caused by their exchange of inherited cultural meanings for a new identify shaped by the gospel ethics and world view.[38]

This perspective liberates believers by "[freeing] redemption from the cross and [freeing] the cross from the 'sacred aura' put around it by existing patriarchal responses to the question of what Jesus' death represents."[39] Baker-Fletcher concurs that "because the cross for Williams is an image of defilement—human sinfulness—to glorify it is to glorify suffering and render exploitation sacred. To ask Black women to glorify the suffering of Jesus and to focus on the sacredness of their own suffering is to render their exploitation sacred."[40] This does not mean that the cross has no significance; indeed, its significance lies in knowing that there is a risk involved in living authentically the gospel of Jesus. But, as Baker-Fletcher assures,

> Resisting the powers of systemic injustice that may result in persecution or assassination is based in faith and hope, not in a fatalistic vision of death and sacrifice. The will and desire of those who engage in an ethic of risk are a will and desire not for death but for abundant life in the immediate future. Williams' preachment that Jesus came for life, not for death is central to a theology that is consistent with a Gospel message of healing, deliverance, survival, and wholeness.[41]

---

[37]Delores S. Williams, *Sisters in the Wilderness: The Challenge of Womanist God Talk* (Maryknoll, NY: Orbis Books, 1993), 164.

[38]Williams, *Sisters in the Wilderness*, 164.

[39]Williams, *Sisters in the Wilderness*, 164.

[40]Baker-Fletcher, "The Strength of My Life," 133; see also Williams, *Sisters in the Wilderness*, 164–166.

[41]Baker-Fletcher, "The Strength of My Life,"135.

In this new liturgical paradigm, then, salvation is not an individual accomplishment based on one's personal relationship with God, nor is the goal or "prize" of salvation a one-way ticket to heaven after death. Rather, salvation is grounded in the redemption of creation through Jesus's "ministerial vision of righting relations between body (individual and community), mind (of humans and of tradition) and spirit . . . giving humankind the ethical thought and practice upon which to build positive, productive quality of life."[42] Not only does this perspective address and critique oppressive, patriarchal theologies, it also helps dismantle the ways these theologies compromise Black liturgy and the integrity and self-determination of Black worshippers. Adopting this new liturgical paradigm means divesting our theologies of "cruel, imperialistic, patriarchal power" that uphold the sadistic idea that God required the death of Jesus in order to save humanity. How liberated and whole would congregations become if people no longer had to reconcile opposing views of God as loving and cruel? How liberated and whole would people become if they no longer had to wrestle with the notion of God calling for the death of an innocent man, which is problematic enough, but becomes even more so in light of wrongful deaths of innocent Black women and men each day in this country?

These death-dealing theologies have wreaked havoc on Black churches and communities since their emergence, causing many to believe the "cross" they bear is a holy, divine sacrifice, because Jesus had to bear his, also. Internalizing these theologies of atonement have also caused persons guilt, grief, and feelings of unworthiness, which further exacerbate Black struggles with self-identity in a society that already deems them unworthy. This liturgical paradigm presents a way of dismantling these theologies and their stranglehold on the Black church.

The Holy Spirit, the Ancestors, and African Spirituality

Peter Paris asserts that "Africans in the diaspora were able to preserve the structural dimensions of their spirituality: belief in a spirit-filled cosmos and acceptance of moral obligation to build a community in harmony with all the various powers in the cosmos."[43] For our ancestors in the antebellum period, the notion of a "Holy Spirit" was redundant, since the concept of spirit was foundational to their understanding of the sacred cosmos. As Paris notes, this would include "the realm of spirit (inclusive of the Supreme Deity, the sub-divinities, the ancestral spirits), which is the source and preserver of all

---

42 Williams, *Sisters in the Wilderness*, 164–165.

43 Peter J. Paris, *The Spirituality of African Peoples: The Search for a Common Moral Discourse* (Minneapolis: Fortress Press, 1995), 35.

life."[44] As Black people became familiar with Euro/Anglo understandings of a "Triune God," they syncretized African cosmologies of Spirit, believing that the Holy Spirit and the Spirit of God were one and the same, inspiring and empowering them to do God's will as they traversed an inhumane societal experience. Baker-Fletcher suggests that a womanist way of employing the term *Spirit* would be, first, in reference to God who is a spirit, and second, among Christian womanists and Christians, in general, in reference to the Holy Spirit.[45] She asserts that the Holy Spirit is comforter, teacher, and guide, advocate, power of life, divine witness to the Word and Wisdom of God, intercessor, and "hypostasis of the One God who makes church a reality."[46] She states:

> The Holy Spirit is a distinctive, relational action or mode of being in the Trinity. Or, to emphasize the dynamic movement of the Holy Spirit, one might say that "she" is the dynamic agent of divine healing revealed by Jesus the Christ. Her constant unchanging nature is to comfort, heal, renew or recreate, and instruct. She is the power through which God "creates a new thing."[47]

The related subjects of sub-divinities, intermediaries, and ancestors have been fraught with tension and caused division in Black churches. Many Black Christians espouse the position that African Traditional Religions (ATR) or African Derived Religions (ADR) are demonic, and any use of or reference to these religions or religious practices is strictly forbidden. This is a result of how Europeans historically demonized ATR/ADR and belief systems out of white supremacist hegemony, ignorance, and fear and passed on this prejudice against ATR/ADR to Black worshippers. Charles Long's words are particularly apt here: "The slaves, out of fear and for the sake of self-preservation (survival), assimilate themselves to the master's definition of their role and function, immersing themselves in nature and work."[48] This could also extend to—as Long possibly intends—assimilating themselves to the master's religion. Attempts to placate or appease white folx have hampered Black liberation and wholeness for millennia, including the need for spiritual liberation and wholeness that emerges from a freedom to worship God in Spirit and in truth. Part of this Spirit and truth is located in Black ancestral

[44]Paris, *The Spirituality of African Peoples*, 25.

[45]Karen Baker-Fletcher, "More Than Suffering: The Healing and Resurrecting Spirit of God," in *Womanist Theological Ethics: A Reader*, ed. Katie Geneva Cannon, Emilie M. Townes, and Angela D. Sims (Louisville, KY: Westminster John Knox Press, 2011), 173.

[46]Baker-Fletcher, "More Than Suffering," 172.

[47]Baker-Fletcher, "More Than Suffering," 173.

[48]Charles H. Long, *Significations: Signs, Symbols, and Images in the Interpretation of Religion* (Aurora, CO: Davies Group, 1999), 182.

ways of worshipping which need to be discovered, re-discovered, uncovered, researched, discussed, and given serious consideration by Black Christians.

Who are ancestors and who are they to us? As noted earlier, the acknowledgment of ancestors is an essential facet of life in African nations, tribes, and cultures. Geoffrey Parrinder writes:

> Belief in the continued existence and influence of the departed fathers of the family and tribe is very strong in all West Africa. Not only are the ancestors revered as past heroes, but they are felt to be still present, watching over the household, directly concerned in all the affairs of the family and property, giving abundant harvests and fertility. They are the guardians of the tribal traditions and history.[49]

And John Mbiti also notes:

> The departed of up to five generations are in a different category from that of ordinary spirits. . . . They are still part of their human families, and people have personal memories of them. . . . They know the needs of men, they have "recently" been here with men, and at the same time they have full access to the channels of communicating with God directly, or according to some societies, indirectly through their own forebearers.[50]

Many Black people brought to the Americas (particularly from the Caribbean) continued to observe African customs and rituals concerning ancestors, believing that "ancestors rewarded or reprimanded their descendants through visitations from the other world, and that they could reincarnate themselves in their descendants."[51] Will Coleman asserts that the notion of reincarnation, while based on an "Afrocentric belief in a cyclical process of regeneration through birth, death, and rebirth," had a counterpart in "the Judeo-Christian tradition, as 'the new birth' on the one hand, and as the 'resurrection' on the other."[52] Akasha Gloria Hull in examining the role of ancestors in the lives of African American women claims that "calling on ancestors has always empowered African American struggle in the world."[53]

Although many Black Christians continue to avoid and perhaps demonize communicating with ancestors, the Bible speaks directly to the presence of

---

[49]Geoffrey Parrinder, *West African Religion: A Study of the Beliefs and Practices of Akan, ewe, Yoruba, Ibo, and Kindred Peoples* (Eugene, OR: Wipf and Stock Publishers, 2014), 115.

[50]Mbiti, *African Religions and Philosophy*, 81–82.

[51]Will Coleman, *Tribal Talk: Black Theology, Hermeneutics, and African/American Ways of "Telling the Story"* (University Park: Pennsylvania State University Press, 2000), 35.

[52]Coleman, *Tribal Talk*, 35.

[53]Akasha Gloria Hull, *Soul Talk: The New Spirituality of African American Women* (Rochester, VT: Inner Traditions International, 2001), 55.

ancestors, and infers their work on our behalf as we run the race of Christian discipleship: "Since we are surrounded by so great a cloud of witnesses, let us also lay aside every weight and the sin that clings so closely, and run with perseverance the race that is set before us, looking to Jesus, the pioneer and perfecter of our faith" (Heb 12:1). Regarding this mention of "witnesses," biblical scholar W. Trent Foley suggests:

> As witnesses, these exemplars of faith give us testimony of what they see. First, they see by faith, and certainly not by sight, God's promises (11:13), their heavenly homeland (11:16), and even God's very self (11:27). Secondly, the passage suggests that they see not only God's redeeming work, but also us, as we struggle through the race they have already completed. As though in the stands of an arena, they surround the runner of faith, offering encouragement and support as she races toward the finish line. Their presence inspires the runner. He does not regard them as simply dead and gone. He must not only imitate their ancient example, but sense their supportive presence in the here and now.[54]

Hull relates the story of Lucille Clifton, an African American writer, who began experiencing her late mother's presence years after her mother's transition. Once she recovered from the initial shock, she began to listen for whatever wisdom or assistance her mother might offer her from the other side. Hull, along with other scholars, suggests that this is very much a part of African and African American culture.[55] Many Black Christians, regardless of their formal religious beliefs, recount similar experiences with loved ones who have transitioned, testifying that their family members are still present and interceding for them, with the Supreme Deity, in life-and-death situations, or just in ordinary everyday circumstances. Acknowledging and affirming the presence and intercession of ancestors, as a great cloud of witnesses surrounding and supporting those on this side, is an extremely powerful and liberating spiritual connection that can enhance liturgical and worship performance and participation.

Carlyle Stewart characterizes African American spirituality as "an expression of human freedom," noting that "it is not simply a collective social goal; it has been a process, a style of existence, a mode of consciousness and being, which has enabled black Americans to survive amid subtle and flagrant forms

---

[54]W. Trent Foley, "Hebrews 12:1–3: Theological Perspectives," in *Feasting on the Word: Preaching the Revised Common Lectionary, Year* B, ed. David Bartlett and Barbara Brown Taylor, vol. 2 (Louisville, KY: Westminster John Knox Press, 2008), loc. 8819–8825 of 19547, Kindle.

[55]Hull, *Soul Talk*, 54–59.

of racism and oppression."[56] He names *creative soul force* and *resistant soul force* as "the two essential elements that shape and compel African American spiritual belief and praxis."[57] As praxis, "African American spirituality has always worked to translate the language and symbols of white racism, oppression, and Anglo culture into systems of power and meaning for African Americans."[58] It is African American creativity, invention, and an intent to survive that compelled Blacks in America to produce their own culture. Stewart offers five functional dynamics, or components, of African American spirituality: "the formation of black consciousness; black *communitas* and black culture; the unification of self and community; the corroboration of value, meaning, and existence for African-American people; and the transformation and consecration of black life as sacred reality."[59] Since the arrival of Africans on these shores, they and their descendants have been in a struggle for *sur-thrival*, striving for wholeness, mentally, physically, psychologically, and spiritually.

The formation of Black consciousness in a white supremacist society required and continues requiring construction of alternative realities and identities than what has been assigned to Black people by the dominant culture. Black spirituality has empowered Black people to accomplish this formation and transformation, through the creation of Black *communitas*,[60] providing spiritual resources that reinforce positive aspects of Black community and identity. This creation of alternate, life-giving culture in and by Black *communitas* shares a reciprocal relationship with Black spirituality. Stewart contends, "We cannot fully conceive of African-American cultural formations without considering the role of spirituality and soul force in shaping black behavior, consciousness, and community through the cultivation of black cultural hermeneutics."[61] As has already been noted, the influence of African/Black spirituality on our ancestors led to the creation of music, art, literature, and other idioms directly out of the Black experience and aesthetic, meant to exhibit the beauty, majesty, power, and unique worth of Black people, not for the approval or acceptance of white gazes, but for the edification of Black people themselves.

---

[56]Carlyle Fielding Stewart III, *Soul Survivors: An African American Spirituality* (Louisville, KY: Westminster John Knox Press, 1997), 20.

[57]Carlyle Fielding Stewart III, *Black Spirituality and Black Consciousness: Soul Force, Culture and Freedom in the African-American Experience* (Trenton, NJ: Africa World Press, 1999), 2.

[58]Stewart, *Soul Survivors*, 21.

[59]Stewart, *Black Spirituality and Black Consciousness*, 27.

[60]Victor Turner defines Black *communitas* as a "community of healing and belonging." Particularly helpful is his exposition on *communitas* in his text *The Ritual Process: Structure and Anti-Structure* (Ithaca, NY: Cornell University Press, 1969), 94–165. He asserts: "*Communitas* . . . is almost everywhere held to be sacred or 'holy,' possibly because it transgresses or dissolves the norms that govern structured and institutionalized relationships and is accompanied by experiences of unprecedented potency" (128).

[61]Stewart, *Black Spirituality and Black Consciousness*, 38.

A womanist liturgical theology must be imbued with Spirit and a spirituality that manifests what Townes calls the womanist concern for "physical and spiritual is-ness in the context of African American life."[62] She also notes that "it is consonant with African cosmology that understands all of life is sacred," and "seeks to rediscover this apprehension in Black life in the United States."[63] Therefore, this liturgical paradigm is not rooted in practices that center other-worldly perspectives; rather it is grounded in the material, lived realities of Black women and men and "succored in the flawed transcendent powers of our spirituality."[64] There is no way to separate the two and still practice liberative, holistic liturgy and worship.

Cheryl Kirk-Duggan also offers a definition and description of womanist spirituality and theological aesthetics that is helpful for the construction of this liturgical paradigm:

> Womanist spirituality is a vital, expressive, revolutionary, embodied, personal, and communal resistance-based way of life and theoretical discourse, based upon the rich lived, yet oppressed, experiences of black women descended from the African diaspora, who as social beings in relationship with the Divine, celebrate life and expose injustice and malaise.[65]

As Townes, Kirk-Duggan, and other womanist scholars have described it, womanist spirituality embodies the "hidden wholeness," "creative," and "resistance soul forces" and Black *communitas* of African and African American spiritualities within a uniquely inclusive, liberative, holistic spirituality and aesthetic for the doing of both primary and secondary liturgical theology.

Affirming Embodiment without Qualification

What does the term *embodiment* mean and why is embodiment essential to liturgy and worship? The root word "embody" literally means "to give a body to."[66] The concept of embodiment, or "the state of being embodied," requires the existence of something in visible, tangible form. Embodiment

---

[62]Townes, *In a Blaze of Glory*, 48.
[63]Townes, *In a Blaze of Glory*, 48.
[64] Townes, *In a Blaze of Glory*, 65.
[65]Cheryl Kirk-Duggan, "Quilting Relations with Creation: Overcoming, Going Through, and Not Being Stuck," in *Deeper Shades of Purple: Womanism in Religion and Society*, ed. Stacey Floyd-Thomas (New York: New York University Press, 2006), 178.
[66]*Merriam-Webster*, s.v. "embody," accessed December 16, 2020, https://www.merriam-webster.com/dictionary/embody.

is essential for liturgy and worship because worship is action, and the performance of liturgy requires physical action, not just mental, emotional, or spiritual engagement. Both need full personhood to be complete, and so, the body, as well as the mind, soul, and spirit must be involved. While that may seem self-explanatory, embodiment as a concept raises issues. Most of these arise from the development of Christian theologies and doctrines concerning incarnation, particularly the persistent struggle with Platonic dualism—the idea that the spirit is divine while the flesh, or body, is sinful. As discussed earlier, this led to theologies and doctrines that demonized the flesh, and certainly demonized Black flesh. The theological justification of violence that occurred against Jews and persons of other faiths who refused to convert to Christianity under Constantine's rule was the same justification used to perpetrate violence against Africans and their descendants in Africa and the Americas.[67] As Orlando Patterson notes, "Afro-Americans became to the body politic what Satan was to the individual and collective soul of the South. For both the same metaphor of a 'black' malignancy to be excised was employed."[68] Africanness, as well as Blackness, became a liability on American shores, something to be ashamed of—to be marginalized or hidden—as much as possible. Black worship has always struggled in this country, and being Black, *embodying* Blackness, is still perceived as a liability. The tendencies of independent Black denominations, churches, and fellowships to imitate white ways of worshipping by adopting, for example, theological and doctrinal statements of Euro/Anglo/white religious institutions caused the minimization, if not disappearance, of many African/Black liturgical elements and worship practices. Regarding this issue, Rosetta Ross inquires:

> The determination of black churches to maintain theological and doctrinal continuity with white Christianity stagnated development of critical theological thinking within much black Christianity, eclipsing responses to questions such as: What was or may have been the systematic theological contribution to black Christianity that derived from continuity of religions of enslaved peoples and African religions? What rituals and creedal affirmations might be developed to address the enormous need for healing the wounded black consciousness?[69]

---

[67]Kelly Brown Douglas, *What's Faith Got to Do with It? Black Bodies/Christian Souls* (Maryknoll, NY: Orbis Books, 2005), "Closed Monotheism and Power," loc. 867–993 of 4485, Kindle.

[68]Orlando Patterson, *Rituals of Blood: Consequences of Slavery in Two American Centuries* (Washington, DC: Civitas/Counterpoint, 1998), 221–22.

[69]Rosetta Ross, "Lessons and Treasures in Our Mothers' Witness: Why I Write about Black Women's Activism," in *Deeper Shades of Purple: Womanism in Religion and Society*, ed. Stacey Floyd-Thomas (New York: New York University Press, 2006), 117.

A second problem with embodiment, closely related to the first, is the notion of unequal Black bodies. Because Platonic dualism demonizes the flesh as sinful, then the activities of the flesh, particularly those involved with the body's reproductive organs, were deemed sinful. Scriptures that reflect this dualism, especially Pauline texts, became the foundation for theologies and doctrines limiting the expression of acceptable sexuality to that which occurred only within heterosexual marriage for the purposes of procreation. Furthermore, many early Patristics viewed women as evil—because of their interpretations of the Fall as Eve's fault, second-class citizens—because of their creation out of man, or at the very least, the weaker sex (intellectually as well as physically), and therefore relegated to roles and tasks suited to their lesser abilities. From these ideologies came the institutionalization of sexism and misogyny across society, including the church. Marvin Ellison and Kelly Brown Douglas address these two perspectives:

> A male-female or gender dualism reflects a patriarchal hierarchy of value, status, and power in which good order requires male control of women's lives, including their procreative power. Under the influence of these twin dualisms, Christianity has never fully debunked the troubling notion that sex is unclean and should be avoided or, at least, restricted as a necessary evil.[70]

For Black women, this has been a multilayered issue, affecting us as both a racialized sexism and a sexualized racism in the larger society. Cheryl Townsend Gilkes offers an in-depth treatment of this "multiple jeopardy,"[71] stating that "racialized sexism, particularly in the form of the specialized sexism that assaults African-American women, compounds our own community's ambivalence about the meaning of being Black and female in America."[72] Kelly Brown Douglas notes, "Vulnerable to both the racist and sexist ideologies of White culture, Black women provide the gateway for the White cultural assault upon Black sexuality."[73] M. Shawn Copeland speaks directly to this phenomenon and how it imbued chattel slavery:

---

[70]Marvin M. Ellison and Kelly Brown Douglas, Introduction to *Sexuality and the Sacred: Sources for Theological Reflection*, ed. Marvin M. Ellison and Kelly Brown Douglas (Louisville, KY: Westminster John Knox Press, 2010), loc. 217 of 10577, Kindle.

[71]"Multiple jeopardy" is a phrase and model used by sociologist Deborah King for examining the "multiplier effects" of simultaneous and interacting oppressions affecting Black women. See Deborah K. King, "Multiple Jeopardy, Multiple Consciousness: The Context of a Black Feminist Ideology," in *Black Women in America: Social Science Perspectives*, ed. Micheline R. Malson, Elisabeth Mudimbe-Boyi, Jean F. O'Barr, and Mary Wyer (Chicago: University of Chicago Press, 1988), 265–295.

[72]Cheryl Townsend Gilkes, *If It Wasn't for the Women: Black Women's Experience and Womanist Culture in Church and Community* (Maryknoll, NY: Orbis Books, 2001), 184.

[73]Kelly Brown Douglas, *Sexuality and the Black Church: A Womanist Perspective* (Maryknoll, NY: Orbis Books, 1999), loc. 713 of 2942, Kindle.

> The colonization of black women's bodies began in slavery. . . . The enslaved black woman's body was held, at once, in contempt and in contemptuous value. On the one hand, the black woman was thought to be "sly," "sensual," and "shameless"; but these characteristics were valued in relation to a libidinous economics: after all, such a woman made a good brood-sow. On the other hand, those same characteristics only reinforced negative stereotypes about the black woman's lasciviousness and immorality. . . . The black woman was reduced to body parts—parts which allowed white men pleasure, however unsettling; parts which afforded white men economic gain; parts which literally nursed the heirs to white racist supremacy.[74]

Another layer to this multiple jeopardy is the struggle Black women have had being treated as full persons in our own communities. The effects of patriarchy and paternalism (white and Black) are far-reaching and have had deleterious consequences on Black communities and Black churches. Copeland addresses the troubled relationship Black women historically have had in Black churches:

> On the one hand, black Christian churches have been places of spiritual, psychological, and social refuge from the burdens in black women's lives. On the other hand, those same churches in "their patriarchally and androcentrically biased liturgy and leadership have been primary agents" of the colonization of black women's bodies and minds.[75]

Here, Copeland quotes Delores Williams who calls to account the ways in which African American denominational churches "have acted as colonizing agents with regard to the minds and culture of African-American females."[76] Williams denotes three primary ways this has taken place: (1) an uncritical reliance upon the Bible for theological articulation—"a thoroughly patriarchal and androcentrically biased text" whereby Black women in the church have been conditioned to regard this bias as sacred; (2) little to no attention given to the "ancient cultural and egalitarian way" African American slaves appropriated biblical figures and stories that present God's positive relation to both Black male and Black female experience into a sacred oral canon of their own (this, Williams argues, has prevented Black women from "knowing how the black community historically has understood the character of black women's experience in relation to God and the community"); and (3) the use

[74]M. Shawn Copeland, "Body, Representation, and Black Religious Discourse," in *Womanist Theological Ethics: A Reader*, ed. Katie Geneva Cannon, Emilie M. Townes, and Angela D. Sims (Louisville, KY: Westminster John Knox Press, 2011), 100–102.

[75]Copeland, "Body, Representation, and Black Religious Discourse," 106.

[76]Williams, *Sisters in the Wilderness*, 242.

of social and theological assessments of male scholars and preachers that do not reflect the overwhelmingly Black female population and cultural foundation of its churches. This results in theologies, worship practices, liturgical elements, and Christian education materials that are bereft of Black female culture. Moreover, Williams contends that Black churchwomen "are not encouraged to think seriously about their oppression and to use the symbolism of black female culture to shape questions and design strategies to challenge sexist oppression in the church. Rather, many black churchwomen ingest male culture through scripture, sermon and liturgy."[77]

Two primary ways Black women have been categorized in church, and which often function as a dialectic, is as Mammy/Jezebel, reflective of the larger society's Madonna/Whore conundrum. "Mammy" was the created image of the perfect female slave, loyal to the white plantation owner and his family, sometimes over and above her own—a persona produced by the slaveocracy both to allow white women to appear as perfect mothers and Black women to appear as maternal asexual servants to white men and their families.[78] In stark contrast to "Mammy" was "Jezebel." Douglas expounds on this character:

> "Jezebel" has come to symbolize an evil, scheming, and seductive woman. This symbol no doubt owes its meaning to the ninth-century Phoenician princess and wife of the Israelite king Ahab, who was accused of destroying the kingdom with her idolatrous practices and otherwise diabolical ways. (1 Kings 16:29—22:53)[79]

Douglas notes that "the Black woman as a Jezebel was a perfect foil to the White, middle-class woman who was pure, chaste, and innocent."[80]

Townes notes that during the nineteenth century, "rigid social roles for men and women remained intact," and that "white men found the cult of womanhood with its values of piety, submissiveness, purity, and domesticity convenient in an increasingly industrial economy where more men were forced to leave farming and enter occupations previously held by middle-class White women."[81]

It is not difficult to see how the legacy of female "respectability" (as evinced by women who lived pious, pure, and submissive domesticated lives) became juxtaposed in the Black church with women with a "Jezebel" spirit. This

---

77 Williams, *Sisters in the Wilderness*, 242.
78 Douglas, *Sexuality and the Black Church*, loc. 810–885 of 2942, Kindle.
79 Douglas, *Sexuality and the Black Church*, loc. 722 of 2942, Kindle.
80 Douglas, *Sexuality and the Black* Church, loc. 774 of 2942, Kindle.
81 Townes, *In a Blaze of Glory*, 37.

legacy lives on in the twenty-first-century church in the form of lap cloths, appropriate dress size, color, length and neckline, hair color and length, shoe heel height, foundation undergarments, nail length and color, lipstick shade, makeup application, jewelry, vocal tone, decibel level of laughter and speaking voice, walking stride, perceived chastity in singleness and submission in marriage, well-behaved children, and deference to male clergy and church leaders, even by female clergy. Any deviation from this paradigm, especially in personal appearance or independence of thought/action, places a woman at risk of being labeled "Jezebel" or having a "Jezebel" spirit.

Two issues with embodiment that directly affect Black women involve how Jesus is viewed or perceived. The first involves the theological understanding of Jesus as the ultimate surrogate figure, standing in the place of sinful humanity as sacrificial offering. Williams raises the question, "Can there be salvific power for black women in Christian images of oppression (for example, Jesus on the cross) meant to teach something about redemption?"[82] Whether "coerced" or "voluntary," surrogacy as sacred or redemptive is problematic as it invites exploitation, particularly of Black women, who are already at multiple risks for exploitation. But Black communities and Black churches request, if not require, Black female surrogacy constantly. Black women "stay capin' " for Black men and Black communities that, too often, do not reciprocate this sacrificial stance. Black women are constantly placing themselves on the line, literally and figuratively, to save the people and communities they love. If not for Black women, Black churches would cease to exist, as pews, choir stands, church boards, and coffers would be empty. But this often causes deep inner conflicts for Black women, which become dis-ease, and finally, disease.

The second issue is the complete masculinization of the Deity, even as the Triune God. In most denominations, God, Jesus, and the Holy Spirit are viewed anthropomorphically as male. Moreover, quite often God and Jesus are conflated, and their names/roles used interchangeably. This further underscores the maleness of both entities, which works both to imply the divinity of men while simultaneously denying the divinity of women, a perspective that has been used to justify church doctrines prohibiting women's ordination or church leadership of any kind. Biblical translations that consistently refer to the Hebrew deity as "He," "Father," "Lord," and other male appellations have been instrumental in laying an almost indestructible foundation of male divinity and superiority, and, conversely, female humanity and inferiority. One particularly notable biblical source of this etiology is one that recounts how the "sons of God" went in to the "daughters of humans, who bore children

[82]Williams, *Sisters in the Wilderness*, 144.

to them" (Gen 6:1–4). Immediately following this pericope, the biblical text proclaims in part that "the Lord saw the wickedness of humankind was great in the earth" (Gen 6:5). Note, it does not call the "sons of God" wicked, but humanity, which includes the offspring of the "sons of God" and the "daughters of humans." Therefore, one may infer it is the humanity (stemming from the daughters) that is wicked, not the divinity (from the "sons").

Williams asks three salient questions regarding this issue:

> Why has this female-mother-God aspect of African-American culture not been efficacious enough historically to make unnecessary the arguments black women have had to wage for women's ordination and for women to be put on deacon boards? Why is it that not a single likeness of "God or Jesus as Mother" (that is, as female image) appears on the stained glass windows in black churches where pictures of white male and sometimes black male Jesuses do appear? Did our African heritage, our American heritage and our African-American strategies for establishing a black biblical tradition together create a split-consciousness granting power to mothers but investing all the authority in males?[83]

The insistence on a male deity (and subsequently, a predominantly male authority) in Black churches creates and undergirds this split-consciousness which contributes to an already problematic sense of embodiment in Black churchwomen.

Another struggle with embodiment in the Black church, also emanating from Platonized Christianity, is that of demonized sexuality. Douglas writes,

> In effect those judged driven by sexual desire and passion are seen as enemies of God. They are effectively demonized just as sexuality itself is demonized. Platonized views on sexuality essentially served to reify the distinctions demanded by Christianity's paradoxical christological core and monotheistic nature.[84]

Just as the Christian Church inherited these Platonic ideas/ideals from Hellenistic Greek thought and culture, the Black church "inherited a body-negating sexual ethic"[85] from the Western/white culture and religious traditions that preceded it. In response to the hypersexualization of Black people by Euro/Anglo/white theorists, philosophers, theologians, and landowners, Black churches used this ethic as "sacred cover for the black community's standard of

---

[83]Williams, *Sisters in the Wilderness*, 191–192.

[84]Douglas, *What's Faith Got to Do with it? Black Bodies/Christian* Souls, 50.

[85]Douglas, "Black and Blues: God-Talk/Body-Talk for the Black Church," in *Womanist Theological Ethics: A Reader*, 123.

hyperproper sexuality, making violation of this hyperproper sexual standard not simply a social breach, but also a sin against God."[86] In this attempt to make itself acceptable to the dominant culture, the Black church becomes oppressor, "seizing an effective tool of oppressing power, the sexuality of those it opposes, and maligns it."[87] Just as Black women are hypersexualized as temptresses, each one a potential "Jezebel," gay and lesbian persons are hypersexualized as "controlled by an abnormal, homoerotic libido."[88]

While Douglas reminds us that Black people did not arrive in this country *tabula rasa* (blank slates), white racism has had its most "penetrating impact on Black sexual discourse,"[89] adding to, if not causing outright, the Black church and community's reticence toward addressing sexual topics. Sex, especially same-gender/same-sex physical intimacy and sexual activity, has certainly been a taboo subject in most Black churches, because of prevailing and internalized white stereotypes of Black hypersexuality. Douglas notes how many Black churches and Black clergy, particularly, have publicly denounced same-gender/same-sex sexuality and marriage, supported constitutional amendments and state laws that limit marriage to heterosexual definitions, labeled HIV/AIDS as a "gay" disease and blamed LGBTQIA persons for the AIDS crisis, and refused to recognize the issues of the LGBTQIA community as civil rights issues.[90]

This marginalization is problematic enough on its own, but it is doubly problematic given the hypocrisy practiced by these same Black churches and clergy who have no problem accepting the gifts, talents, and money of LGBTQIA church members and attendees. The prevailing response in Black churches is: "As long as 'they' are quiet about it, I/we don't have any problems with 'their' sexuality." But this position, as Horace Griffin points out, is "necessarily contradictory." He emphasizes that "to say that a gay person is accepted as long as she/he does not demonstrate the very thing that makes her/him gay is no acceptance at all"—an attitude strikingly similar to that of white racists who were accepting of Blacks as long as they stayed in their place or exhibited behaviors that did not reflect Black cultural thoughts or practices:

> The expectation for gays to be invisible . . . reflects the shame and embarrassment that Africans Americans harbor about bodily expression between the same sex. . . . This reaction is more than cultural modesty of

[86]Douglas, "Black and Blues," 123.

[87]Douglas, "Black and Blues," 125.

[88]Douglas, "Black and Blues," 125.

[89]Kelly Brown Douglas, "Daring to Speak: Womanist Theology and Black Sexuality," in *Embracing the Spirit: Womanist Perspectives on Hope, Salvation, and Transformation*, ed. Emilie M. Townes (Maryknoll, NY: Orbis Books, 1997), 240.

[90]Douglas, "Black and Blues," 114.

sexual relationships. Rather, this kind of silencing is a means of control over gays, and like all silencing, works toward the death of a people.[91]

Townes also addresses embodiment and sexual repression in the church:

Our sexuality is who we are as thinking, feeling, and caring human beings. It is our ability to love and nurture. To express warmth and compassion. It is not only our gonads. Heterosexism encourages the objectification of our bodies—male and female. . . . Too often we do not see or want to discover the care and nurture that lesbians and gay men can and do have for each other. We must raise some exacting questions about an ethic that insists that homosexuals should either try to engage in heterosexual relationships unhappily or remain celibate. An ethic is suspicious when it allows some to impose on others obligations that they are unwilling to accept for themselves.[92]

One final issue regarding embodiment concerns ableism, which refers to a set of beliefs or practices that devalue and discriminate against people with physical, intellectual, or psychiatric disabilities and often rests on the assumption that disabled people need to be "fixed" in one form or the other and are often not included at the table for key decisions.[93]

Just as marginalization of Black women and members of the LGBTQIA community occurs in the Black church, so too does the marginalization of persons considered physically and/or mentally disabled. Just as the marginalization of Black women and LGBTQIA persons is based on the idea that something is inherently inferior, sinful, or "wrong" with them, so too, are differently abled persons often perceived by religious/church people as inferior, "wrong," and possibly the product of sinful behavior. However, Thomas Reynolds, a scholar and the father of a differently-abled son, claims that disability has theological power that "opens up a range of possible resources and interdisciplinary approaches to the vulnerable and relational character of human existence, bringing to the fore issues of difference, normalcy, embodiment, community, and redemption."[94]

---

[91]Horace Griffin, "Toward a True Black Liberation Theology: Affirming Homoeroticism, Black Gay Christians, and Their Love Relationships," in *Loving the Body: Black Religious Studies and the Erotic*, ed. Anthony B. Pinn and Dwight N. Hopkins (New York: Palgrave Macmillan, 2004), 148.

[92]Townes, *In a Blaze of Glory*, 81.

[93]Leah Smith, "Ableism," Center for Disability Rights, https://www.cdrnys.org/blog/uncategorized/ableism/.

[94]Thomas Reynolds, *Vulnerable Communion: A Theology of Disability and Hospitality* (Grand Rapids, MI: Brazos Press, 2008), 13.

Nancy Eiesland identifies three "carnal sins" that contribute to the marginalization and exclusion of persons with disabilities. First, there is the implicit or explicit belief in a causal relationship between sin and disability—the "sin-disability conflation"—which holds that persons with disabilities are evidence of the sinfulness of the created world that God seeks to heal and transform. Second, there is the concept of "virtuous suffering," in which the church sees the suffering of those considered disabled a means of divine work in the world. Finally, there is the notion of "segregationist charity," which occurs when congregations maintain a "safe distance" from those whose disabilities challenge their theologies, even while attempting to help them. Each of these represent a persistent problematic theology: persons with disabilities are "either divinely blessed or damned: the defiled evildoer or the spiritual superhero."[95]

Biblically, Christians wrestle with the reality of disabilities in light of texts centered on miraculous healings, especially those of Jesus. Christians wonder: "If Jesus healed then, and we believe in a resurrected Jesus who has all power in his hands, then why won't Jesus heal those who are in need, now?" "Does the person not want to be, or believe she can be, healed?"

Theologically, Christians wrestle with questions of theodicy: "Why would God allow someone to be born that way?" or "Why would God allow someone to lose their abilities?" "Why doesn't God allow this person to be healed?" "Where is God?" Reynolds examines rationales for asking these questions and how they speak to personal and group discomfort with disability, concluding that most non-disabled persons are unsure of how to make sense of disability. First, disability confronts non-disabled persons with their own tenuous humanity. Second, because non-disabled persons are unsure of how to be comfortable in the presence of disability, they feel they must hide it or make it go away. Last, disability makes people see the ways their communities include some and exclude others, and rather than admit and address these inequities, they attempt to neutralize them by fixing what they perceive is broken in others, so that persons with disabilities reflect what they perceive themselves to be, normal.[96] Unfortunately, these perceptions and perspectives keep non-disabled persons from truly knowing and sharing "the ordinary lives and lived realities of most people with disabilities."[97]

Why is the concept of embodiment crucial to Christian worship? First,

---

[95]Nancy Eiesland, *The Disabled God: Toward a Liberatory Theology of Disability* (Nashville, TN: Abingdon Press, 1994), 71–74. See also Rebecca Spurrier, *The Disabled Church: Human Difference and the Art of Communal Worship* (New York: Fordham University Press, 2019), 29, in which she asserts, "In such a theological framework, disabled lives provide others with inspirational examples of suffering and overcoming. Such theologies have been used to isolate people with disabilities and to encourage them to adjust to unjust circumstances."

[96]Reynolds, *Vulnerable Communion*, 29.

[97]Eiesland, *The Disabled God*, 71.

because Christianity is an incarnational faith; it is not based on a book of scriptures about a deity nor is it merely a set of proverbs about how one should live. It is a faith tradition rooted and grounded in the life, death, and resurrection of Yeshua Hamashiach—Jesus, the Anointed One—who was flesh and lived on earth. He was born to a teenage mother, lived under Roman occupation, was baptized by his cousin, endured hunger in the wilderness, walked with crowds, lived with disciples, debated with religious scholars, ate with outcasts, touched, and was touched by those who wanted to be made whole, experienced emotions, cried, suffered brutal torture, died, and was buried, as a human being. All these acts define Jesus as fully human, and in them, Jesus brought his full humanity with him. He did not separate his mind from his emotions, his emotions from his body, or his body from his spirituality.

Moreover, in his male embodiment, Jesus turned the notion of male and masculine power and dominance on its head. Copeland writes:

> Through his oppositional appropriation of masculinity, Jesus countered many gendered cultural expectations. He overturned patriarchal family structure, releasing family members from the denotation as property of the male head of household. . . . He chose women as disciples and taught them as he taught the men, defending them against those who questioned, attacked, or belittled them, and he affirmed their agency over against those narrow and constricting roles set for them by culture, religion, and empire. Jesus's performance of masculinity was *kenotic*: he emptied himself of all that would subvert or stifle authentic human liberation.[98]

In other words, Jesus's incarnation frees the world from patriarchal, hierarchical, and heteronormative notions of what it means to be both divine and human. His life is an example of how divestment from these false constructions can liberate and make individuals and communities whole.

Furthermore, embodiment in worship is essential because Jesus instituted bodily acts for his disciples. Jesus instructs his disciples to baptize all nations; baptism is a tangible, physical act that symbolizes an intangible transformation. It is incarnational; it must be expressed bodily. Holy Communion is a tangible, physical act of consuming elements that represent Jesus's body and blood, during which one becomes a member of Jesus's body—the body of Christ. It is incarnational; it must be expressed bodily. Moreover, engaging in

[98] M. Shawn Copeland, *Knowing Christ Crucified: The Witness of African American Religious Experience* (Maryknoll, NY: Orbis Books, 2018), 94–95.

the act of Holy Communion imbues those who partake with the responsibility to go and be Christ's body for the whole world. Disciples embody Jesus the Christ, incarnating him again and again, until he comes. This is done in the full, bodied humanity of those who come—the full Black bodied humanity; the full female bodied humanity; the full lesbian, gay, bisexual, transgender, and queer bodied humanity; the full differently abled bodied humanity; and Jesus meets all of us in these acts, in our bodies.

Finally, embodiment is crucial in worship because it is how Jesus instructs worshippers to encounter the Holy. He tells his disciples and the crowds that they are to love the Lord their God with all their mind, soul, strength, and heart. These four facets represent the four quadrants of personhood. The *mind* is the intellect, where cognitive processing occurs. One cannot worship fully without intellectual engagement, meaning without registering mentally what is happening and responding, in some sense, cerebrally. The *soul* is the seat of the emotions, which are also needed for an authentic worship experience. Whatever state one may be in, emotionally, or whatever emotions one may experience while in worship, all of those are brought to bear in the worship encounter. *Strength* represents the physical body which is often the quadrant most overlooked in worship. Much of our worship, unfortunately, happens from the neck up; once we are seated after the opening hymn, we remain there until the benediction. Even in churches where movement occurs, it is often repetitive and does not register intentional meaning. But in moving our physical bodies, we have an opportunity to practice movement that carries significant meaning, both theologically and ontologically. Finally, the *heart* is where one's will, or volition, is located. Whatever occurs in worship, the call for a response requires a choice. The heart is where one chooses to become a disciple, to act, to make a change in one's life, and to decide to embody Jesus Christ.

To worship God with mind, soul, strength, and heart requires one's full embodied humanity. Therefore, we need a liturgical paradigm that honors our full embodiment, does not shame or exclude any bodies, acknowledges the beauty of each one's humanity and divinity, and does not require any to divest herself, himself, or themselves from their bodies to be seen as God's divine, human creation.

A womanist liturgical theology is founded on the desire for wholeness, a wholeness that, in many ways, has remained hidden in the Black church. Studying and employing primary and secondary liturgical theology can assist Black congregations in examining their current worship practices for meaning, as well as explore new frontiers for more liberative liturgical frameworks. One such framework is a womanist liturgical paradigm that employs ancestral African cosmologies and spirituality within Black Christian worship and liturgy, divested of androcentric patriarchy and problematic notions of exclusive embodiment, while empowering worshippers to become participants, not merely spectators, in liturgical expression and activity. The next chapter explores this new womanist liturgical paradigm and how congregations can engage these ways of worshipping.

10

A Womanist Liturgical Theology

We have a real comfort zone in our worship lives. We only notice our complacency when it's challenged by the new, the different.

—Emilie Townes

What would it mean to worship in a womanist way? What would womanist liturgies look like? In light of what has been discussed, worshipping through a womanist lens would include critical engagement and employment of womanist ethics and hermeneutics of liberation, suspicion, and incarnation, as well as womanist spirituality in all aspects of liturgical and worship planning, performance, and evaluation.

Womanist Ethics and Hermeneutics in Liturgy and Worship

Most published scholarship in the disciplines of womanist ethics and hermeneutics has been in the arenas of biblical interpretation, biblical hermeneutics, and homiletics. Though womanist scholars, including Delores Williams and Cheryl Kirk-Duggan, have written articles and book chapters that explore womanist resistance practices in worship, very few monographs, if any, are solely dedicated to applying womanist lenses to liturgy and worship. However, this is a critical need if Black faith communities are going to *sur-thrive* and if the Black church is going to remain viable as a prophetic voice and force in this century.

Ethics and Hermeneutics of Liberation

Mother of womanist ethics Katie Geneva Cannon insists that "womanist ethics examines the expressive products of oral culture that deal with our perennial quest for liberation, as well as written literature that invites African Americans to recognize 'the distinction between nature in its inevitability and culture in its changeability.'"[1] She offers four areas of focus for her work: (1) *the creation of womanist pedagogical styles*—inviting a more serious encounter with Black contributions to theological and religious studies; (2) *the emergence of distinctive investigative methodologies*—constructing cognitive maps that set perimeters for the intelligibility and legitimacy of race, sex, and class oppression to discern hierarchical, mechanistic patterns of exploitation that need altering for justice's sake; (3) *reconsideration of the established theories, doctrines, and debates of Eurocentric, male-normative ethics*—defining, elaborating, exemplifying and justifying the integration of being and doing; and (4) *the adjudicative function of womanist scholars*—formulating fresh ethical controversies relevant to the particular existential realities of Black women as they are recorded in the writings of African American women.[2] Importantly, Cannon lays the groundwork for constructing alternative sites of ethical and theological authority that inform a more liberative liturgical paradigm. Her areas of focus assist liturgical theologians—primary and secondary—in seeing the ways worship has been beset by androcentric, patriarchal, and ableist patterns, and they give us a framework within which to question, evaluate, reform, and replace those patterns that are death-dealing and antithetical to the goal of a holistic justice agenda in private and public spheres.[3]

Cannon notes several pressing concerns in the African American women's literary tradition that parallel problematic issues in liturgical traditions. One concern is *colorism*, an "interiorized color consciousness" based on skin complexion, hair texture, and other physical features that are used to promote and practice discrimination against Black women.[4] This correlates directly to the anti-Africanness and anti-Blackness found in Euro/Anglo/white religious and theological traditions. As previously noted, anti-Blackness pervades liturgy in most Protestant traditions, including its hymnody, sacramental liturgies, and biblical interpretations. A second concern that has potential for helping construct a womanist liturgical paradigm is that of "Black women's bodies as texts."[5] Cannon writes, "Flesh houses memories—the color of flesh, the reproductive character of flesh, and the manifold ways that the flesh of African women is the text on which androcentric patriarchy is written."[6] How much richer, deeper, more meaningful, liberative, and holistic would liturgies in Black churches be if they emanated from the memories of Black women, if

[1]Katie Geneva Cannon, *Katie's Canon* (New York: Continuum, 2003), 69.

[2]Cannon, *Katie's Canon*, 69–70.

[3]Cannon, *Katie's Canon*, 72.

[4]Cannon, *Katie's Canon*, 72.

[5]Mae Henderson, "Toni Morrison's *Beloved*: Re-Membering the Body as Historical Text," in *Comparative American Identities: Race, Sex and Nationalities in the Modern Text*, edited with an introduction by Hortense Spillers (New York: Routledge, 1991), 62–86.

[6]Cannon, *Katie's Canon*, 75.

the words, thoughts, memories, lived experiences of Black women carried as much (if not more) weight as those of Jewish and European characters of the biblical text and the European/Euro-descended theologians who developed and wrote most of the liturgies in our churches?

New Testament scholar Clarice J. Martin outlines three assumptions about the Bible that undergird womanist biblical interpretations: (1) the Bible is a primary source for how African Americans understand God; (2) the Bible is a liberative and empowering resource for African Americans; and (3) there are multiple, interlocking ideologies and systems of hegemony within the biblical tradition.[7] Martin notes four primary tasks for womanist biblical interpreters: (1) the recovery, analysis, and reconstruction of texts and their worlds; (2) reclaiming neglected histories and stories of Black peoples within divergent biblical traditions; (3) challenging the persistent narrow vision of feminist theologians and biblical interpreters on issues of race; and (4) analyzing and documenting the effects of biblical interpretation on African and African diasporic peoples.[8] With these directives, liturgical theologians have a clear path on how to engage processes of womanist biblical interpretation.

Delores Williams makes a distinction between Black liberation theology, which "provides the theological explication of the liberation principle of black biblical interpretation," and womanist survivalist/quality-of-life theology, which "provides the theological explication of the survival principle of African-American biblical interpretation." The latter holds liberation as the goal, but acknowledges that, while striving to achieve liberation, Black women—and the communities they uplift—must experience survival and prosperity, even in the midst of their oppressors. This hermeneutic helps preachers and teachers who wrestle with biblical texts in order to provide faith communities with sermons and lessons that do not gloss over, excuse, or defend a deity that is not always liberative for women. It can provide Black faith communities a lens to critique "the liability of its habit of using the Bible in an uncritical and sometimes too self-serving way."[9]

Another liberative womanist hermeneutic Williams offers is *identification-ascertainment*, which involves three modes of inquiry: subjective, communal, and objective.[10] The *subjective* mode requires a personal analysis of one's faith journey regarding its biblical foundations to discover with whom one personally identifies in the text. The *communal* mode attempts to uncover

---

[7]Clarice J. Martin, "Womanist Biblical Interpretation," in *Dictionary of Biblical Interpretation*, ed. John H. Hayes (Nashville, TN: Abingdon Press, 1999), 656–657.

[8]Martin, "Womanist Biblical Interpretation," 657–658.

[9]Delores S. Williams, *Sisters in the Wilderness: The Challenge of Womanist God Talk* (Maryknoll, NY: Orbis Books, 1993), 150.

[10]Williams, *Sisters in the Wilderness*, 149.

this meaning for the faith community by analyzing liturgy, ritual, and the socio-political-cultural affiliations it holds. Following those two analyses, theologians then engage the *objective* mode, which determines with whom the biblical writers have and have not identified, and who are the victims of those with whom the biblical writers have identified. This hermeneutic can not only assist Black liberation theologians with critiquing ways of using the Bible, but the methodology can be used to help liturgical theologians critique other foundational areas of worship, including historical, theological, and psychological, in addition to biblical foundations.

Feminist scholar Phyllis Trible offers a helpful hermeneutic for reading biblical texts. Labeling her work as "feminist hermeneutics," she describes a similar methodology to that used in womanist biblical hermeneutics, stating, "By feminism I do not mean a narrow focus upon women, but rather a critique of culture in light of misogyny."[11] Trible's work focuses on what she calls "texts of terror," exegeting and analyzing biblical texts to "tell sad stories as I hear them."[12] Another feminist scholar whose work employs liberative hermeneutics is Elisabeth Schüssler Fiorenza, who describes a "hermeneutics of liberative vision and imagination," as one that "seeks to actualize and dramatize biblical texts differently."[13] One of the ways it resonates with womanist biblical hermeneutics is that "it retells biblical stories from a different perspective and amplifies the emancipatory voices suppressed in biblical texts."[14]

Pioneering womanist biblical scholar Renita J. Weems is careful to press the distinctions between feminist and womanist readings of the biblical text. For Weems, womanist biblical interpretation does not begin with the Bible, but with Black women's experiences, particularly the experiences of Black women who have faced intersectional oppression. She asserts, "Victimized by multiple categories of oppression (e.g., race, gender, class) and having experienced these victimizations oftentimes simultaneously, women of color bring to biblical academic discourse a broader, and more subtle, understanding of systems of oppression."[15] Weems has authored several texts that offer liberative strategies and critical approaches for reading the biblical text. In "Re-Reading for Liberation: African American Women and the Bible," Weems notes that "womanist biblical criticism is interested in the ways in which African Americans read the Bible, the strategies they use in negotiating meaning

[11]Phyllis Trible, *God and the Rhetoric of Sexuality* (Philadelphia: Fortress Press, 1978), 7.

[12]Phyllis Trible, *Texts of Terror: Literary-Feminist Readings of Biblical Narratives* (Philadelphia: Fortress Press, 1984), 1.

[13]Elisabeth Schüssler Fiorenza, *But She Said: Feminist Practices of Biblical Interpretation* (Boston: Beacon Press, 1992), 54.

[14]Schüssler Fiorenza, *But She Said*, 55.

[15]Renita J. Weems, "Womanist Reflections on Biblical Hermeneutics," in *Black Theology: A Documentary History*, ed. James H. Cone and Gayraud S. Wilmore (Maryknoll, NY: Orbis Books, 1993), 220.

and identity from stories, and those they use when resisting the meaning(s) and identities attached to certain stories."[16]

Womanist biblical scholar Mitzi J. Smith offers new voices, methodologies, and approaches to womanist biblical hermeneutics. Referring to insight she received from Weems, Smith reminds the reader that "no matter our station in life, we all may at any time find ourselves in a position to exploit or oppress another human being; we all have potential victims. And we can be passive participants in our own exploitation."[17] She notes the influence of both Black liberation theology and feminist biblical criticism on womanist biblical interpretation, asserting that the latter "is engaged in a political liberationist project aimed at dismantling oppressive structures and obliterating racism, sexism, classism, heterosexism, and other isms."[18]

Ethics and Hermeneutics of Suspicion

Another essential hermeneutic for critically assessing and employing liturgical elements, particularly biblical and doctrinal texts, is the "hermeneutics of suspicion." According to biblical scholar Nyasha Junior, "the notion of a 'hermeneutics of suspicion' stems from the work of philosopher Paul Ricoeur, who identifies Karl Marx, Friedrich Nietzsche, and Sigmund Freud as thinkers within a school of suspicion that examines the ways in which discourse both reveals and conceals meaning."[19] Schüssler Fiorenza details this hermeneutic in her text, stating, "A *hermeneutics of suspicion* seeks to explore the liberating or oppressive values and visions inscribed in the text by identifying the androcentric-patriarchal character and dynamics of the text and its interpretations."[20] She also notes, "Rather than presuppose the feminist character and liberating truth of biblical texts, a hermeneutics of suspicion rests on the insight that all biblical texts are articulated in grammatically masculine language—a language which is embedded in patriarchal culture, religion, and society, and which is canonized, interpreted, and proclaimed by a long line of men."[21]

Although Schüssler Fiorenza and other feminist writers may have been first to use the phrase *hermeneutics of suspicion* with regard to alternate readings

---

[16]Renita J. Weems, "Re-Reading for Liberation: African American Women and the Bible," in *Feminist Interpretation of the Bible and the Hermeneutics of Liberation*, ed. Silvia Schroer and Sophia Bietenhard (New York: Sheffield Academic Press, 2003), 29.

[17]Mitzi J. Smith, Introduction to *I Found God in Me: A Womanist Biblical Hermeneutics Reader*, ed. Mitzi J. Smith (Eugene, OR: Wipf and Stock, 2015), 2.

[18]Smith, *I Found God in Me*, 7.

[19]Nyasha Junior, *An Introduction to Womanist Biblical Interpretation* (Louisville, KY: Westminster John Knox Press, 2015), chap. 4, footnote 37, loc. 2086-2106 of 4442, Kindle.

[20]Schüssler Fiorenza, *But She Said*, 57.

[21]Schüssler Fiorenza, *But She Said*, 53.

of biblical texts, this method of critical analysis is inherent in the methods of womanist ethics and biblical hermeneutics employed by Cannon, Williams, Grant, Martin, Weems, and other early womanist scholars. Indeed, Martin uses the phrase in describing how enslaved Blacks rejected preaching and teaching that upheld oppressive interpretations of biblical texts regarding slavery. She asserts:

> Black slaves . . . brought a "hermeneutics of suspicion" to bear against prevailing arguments that the *doulos* verses should be a normative guide for their behavior. The slaves promulgated a gospel that averred that God is liberator of all oppressed peoples, and that God is opposed to all persons determined to maintain oppressive social systems.[22]

Weems refers directly to the application of this type of lens in 1991. In discussing why, despite its historic use to subjugate and enslave, the Bible continues to be authoritative for Black women, she notes that many still believe it "provides insight into African American women's particular dilemmas of existence and reflects values and advocates a way of life to which African American female readers genuinely aspire."[23] Her caveat follows: "But the fact that it has been used most often in American society to censure rather than empower women and African Americans has forced them to approach the task of reading the Bible with extreme caution."[24] Williams also employs the phrase when exploring the "organic relationship" womanist and feminist theologies have with each other. She advocates womanists engaging a "hermeneutical posture of suspicion, just as their feminist sisters do,"[25] when reading and looking for meaning within the biblical text.

Ethics and Hermeneutics of Incarnation

Alongside ethics and the hermeneutics of liberation and suspicion, liturgical theologians who seek to practice liberative, holistic worship must also employ a *hermeneutics of incarnation*. The doctrine of the Incarnation, the theological belief that Jesus, as the second person of the Trinity, the *Logos*, was both fully human and fully divine, was established by the Council of Chalcedon in 451 AD. This defining moment in Christendom emerged after intense struggles and debates over the nature of Jesus, which had resulted in

---

[22]Clarice J. Martin, "Womanist Interpretations of the New Testament: The Quest for Holistic and Inclusive Translation and Interpretation," in *I Found God in Me: A Womanist Biblical Hermeneutics Reader*, 37.

[23]Renita J. Weems, "Reading Her Way through the Struggle: African American Women and the Bible," in *Stony the Road We Trod: African American Biblical Interpretation*, ed. Cain Hope Felder (Minneapolis: Fortress Press, 1991), 63.

[24]Weems, "Reading Her Way through the Struggle," 63–64.

[25]Williams, *Sisters in the Wilderness*, 187–188.

many divergent beliefs, branded heresies after confirmation of the *Chalcedonian Definition of Faith*. While this event offered a decisive conclusion to Christological conundrums, the ways it has since been lived out in Christian churches evinces continued struggle, even "radical disjunction between who the church says it is (Christian identity) and what the church actually does (Christian ethics)."[26] Womanist ethicist Eboni Marshall Turman argues:

> Christian communities often find themselves unable to escape the circularity of human oppression because they are rooted in a narrative that seemingly suggests that the body that defies normative wholeness must be dehumanized and choreographed to adhere to a specific narrative, one that ascribes to a binary hierarchy of sorts that too often divinizes certain kinds of flesh, while demonizing others.[27]

It is this demonization of flesh—Black, female, LGBTQIA, and differently abled flesh—that makes necessary a lens for critically assessing how texts, acts, and elements in and of worship actually exclude, rather than invite, some bodies into liturgical practice. M. Shawn Copeland centers this discussion on theological anthropology and the *enfleshing* of created spirit. Considering Genesis 1–3, she presents three convictions regarding theological anthropology: (1) that human beings, created in the image and likeness of God (*imago Dei*), have a distinct capacity for communion with God; (2) that human beings have a unique place in the cosmos God created; and (3) that human beings are made for communion with other living beings.[28] Copeland argues for the inclusion of all bodies in this theological anthropology, acknowledging the risks of absolutizing or fetishizing what can be seen, constructed, represented, expressed and regulated in bodies, but maintaining the necessity of taking such risks because the Word (Jesus of Nazareth) "made flesh was subjugated in empire."[29] She refers to the body as "the medium through which the person . . . realizes selfhood through communion with other embodied selves."[30] Copeland offers liberative and holistic ways of viewing Black, female, homosexual, and queer bodies as full participants in the body of Christ:

> As the flesh of the church is the flesh of Christ in every age, the flesh of the church is marked (as was his flesh) by race, sex, gender, sexuality, and culture. These marks differentiate and transgress, they unify and

[26]Eboni Marshall Turman, *Toward a Womanist Ethic of Incarnation: Black Bodies, the Black Church, and the Council of Chalcedon* (New York: Palgrave Macmillan, 2013), 38.

[27]Turman, *Toward a Womanist Ethic of Incarnation*, 38.

[28]M. Shawn Copeland, *Enfleshing Freedom: Body, Race, and Being* (Minneapolis: Fortress Press, 2010,) 24.

[29]Copeland, *Enfleshing Freedom*, 56–57.

[30]Copeland, *Enfleshing Freedom*, 24.

> bond, but the flesh of Christ relativizes these marks in the flesh of the church. These marks may count; but the mark of Christ, the baptismal sign of the cross, counts for more, trumps all marks.[31]

Noting the ways Jesus embodied "openness, equality, and mutuality in his relationships with women and men," Copeland advocates for full inclusion of all bodies, stating that "in Jesus, God critiques any imperial or ecclesiastical practice of body exclusion and control, sorrows at our obstinacy, and call us all unceasingly to new practices of body inclusion and liberation."[32]

Nancy Eiesland has noted that full inclusion of all bodies has also eluded differently abled bodies in the church:

> The history of the church's interaction with the disabled is at best an ambiguous one. Rather than being a structure for empowerment, the church has more often supported the societal structures and attitudes that has treated people with disabilities as objects of pity and paternalism. For many disabled persons the church has been a "city on a hill"—physically inaccessible and socially inhospitable.[33]

Eiesland has developed a liberatory, incarnational theology of disability based on a symbol of Jesus Christ, not as suffering servant or conquering lord, but as a disabled God. Her theological method combines the political actions of "acting out" (doing the work of revolutionary resistance) and "holding our bodies together" (keeping solidarity with one's own body, other persons with disabilities, and other marginalized groups) in the struggle against discrimination and "deconstructing symbolic order of 'normal' attitudes and unconscious prejudice."[34] The symbol of the resurrected Christ with impaired hands and feet as the disabled God rejects theologies of disability as consequence for individual sin, alters taboos of physical avoidance of disability, embodies practical interdependence and interrelatedness, makes possible hope in the face of bodily limitations, and emerges from Jesus Christ's lived commitment to justice within right relationship.[35]

What impact does this theology have on liturgical practice? Liturgical theologian Don Saliers asserts:

---

[31]Copeland, *Enfleshing Freedom*, 81.

[32]Copeland, *Enfleshing Freedom*, 80–81.

[33]Nancy Eiesland, *The Disabled God: Toward a Liberatory Theology of Disability* (Nashville, TN: Abingdon Press, 1994), 20.

[34]Eiesland, *The Disabled God*, 94–95.

[35]Eiesland, *The Disabled God*, 101–103.

> The reverberating character of liturgy is found in the freedom from captivity to the unreal, to the projected fantasies; it is to live without the denial of limit and mortality. This is why the presence and gifts of persons with disabilities are crucial. The invitation for all is for all but waits upon our inclusion of those who know and share access to the power of life and its brokenness. . . . God embraces the human bodily form of life so that the significance of Christian liturgy thus lies in its narrative of death and resurrection as the story of human existence: not avoiding, not denying or merely appearing, but rendered palpable, tangible, what it is to be human at full stretch. . . . If "inclusiveness" is to be more than a slogan, our practice must lead to acknowledgment of common humanity in the image of God and to the discovery of what it means to be "present" to one another.[36]

Harold Trulear addresses how liturgy is an especially effective method for ensuring the inclusion of persons with disabilities in the Black church. Arguing that the context of worship is where themes of human wholeness and egalitarianism are most often engaged, he uses liturgical elements of preaching, music, dance, and sacred space as points of departure in advocating for full inclusion of all bodies in worship.[37] Trulear asserts that in these elements, African American Christian worship offers historical ethical resources that critique current practices of inclusion while offering hope for the construction of a new communal vision of a church welcoming of all persons.[38]

Kelly Brown Douglas calls the Black church, in particular, to account on the notion of embodiment and incarnation. She proclaims, "The reality of the incarnate God marked as heretical any notion that God was not *en sarki*, that is, a fully embodied presence in Jesus. The divine incarnation seemingly precluded as acceptable to Christianity any belief that reviled the human body/flesh. Yet there has been a prominent Christian tradition that has denigrated and demonized the body."[39] Noting the irony of a people who emerged from an African consciousness that recognized "no contradiction between flesh and divinity" becoming purveyors of Evangelical Protestantism, Douglas reminds the reader of the "devastating consequence when a *platonized* Christian tradition shapes Black life—a life already put upon by

---

[36]Don E. Saliers, "Toward a Spirituality of Inclusiveness," in *Human Disability and the Service of God*, ed. Nancy L. Eiesland and Don E. Saliers (Nashville, TN: Abingdon Press, 1998), 28.

[37]Harold Dean Trulear, "To Make a Wounded Wholeness: Disability and Liturgy in an African American Context," in *Human Disability and the Service of God*, 235–246.

[38]Trulear, "To Make a Wounded Wholeness," 236.

[39]Kelly Brown Douglas, "The Black Church and the Politics of Sexuality," in *Loving the Body: Black Religious Studies and the Erotic*, ed. Anthony B. Pinn and Dwight N. Hopkins (New York: Palgrave Macmillan, 2004), 351.

sexualized racist ideology." She advocates a return to the Black church's "own enslaved religious heritage—one that defied body/soul splits and protected the sanctity of sexuality" to repudiate what she calls the "religiously racist tradition" of *platonized* Christianity.[40]

Eboni Marshall Turman argues that "the wholeness and future of the body of Christ, the black church specifically, can only be realized insofar as the church commits itself to dismantling the binary hierarchy of personhood that informs its moralscape."[41] She offers a "womanist ethic of incarnation" that starts with "flipping the script" of images of Jesus Christ and Black women, "employing the broken bodies of black women as the *not-boundary*, rather than *exclusive inclusivity*, which can serve as a primary resource for approximating intracommunal wholeness."[42] Rather than continuing to perpetuate exclusionary hierarchical standards of embodiment and incarnation, Turman presses the Black church to "embrace and act in accordance with an 'in the flesh' body ethic that engenders justice for *every body*, and not just some of them."[43]

Employing these various ethics and hermeneutics of liberation, suspicion, and incarnation in liturgical theology—the studying, writing, and doing of it—has the potential to produce richer, more meaningful, holistic, and transformative worship experiences for all attendees. Exploring, analyzing, and critiquing liturgical elements through these lenses serve to assist the worshipper, worship leader, and worship planner in four distinct ways. First, they give pause to the sometimes busied (and therefore uncritiqued and typical) order of liturgies and worship services. It makes those who are worshipping and planning worship reflect and ask questions about how and why the service is ordered in a particular manner, questions that might not have arisen in previous instances. Second, it creates opportunities for extensive dialogue between clergy and laity. As these ethics and hermeneutics are applied to liturgical elements, there is the potential for fruitful, albeit uncomfortable, conversations, theological discussions, exegetical questions, and opportunities for participants to engage in worship planning as a way of employing new understandings in worship. Third, it potentially inspires further study and research. Introducing new concepts in an inclusive, non-threatening communal forum often stimulates the desire to know more about a given topic. This can deepen the connections between worship and Christian education, making stronger and more likely continuation of these processes of inquiry. Last, engaging in dialogue strengthens communal fellowship and congregational engagement. When people work together on common interests, they

---

[40] Douglas, "The Black Church and the Politics of Sexuality," 356–360.
[41] Turman, *A Womanist Ethic of Incarnation*, 159.
[42] Turman, *A Womanist Ethic of Incarnation*, 159–160.
[43] Turman, *A Womanist Ethic of Incarnation*, 160.

learn each other as they learn *from* each other. Hearing different perspectives and personal narratives, sharing stories of life-changing events, and confessing one's struggles to understand particular concepts and beliefs, again, in non-threatening spaces, with the common goal of producing life-giving, life-affirming liturgies that *every body* can proclaim without marginalization can transform a church into the body of Christ.

Womanist Spirituality in Liturgy and Worship

It is impossible to include every aspect of womanist spirituality in one text. It is also impossible to include an analysis of every potential liturgical practice through a womanist lens. This section presents a broad overview of how womanist spirituality infuses this new liturgical paradigm holistically.

Townes notes that during the nineteenth century Black women's religious experience evinced a connection between their deep faith and piety and the active witness and work they were called to engage in as they sought (and fought) to reform society. She notes that they developed a relational and contextual spirituality: "Their public work was deeply wedded to their inner and intense reflection. The goal was salvation on earth. . . . African American women began with an intense personal experience of the divine in their lives and took that call to salvation into the public realm to reform a corrupt moral order."[44]

This "intense personal experience of the divine" reflects the intense, personal experiences their ancestors engaged during worship in praise/pray's houses, br(h)ush arbors, and in forests and fields of the African countries from whence they came. From these varied yet common and communal experiences emerged the foundations of what is now being referred to as womanist spirituality. For Townes a womanist spirituality is "concrete, particular, universal, relevant, relentless, self-critical, and communal." She asserts:

> Womanist spirituality holds all these individual and corporate realities in a rigorous hermeneutical circle that moves beyond the known to the unknown and pushes for a rock-steady testament of the faithful who refuse to accept a world as interpreted through the eyes of those who are the key masters and mistresses of hegemony.[45]

---

[44]Emilie M. Townes, *In a Blaze of Glory: Womanist Spirituality as Social Witness* (Nashville, TN: Abingdon Press, 1995), 34–36.

[45]Townes, *In a Blaze of Glory*, 121.

A Radical Concern for Is-ness

Is-ness marks us as human beings, with a primary concern for concrete existence and a holistic relationship between body, soul, and creation. Since arriving on these shores, Black people have struggled with physical, psychological, and even spiritual warfare, seeking to "recenter themselves amid these debilitating constraints."[46] The formative function of Carlyle Fielding Stewart's five functional dynamics of African American spirituality addresses this sense of "'I am ness,' [which is] an ontological connectedness to God that repudiates all attempts at black devaluation and destruction."[47] Stewart further notes that African American spirituality has been instrumental in this struggle for liberation as resources of creativity and cultural capacity for self-determination.[48]

The Black church is historically the place where Black people had the freedom to affirm their personal and collective humanity. No matter what they had endured during the week, coming to the "church-house" undergirded and upheld their individual and communal senses of self. Furthermore, at church, they had opportunities to lead, to share their gifts, and offer their wisdom. Liturgically, they participated in calls to worship, sang solos and in choirs, prayed prayers, read scriptures, danced, played instruments, preached, and taught in a multiplicity of ways, collectively praising God in their "is-ness." How is that "is-ness" included and celebrated in today's worship service? How does that "is-ness" reflect liturgy's link with justice, both inside and outside the doors?

First, to live in and celebrate a communal sense of "is-ness," a faith community has to decide who it is—what its true identity is for that time, space, and place. Too many churches are living in historic identities without the contemporary actions to match. Communities around the church may have changed, or perhaps the church has changed its geographic location and is not serving the same demographics it once did. Churches must engage in reality checks about their core values, mission, and vision and how these get lived out in faith communities and the wider community.

Second, faith communities must do the difficult work of exegeting theological and doctrinal standards that infuse liturgical traditions to determine whether they are life-giving or death-dealing. Celebrating liturgies that address contemporary issues can be informative, educational, and even provocative,

---

[46]Carlyle Fielding Stewart III, *Black Spirituality and Black Consciousness: Soul Force, Culture and Freedom in the African-American Experience* (Trenton, NJ: Africa World Press, 1999), 29.

[47]Garth Baker-Fletcher, *Somebodyness: Martin Luther King, Jr., and the Theory of Dignity* (Minneapolis: Fortress Press, 1993).

[48]Carlyle Fielding Stewart III, *Soul Survivors: An African American Spirituality* (Louisville, KY: Westminster John Knox Press, 1997), 23.

but ultimately have little transformational power if there is no sustained analysis of the status quo. This may be controversial, but considering the problematic histories of development of many of our liturgical traditions and documents, it is necessary. To get at the heart of who we are, we must look at who we've been and who we've chosen to be and become, theologically and doctrinally, and ask hard questions about whether these foundational grounds continue to be secure enough for Black folx.

Third, to engender a holistic relationship between body, soul, and creation, faith communities must do the uncomfortable work of deconstructing embedded theologies of embodiment and incarnation. As scholars have stated, the Black church has internalized a *platonized* Christianity that negates the beauty, sensuality, and sexuality of bodies, internalizing instead troubling theologies of surrogacy and suffering as the only acceptable expressions of Christian physicality. This has led to the adoption of a double-consciousness that encourages living from Monday to Saturday and lying about living on Sunday. Part of this work includes re-humanizing Jesus and recognizing his humanity in more than just his suffering and death. As Townes states, "Situations of oppression do not reveal the mystery of God's love. The revelation of God's love manifests itself in work to end oppression."[49]

Liturgically, worship planners and leaders need to include scripture readings that underscore Jesus's emotions and human needs; music that helps congregations ponder what it meant and means to live as a human called to divine purpose; prayers that ask God to forgive our arrogance and replace it with a willingness to listen and love; and creeds that affirm not just Jesus's existence on this earth, but ours as well.

Re-Imaging God

Who is God in our churches? Liturgically, most often God is male: hymns that proclaim God solely as Father, songs and choruses that refer to God as "He," or conflate God and Jesus so that the language used for both is exclusively male; prayers that call on "Father God" to the extent that one wonders if God knows God's name; sacramental liturgies and creeds that never acknowledge anything feminine or maternal about God—all serve to drive home the same point: God may be Spirit, but that Spirit is male. Delores Williams notes that even some Black churches who have rejected a white Jesus still affirm a male God.[50] Moreover, God, as male, is very often described in sermons and lessons as a stern judge, an angry avenger, whose love, grace, and mercy have limitations, depending on the sin and the sinner.

---

[49]Townes, *In a Blaze of Glory*, 121.
[50]Williams, *Sisters in the Wilderness*, 206–219.

In some churches—even Black ones—the image of God is still an old, white man, with a long white beard, sitting high in the heavens waiting to strike down those who dare question or disobey.

These anthropomorphic, androcentric, patriarchal views of God limit our individual and collective abilities to deepen our spiritual and cosmological understandings of who God is, who we are, who God is calling us to be, and who God wants to be with and in us. If we affirm that God is divine Spirit and that we are made in the *imago Dei*, then we, too, are divine Spirit. Cosmologically, therefore, God meets us on a spiritual plane, speaking, listening, and sharing Godself in intimate, creative, and life-giving ways. God then invites us to become co-creators and co-laborers in the divine project of communal reconciliation and restoration. This re-imaging of God has the potential to dismantle false hierarchical notions of the Holy that cause people to fear and avoid relationship with God and one another.

Furthermore, as we have already noted, these views of God serve to alienate and marginalize those who are not male or perceived as male. To refer to God as male privileges maleness as "divine, authoritative, and mystical,"[51] setting it up as a standard to be reached, admired, or worshipped. Those who—either biologically or sexually—are perceived not to measure up to maleness are left with the choice of admiring and deferring to maleness or being categorized as a problematic "other." This precludes meaningful dialogue about the nature, character, and attributes of God, and creates false hierarchies of human worth, while perpetuating patriarchal systems. Often, it leads to abuse and neglect, both of admirers and "others."

Liturgically, churches who view and/or refer to God primarily as male need reform. There must be a clarion call throughout denominations, churches, and fellowships for an intentional change in language and practice. Many will argue this is unnecessary, but if liturgy is to be linked with justice, our liturgies must be just. We must work to deconstruct embedded male language for the Divine, in all aspects of our worship practices. There must be an intentional use of inclusive language in scripture readings, creeds, sacramental liturgies, and other texts, hymns and spiritual songs, prayers, and any other worship elements. If it sounds awkward, that is because it will feel awkward; but justice does not always feel comfortable.

Liturgical leadership must also reflect the inclusive nature and character of God. All bodies must be accepted as worthy of full participation in all liturgical practice—reading, singing, praying, and preaching. Re-imaging God means re-imaging and re-imagining God's people, *all of God's people*, as loved, invited, able, divine representations of God in flesh. There must not be anything liturgical that cannot be done by someone because of the flesh

[51]Townes, *In a Blaze of Glory*, 70.

in which their divine Spirit is wrapped. Townes reminds us, "Our concepts of God either support the oppression of Black folk in gender-based, racist, classist constructs, or they serve as companion and confederate to our struggle for liberation and faithfulness."[52] What concepts of God are guiding Black congregations? Are they lending themselves to obstruction or full incorporation of God's people into the *ecclesia*? How do we know? Our liturgies tell us so, and we must decide whether we are going to struggle for full inclusivity, and "'git man off [our] eyeball' so that we can see a God whose spirit calls us into a spirituality that loves our bodies into wholeness as God holds us in the palm of creation and with creation itself."[53]

Advocating a Self-Other Relationship

Townes asserts that "a womanist spirituality advocates a self-other relationship," in contrast to Western practice of promoting a self-other opposition, "for it is in the relational matrix that wholeness can be found for African Americans."[54] This wholeness encompasses body and spirit, individual and communal well-being. This is an especially important aspect of this womanist liturgical theological paradigm, for it seeks to recapture African cosmologies of holistic being that negate dualities of spirit/flesh and sacred/secular. Furthermore, this paradigm promotes African cosmologies of kinship and divine relationality between the Holy, humanity, and creation. Essential to apprehending these concepts is the adoption of this self-other relation which prevents our spirituality from becoming solely individually focused and driven or so otherworldly that it is no earthly good. To love the Lord our God with all our hearts, souls, minds, and strength also calls us to love ourselves and one another the same ways, as Baby Suggs *holy* instructs us from the Clearing to love our bodies, hearts, and dark, dark livers[55] to ward off the deprecation and destruction wielded by those who insist on living in self-other opposition.

An African cosmology of kinship and relationality undergirds this self-other relation and presents the dangers inherent in individualism and notions of "othering." "Othering" causes separation and alienation, both when we choose to identify as "other," separating ourselves—individually and collectively, in faith communities—from those we identify as problematic and when we actively "other" or make distinctions of persons in our midst because they are not considered "in" our crowd. This occurs in faith communities every week, as ministers, church leaders, and congregants form cliques, "othering" themselves within the church itself, and then "othering" non-members who do

[52]Townes, *In a Blaze of Glory*, 71.
[53]Townes, *In a Blaze of Glory*, 86.
[54]Townes, *In a Blaze of Glory*, 49.
[55]Toni Morrison, *Beloved* (New York: Alfred A. Knopf, 1987), 88–89.

not fit acceptable parameters of potential membership. While this may seem simplistic, it is one of the reasons the Black church has seen such a substantial decline in membership, and why its prophetic voice has been diminished. Self-other relation is not just a matter of cordiality or friendliness; at its core, it is community-building work that "ministers to our souls, lifts our spirits (individually and collectively), assures our connection with one another and to God, pulls us beyond ourselves."[56] Michael Dash and coauthors support this communal concept of interconnectedness, and state:

> When we allow ourselves to see ourselves as private, individual entities in the midst of a multilayered and pluralistic world context, we cannot help but feel frustrated. But we are not private, individual, and isolated people. We are more than an *I*; we are a *we*. And a more holistic perspective is required if we are going to be active participants in a liberating spirituality that dispels this fearful isolationism. . . . We must see ourselves and others as parts of a greater whole.[57]

To live and worship in this sense of wholeness is not limited to religious conversations or the four walls of a church edifice. What womanist spirituality advocates is an inclusive, communal ethic of being and belonging that acknowledges and articulates the full experiences and intricacies of what it means to be Black in countries, societies, institutions, and spaces committed to anti-Blackness, patriarchy, heteronormativity, homophobia, ableism, and "respectability." To adopt or incorporate this spirituality into liturgical practice, then, cannot be limited to worship experiences. To be sure, it must infuse and inform the worship experience, but it must also extend outward beyond typical parameters of church "business," to community business. The Black church cannot be concerned only with the spiritual and material well-being of its members but not concerned with the spiritual and material well-being of the wider community. It cannot be concerned only with the quality of water in its faucets and fountains but not with the quality of water in the sinks and sewers of the communities in which it resides. The Black church is called to care and confront empire on behalf of all who are oppressed and marginalized, not just those who are deemed "acceptable."

The contemporary lynching of transgendered bodies ought to raise as much of an outcry and a call for justice in the Black church as the lynching of Black women and men in previous decades and centuries. The contemporary

[56]Townes, *In a Blaze of Glory*, 86.

[57]Michael I. N. Dash, Jonathan Jackson, and Stephen C. Rasor, *Hidden Wholeness: An African American Spirituality for Individuals and Communities* (Cleveland, OH: United Church Press, 1997), 77.

economic pillaging and plundering of individuals and communities by those in power ought to bring Black faith community members to town councils, city hall, state capitols, and the White House to speak truth to power in the same prophetic tradition as Harriet Tubman, Sojourner Truth, Ida B. Wells-Barnett, Frederick Douglass, Henry Highland Garnett, A. Philip Randolph, Medgar Evers, Rosa Parks, Martin Luther King Jr., Mamie Till-Mobley, Fannie Lou Hamer, and so many other unnamed prophets.

Be not deceived, this is worship, too. The service aspect of worship (*latreuo*) calls on the Black church to use its collective prophetic voice to fight against powers and principalities in high places for the collective well-being of communities. Liturgical and worship practices should bear witness to this mandate each week. Stewart reminds us:

> Black life then is a perpetual invocation of the Spirit power, presence, and work to overcome communal distinction and harmonize its disparate parts into a community of wholeness, strength, and potential. Without the Spirit of God, black people could not overcome the constraints of disintegration, oppression, and dehumanization. Divine Spirit is the basis of the black community and a source of its collective power and strength. Communing in the Spirit overcomes the disparities of the African American community and allows black people to forge a common ground with themselves and others. Practicing the Spirit and creative presence of God is still the most powerful ritual of African American life. Using that Spirit to build community is the paramount focus of African American spirituality. . . . To envelop oneself in the power of God's Spirit and to disseminate that Spirit as a means of creating and sustaining community is very important for the health, wholeness, and vitality of blacks in America.[58]

Prophetic preaching that espouses prosperity as the collective, communal well-being of all creation and critiques and confronts death-dealing policies and practices, in the church and the world, is necessary as an authentic expression of the gospel of Jesus Christ. Liturgical elements that affirm and empower holistic Christian community as the good creation of God called to walk in the life-giving Spirit and Way of Jesus Christ work to transform faith communities from museums and social clubs mired in self-other opposition into collective communities of healthy empowerment and agency, which, in turn, can transform wider communities into the *beloved community*.

[58]Stewart, *Soul Survivors*, 54–55.

Apocalyptic Visions of Hope and Salvation

On Wednesday, January 6, 2021, in broad daylight and live-streamed on network television and social media, a mob of persons, many, if not all, American citizens, some of them armed, stormed the Capitol building in Washington, DC. Many participants were identified by flags, posters, insignia, and other signage as members of white supremacist and/or nationalist groups. Criminal activity and violence raged throughout the building, creating chaos, and causing extensive damage, while participants took pictures and recorded themselves on social media. During and afterward, government officials, newscasters, and political pundits alike characterized it as a failed insurrectionist attempt to overthrow the United States government. What was compelling were the responses of white interviewees versus Black ones. White people reported being shocked, appalled, unnerved, embarrassed, and sickened by the desperate carnage they watched unfolding before their eyes. Black people, on the other hand, felt this was the foregone conclusion of the previous administration's four-year trajectory. Few, if any Black people reported being shocked, appalled, or embarrassed by the events of the day. Even the lack of Capitol police response, though maddening, was not shocking to Black folx in America.

What accounts for the difference in response, and what does this event have to do with spirituality or liturgical theology? What happened on that day is what has been happening in America since its inception. White privilege, supremacy, and nationalism have been on display since America's colonization. Government-sanctioned massacres of Native Americans, the Trail of Tears, enslavement of Africans and African-descended peoples, sharecropping, Black codes, Jim and Jane Crow, segregation, internment camps, red-lining, gentrification, border patrols, and the caging of children and adults—all testify to the evils of whiteness as an underlying ideology. Why would Black people be shocked or surprised that in 2021 this ideology is still undergirding and supporting actions like the one that took place on January 6? But, for many white people, the event was apocalyptic; in the original etymological sense of the word—it was revelatory. Just as the events on the Edmund Pettus Bridge in Selma, the bombing of the 16th Street Baptist Church in Birmingham, the brutal assaults during the Children's March, lynching of civil rights workers, the body of Emmitt Till, the beating of Rodney King, the burning of Black churches, the massacre of the Mother Emmanuel Nine, the killings of Trayvon Martin, Michael Brown, Tamir Rice, Rekeisha Boyd, Eric Garner, George Floyd, Breonna Taylor, Ahmaud Arbery, and so many, many others revealed to America the savagery and barbarism of white supremacy, so, too, did this event reveal that white supremacy is still alive and well.

As we have discussed, white supremacy is not merely a political ideology;

it is grounded in racist and patriarchal religious beliefs about the evils of Blackness and the embodied "other." These beliefs imbue religious, liturgical, and worship practices in both white and Black churches. They are what cause Black people to despise their own histories, African heritages, ancestral ways of worshipping and seeking the Creator Spirit. This is how evangelicalism and prosperity theology became so popular among Black people. Evangelicalism promises to wash Black folx "whiter than snow," and prosperity theology promises to make them rich. The problem with these promises is they are built on faulty premises. Advocating and adhering to theological and doctrinal beliefs built on foundations antithetical to one's being doesn't result in wholeness, but schizophrenia. This same schizophrenia imbues too much of Black liturgy and worship today. It is why many newcomers attend once and never return, and why others continue to live dualistic, fractured lives. To counter this, Townes advocates a womanist spirituality that emerges from apocalyptic visions of hope and salvation.[59]

A revelatory vision of hope and salvation integrates faith and life, in "a context of struggling for faith and justice."[60] In this context, we come to terms with the realities of life for Black people in America and the world, acknowledging the futile dualisms and incessant desire for consumption that constantly bombards us and with which we constantly wrestle. This aspect of womanist spirituality presses us to reject these warring entities, recognizing them as unhealthy and unnecessary, and replace them with a liberative, holistic, apocalyptic vision of who God truly is and who we truly are as God's people. To do this, Townes encourages us to explore the nature of our relationship with God, not as sinful, worthless creatures, but as the *imago Dei*, in our full embodied selves.[61] We must then explore God's presence as "the very fabric of our existence, a divine and sustaining reality in our lives."[62] This frees us to re-image God as our ancestors did—as immanent and transcendent Spirit that is at once present with and within us.[63] That gives us the ability to re-imagine ourselves as co-creators with Spirit, empowered individually and collectively to sing, pray, dance, preach, and work for the good of our communities. Finally, Townes notes, we must accept and internalize God's unconditional love for us.[64] This calls us to purpose and possibility with accountability and acceptance for each other. We are called away from the precariousness of unchecked individualism onto the solid, steady ground of *beloved community*, away from the separate, alien territory of exclusivity into

[59]Townes, *In a Blaze of Glory*, 139.
[60]Townes, *In a Blaze of Glory*, 139.
[61]Townes, *In a Blaze of Glory*, 140.
[62]Townes, *In a Blaze of Glory*, 140.
[63]Townes, *In a Blaze of Glory*, 140.
[64]Townes, *In a Blaze of Glory*, 140.

the wide, welcoming hospitality of communal love, grace, and mercy. This is what God, in dynamic process, seeks with and for us, intimate, sustaining, reconciling relationships that honestly name our struggles and shortcomings, but are ready to do the revelatory work of finding and creating solidarity with God's will for a new heaven and a new earth.

Liturgically, our ancestors broke this ground for us. Spirituals spoke to our questions, our longings, our fears, despair, grief, and even joy at our circumstances. Lined hymns called the community to sing a foreign song in an ancient manner, led by one who knew the way and could be trusted to carry the tune forth without faltering. Imprecatory prayers honestly laid bare the anger, turmoil, and resignation of a people whose only hope was in the Lord, and some days, even that hope was called into question. Preachments brought to life what was remembered of the text, often turning prevailing interpretations on their heads, to see the work of God in a liberative, just way for those who had yet to see justice on this side. Dancing allowed battered, bruised, and torn flesh to move as freely as possible, witnessing to the beauty of the body enveloped in Blackness. And when they were able, a shout rose up, a mighty cry, accompanied by rhythmic footsteps, in circuitous motion, women and men and even children together, one after the other, slide-stomp, slide-stomp, round and round, chanting getting louder now, slide-STOMP, slide-STOMP, every round going higher, higher, SLIDE-STOMP, SLIDE-STOMP, somebody feelin' the Spirit, now, SLIDE-STOMP, SLIDE-STOMP, bodies starting to contort in divine possession, now, SLIDE-STOMP, SLIDE-STOMP, communal chanting and shouting now, worship in full effect, the presence of our God is here!

When Black folx recover this revelation of the living Divine and allow themselves to worship this way once again, without reservation or hesitation, with a communal sense of solidarity and justice, the Black church will witness its own resurrection.

Epilogue

> *Black worship is based on the cultural and religious experience of the oppressed.... Worship in the black tradition is celebration of the power to survive and to affirm life with all of its complex and contradictory realities.*
>
> —William B. McClain

This book, my love letter to the Black church, arose out of a faculty lecture I gave at the Interdenominational Theological Center over a decade ago. The lecture title, "Liturgy, Justice, and the Future of the Black Church," spoke of my concern, angst, and hope for an institution of which I have been a member my entire life. Over the past five decades, I have watched as Black churches of my childhood, youth, and even adulthood have closed while others struggle just to remain open, let alone vibrant and communally engaged.

Recent protest and freedom movements have emerged in the wake of police brutality and vigilante violence against Black people and other people of color in America. Most of these movements have begun outside of the church, leading myself and others to ask, "Why? Why has the Black church as a major institution in Black life seemed to have lost its significance and prophetic voice in American culture and even in Black communities?" There is no one answer to this question, in part, because there is no monolithic Black church. However, there are commonalities across Black churches, particularly in Black denominations and fellowships that offer clues to answering this question.

One of the most salient clues is the worship happening in Black churches—its origins, styles, music, preaching, and congregational participation, encapsulated in the weekly liturgies. As I researched worship services—in person, online, and on television—so much of what I saw troubled me. Worship services often seemed monotonous, repetitious, unplanned, or planned without much congregational input, focused only on the sermon and subsequent praise dancing, with little concrete, communally empowering responses to the Word of God. As I compared these services with historical accounts of services from Black churches since the antebellum period, there was one jarring revelation: the link of liturgy with justice that infused and imbued the worship of the historic Black church is all but missing today. There are preachers who preach justice and liberation in Black churches, to be sure, but do entire worship services in these churches undergird and underscore the important link between worship with justice? If not, what happened to weaken or sever this link and cause the subsequent identity crises that impact Black churches now? Does the Black church still equate liturgy with justice? If so, how do these liturgies evince this link communally?

This book addresses these questions, while uncovering, rediscovering, and recovering liturgical and worship traditions of Black churches and communities throughout American history. Research has shown that authentic Black worship, at its core, is communal—in practice, as well as in theory. To thrive again, the Black church must first recover and restore its prophetic identity as community representative, and its authority, not just spiritually, but also physically and politically. If the Black church is to be representative of and authoritative in our communities, it must be part of the everyday life of the residents of communities in which it resides. It must invest in the economic, educational, political, and social lives of the people it is called to serve. It cannot afford to remain contained within walls while the communities outside its doors perishes.

Second, the Black church must be intentional about inviting communities in which it resides. It is not enough to place this week's sermon title on the marquee and hope the community is intrigued enough to visit, nor is it enough to schedule program after program and hope the community values the information enough to attend. The Black church must create an environment of hospitality to those who may never have been welcomed in worship settings. It must be intentional about breaking the silence on issues that directly affect Black communities. The Black church must take the gospel of liberation back into the streets whence it emerged when Jesus went from place to place teaching, healing, and proclaiming the prophetic message of God's kin-dom come on earth.

Third, the Black church must be intentional about worship planning—the who, what, when, where, why, and how of worship. If there is to be vital, meaningful worship, it must stem directly from whatever issues and problems the community identifies. One of the best ways to know that is to invite the community to help plan worship—to share stories and testimonies, sources of despair and hope—so as to shape worship into transformative encounters with the Divine that acknowledge these stories of struggle and triumph and offer hope to those still in despair.

It is not enough to attend worship each week for our own personal gain or benefit; indeed, that is not, nor has that ever been, the purpose of worship. Worship exists for God and God alone and, when Black people assemble to worship, it is for the sake of worshipping God alone, the God who brought us up out of the house of bondage, out of the house of slavery, who has kept and continues to keep us, and who has sent Jesus as the example of how to live and be in community in the world. Therefore, as James Cone asserts, an authentic ecclesiology of the Black church flows out of our participation with God in proclaiming the reality of divine liberation, sharing in the liberation struggle, and understanding ourselves as a visible manifestation of the reality of the gospel.[1]

Finally, we have to recover the foundational concept that liturgy is inextricably tied to justice. This is at the root of Black and womanist theology, African and Black worship, and the Black church itself as a follower of Jesus—the One who comes to liberate creation. To paraphrase Kelly Miller Smith, being a Black follower of Jesus means to act out the story of Black theology, to participate in the message and meaning of that story in proclamation and demonstration, integrating our Blackness and faith in a way that not only bestows wholeness and healing upon individuals and families, but engages communities in corporate ministries of intervention and transformation of the structures of social, economic, and political life.[2]

It has been my intention throughout this text to find answers to the questions posed. As with any text, it is impossible to include every reference on a topic, address every issue or scenario, but I have attempted to present and lay historical, theological, and liturgical foundations that help answer these questions and provide a framework for future researchers to continue seeking answers. Moreover, I have provided a womanist liturgical paradigm for worship that can help deconstruct unhealthy, even death-dealing tenets of theology and liturgy that plague our churches and keep our people spiritually bound. It is intended to be reconstructive and reconstitutive of ancestral liturgical models that affirmed and empowered a people throughout history and across continents. Were these models perfect? No, and neither is this one, but it is offered for consideration to churches of every hue and identity who desire to be wide, welcoming spaces of liberative, holistic transformation, and to scholars who understand and are committed to the necessity of continuing this work.

If our liturgies are to be transformative, they must be grounded in the biblical commands to do justice, love kindness, walk humbly with God, and love neighbor as self, and in African ancestral heritages of sacred cosmos, community, and kinship, and liberative, holistic hermeneutics. Then, and only then, can we become fully engaged in the transformation of our communities and the persons who live therein. Otherwise, we are playing church while Black America continues to burn. *Ashe.*

---

[1]James Cone, *A Black Theology of Liberation, Fortieth Anniversary Edition* (Maryknoll, NY: Orbis Books, 2010), 138–139.

[2]The Kelly Miller Smith Institute, "What Does It Mean to Be Black and Christian?" in *Black Theology: A Documentary History*, ed. James H. Cone and Gayraud S. Wilmore (Maryknoll, NY: Orbis Books, 1993), 168.

Index

16th Street Baptist Church (Birmingham), 216
2021 US Capitol riot, 216
700 Club, The, 117

abolitionism, 82–83, 125–26. *See also* slavery
Abyssinian Baptist Church (New York), 77, 133–34
Adams, Charles G., 78, 83
affirmation, 61–62
African ancestral worship, xiv, 16, 221
African Benevolent Society, 80
African Derived Religions (ADR), 182
African Methodist Episcopal (AME) Church, 81–83
African Methodist Episcopal Zion (AMEZ) Church, 83, 126
African Religions and Philosophy (Mbiti), 88
African Traditional Religions (ATR), xi, 20, 53–56, 182
Afro-Baptist churches, 77–81
Agenda for Public Action, 117
Alabama Christian Movement for Human Rights (ACMHR), 138, 140
Ali, Noble Drew, 114
All Saints Day, 92
"All the Way My Savior Leads Me" (Crosby), 81
Allen, Asa Alonso, 116, 119
Allen, Richard, 43, 81–83, 107, 108, 126
American Negro Spirituals (Johnson and Johnson), 132
anamnesis, 10
ancestors, presence of, 183–84
Anderson, Robert, 32
Anglicanism, 45, 98–99, 112, 157
anti-Blackness, 94–96, 100–101, 105–6, 107, 108, 157, 166, 172
Arbery, Ahmaud, 216
Asante, Kariamu, 88
Asante, Molefi, 88
Asbury, Francis, 82
assimilationism, 154–56
atonement, 181
authenticity. *See* worship, authentic
authority, xviii, 220
Azusa Street Revival, 84, 128–29

Bailey, Richard, 97
Baker-Fletcher, Karen, 176–77, 178, 180, 182
Bakker, Jim, 117
Bakker, Tammy Faye, 117
baptism, 14–15, 89–90, 124
Baptist Ministers' Alliance (Montgomery, AL), 139
Barnett, John, 112
Barrett, Leonard, 17, 18–19, 23, 25, 41
Baton Rouge Movement, 138
Battle, Michael, 61, 112
Bay Psalm Book, 79
Beloved (Morrison), 213
Bernard, George, 81
Best, George, 96
Bibb, Henry, 37
Birmingham Campaign, 140
Black aesthetics, 62–70, 72
Black Arts Movement, 62
Black Baptist Church (Williamsburg, VA), 77
Black Baptist churches, 77–81, 108, 127–28
Black Brotherhood of Sleeping Car Porters Union, 140
Black Church Freedom Movement, 155

"Black Church Is Dead, The" (Glaude), xviii
Black Entertainment Television (BET), 120
Black exceptionalism, 153–54, 155
Black feminism, 158–59
Black humanism, 156–57
Black Jews, 114
Black Lives Matter, xvii, 150–51
Black Manhattan (Johnson), 132
Black Manifesto, The, 158
Black marginalism, 156
Black Messiah, The (Cleage), 158
Black Methodism, 81–83, 107, 126–27
"Black Power and the American Christ" (Harding), 158
Black Power movement, 154, 158
Black, Daniel P., 42
"Blessed Assurance" (Crosby), 81
Bliss, Philip, 81
blues, 72
Bluestone African Baptist Church (Mecklenburg, VA), 76–77
Bodin, Jean, 96
Bonhoeffer, Dietrich, 134
Book of American Negro Poetry, The (Johnson), 132
Boyd, Rekeisha, 216
Bradbury, William, 81
Bray, Thomas, 98–99
Bridgeman, Valerie, 6
broadcasting ministries, 115–21
Brooks, Gennifer, 54
Brown, John, 11
Brown, Julia, 22
Brown, Michael, 216
Bryan, Andrew, 77
Bynum, Juanita, 120

call to worship, 34–35
Calvinism, 98, 108, 157
Campbell, Lucie, 86
Cane Ridge Camp Meeting, 46
Cannon, Katie Geneva, 28–29, 174, 199–200, 204
catechesis, 24
Chalcedon, Council of, 157, 204–5
Chan, Simon, 4, 167
chant, 77–78
charismatic mainlines, 121–22
Children's March, 216
Christian Broadcasting Network (CBN), 120
Christian Methodist Episcopal Church, 83
Chronicle of the Discovery and Conquest of Guinea, The (Zurara), 95–96
church decline, xi
Church of Christ Holiness, USA, 129
Church of God, 129–30
Church of God in Christ (COGIC), 129
circament, 169
civil disobedience, 117
Civil Rights Movement, xiii–xiv, xvi, 137–41, 149, 155
Cleage, Albert, 158
Clifton, Denzil, 98–99
Clifton, Lucille, 184
Coleman, Monica, 178–79
Coleman, Will, 90–91, 183
Color Purple, The (Walker), 177
Colored Methodist Episcopal Church. *See* Christian Methodist Episcopal Church
Colored Sacred Harp, 80
Colored Union Church (Newport, RI), 80
colorism, 200
Columbia Records, 118
Coming, The (Black), 42
communal identity, 8–9
communion, 14–15, 82, 169, 196–97
Compassion Baptist Church (Chicago), xvii
Concepts of God in Africa (Mbiti), 16
Cone, James H., xvi, 7–8, 22–23, 25, 28, 34, 37, 40, 48, 60, 72
conversion, 25, 76, 90, 124
Copeland, Kenneth, 117
Copeland, M. Shawn, 188–89, 196, 205–6
Cornish, Samuel E., 126
cosmologies, African, xi, xiii, 16–19, 20, 21, 30, 54, 68, 124, 176–77
Costen, Melva Wilson, 4–6, 9–10, 11, 18–19, 20, 34, 39–40, 43–47, 54–55, 73–74, 76, 82, 90

Cotton, John, 95
covenant, 97
COVID-19, 13, 165
Crawford, Percy, 115
"Creation, The" (Johnson), 132
creativity, 64, 67, 70, 185, 186, 210
and God, 6, 24, 176–77, 212, 215
Crisis, The, 130
Crosby, Fanny, 81
Crouch, Andrae, 120
Crouch, Jan, 120
Crouch, Paul, 120
Cullors, Patrisse, 150
Cummings, George, 24–25

dance, 41
Dash, Michael, 214
Davies, Samuel, 111
Davis, Reginald, 159–60
Day of Judgment, 125, 166
deliverance. *See* liberation
depravity, total, 108
Devine, Loretta, 92
Devisse, Jean, 95
Dewing, R. Thomas, 68
dialectics, 70–72
Dickerson, Dennis, 81, 82
disability, 195, 206–7
discipleship, 179, 184
Divine, Father, 115
Dixon, Calvin P., 118
Dixon, Emily, 47
Dixon, Vernon, 71
Docetism, 104
Dollar, Creflo, 120
Dormon, James H., 125, 126
Dorsey, Thomas A., 86
double consciousness, xv, 12, 15, 102–6
double self-negation, 105–6
Douglas, Kelly Brown, 179, 188, 190, 192–93, 207–8
Douglass, Frederick, 125, 126, 141, 215
Du Bois, W. E. B., xv, 34, 37, 43, 47, 55, 102, 130–31, 132
dualistic anthropology, 12, 15, 64, 104–5, 188, 192, 205, 207–8, 211

Earl, Riggins R., 103, 105–6
ecclesiology, 168
Edmund Pettus Bridge (Selma, AL), 216
education, theological, xvii
Edwards, Jonathan, 111–12
Eiesland, Nancy, 195, 206
Eikerenkoetter, Frederick J., II ("Rev. Ike"), 119–20
election, divine, 98, 108
Ellison, Marvin M., 188
Emancipation, 66, 93, 127
Emba, Christine, 152
embodiment, xviii, 103, 186–98, 205–7
and emotions, 196, 197
See also worship, embodied
emotionalism, 84, 107, 108–9, 110
opposition to, 113
empowerment, 6
eschatology. *See* worship, as eschatological
evangelicalism, xv–xvi, 14, 115–23, 217
Evers, Medgar, 215

Falwell, Jerry, 117
Fard, W. D., 114
Farrow, Lucy, 128
Faulkner, William J., 29
feminism, 202
Fifty Years and Other Poems (Johnson), 132
Finney, Charles Grandison, 113
First African Baptist Church (Philadelphia), 77
First Colored Church (Savannah, GA), 77
Fisk Jubilee Singers
Fitzgerald, Frances, 112, 117
Florida Bible Institute, 116
Floyd, George, 149–50, 216
Floyd-Thomas, Stacey, 174–75
Foley, W. Trent, 184
folklore, 19, 28–30, 67–68, 106. *See also* wisdom
Franklin, Clarence LaVaughn, 118, 119
Franklin, Robert, 33
Frazier, E. Franklin, xvi, 21, 32, 40, 44
Free African Society, 82, 107, 126
Free Speech and Headlight, The, 128
Freedom's Journal, 125–26
Freud, Sigmund, 203
Fuller, Charles, 115

fundamentalism, 115
funerals, 91–92

Gabriel, Charles, 81
Gardner, Newport, 80
Garner, Cornelius, 25
Garner, Eric, 216
Garnett, Henry Highland, 215
Garrison, William Lloyd, 125
Garvey, Marcus, 114
Garveyism, 137
Garza, Alicia, 150
Gates, Henry Louis, Jr., 67
Gates, J. M., 118
Genovese, Eugene D., 100
George, David, 77
Gilkes, Cheryl Townsend, 188
Gillfield Baptist Church (Petersburg, VA), 138
Glaude, Eddie, Jr., xviii
God Struck Me Dead (Johnson), 90
God, 16–17, 22–23, 53, 176–78, 201, 211–13
  and gender, 177–78, 191–92, 212–13
  as liberator, 23, 176, 217
  personal view of, 8
God's Trombones (Johnson), 132
Goetz, Rebecca Anne, 99
Goff, James, 46–47
Good Master Well Served, A (Mather), 97
gospel blues, 86
Gospel Hymns and Sacred Songs (Sankey), 81
Gospel Pearls (Townsend), 86
gospels, 79, 145–49, 166
Graça, Marcelino Manuel da (Daddy Grace), 115
Graham, Billy, 116
Grant, Jacquelyn, 178, 204
Great Awakenings, xv, 79
  First, 45, 111–12, 158
  Second, 46, 80, 109, 112–13, 158
Great Depression, 136
Great Migration, 114, 135–37, 141, 155
Griffin, Horace, 193–94
Grimes, Ronald, 9
griots, 38, 39, 68, 78, 103
Gumperz, John, 77

Hamblen, Stuart, 116
Hamer, Fannie Lou, 215
Hampton Institute, 110
Harding, Vincent, 158
Harlem Renaissance, 130–34
Harris, Larnelle, 120
Harrison Street Church (Petersburg, VA), 77
Hearst, William Randolph, 116
Heng, Geraldine, 96
Henry, Prince of Portugal ("the Navigator"), 96
hereditary heathenism, 99–101, 108
hermeneutics
  of incarnation, 204–9
  of liberation, 199–203, 221
  of suspicion, 203–4
Herskovits, Melville J., 21
Higginbotham, Evelyn Brooks, 65, 127
Hill, E. V., 120
Hinn, Benny, 117
"His Eye Is on the Sparrow" (Gabriel), 81
Holiness churches. *See* Sanctified churches
Holy Spirit, 24–25, 48, 53, 69, 91, 104, 181–82, 215, 217
homophobia, 150, 151, 166, 193–94
hooks, bell, 158
Hopkins, Dwight N., 17–18, 20–24, 26–28, 29–30, 33, 36, 47, 58–59, 65–66
Horn, Rosa Artimus, 118–19
hospitality, 70, 218, 220
Howard University, 131
Hughes, Langston, 30
Hull, Akasha Gloria, 183
Hurston, Zora Neale, 30, 85
Hyde, Patsy, 58
Hymns and Spiritual Songs (Watts), 45, 79
hymns, 76
  hymn lining, 46, 79, 108

"I Am Thine, O Lord" (Crosby), 81
imago Dei, 205, 212, 217
incarnation, 196–97. *See also* hermeneutics, of incarnation
independent religious movements, 114–15

individualism, xi, xvi
Inter-Civic Council, 138
Interdenominational Ministerial Alliance (Montgomery, AL), 139
Interdenominational Theological Center (Atlanta), 219
interracial churches, 84–85
intersectionality, 175
invisible institution, xiii–xiv, 16, 32–34, 54–55, 57, 72–74, 103–4
Isaiah (prophet), 144, 148, 165–66
is-ness, 210
"It Is Well with My Soul" (Spafford), 81

Jackson, Jonathan, 214
Jackson, Judge, 80
Jakes, T. D., 120
Jamestown, 98
Jesus, 23–24, 53, 55, 104, 145–49, 166, 178–81, 191, 196–97, 205
  as liberator, 23–24
  and servanthood, 178
  suffering of, 180
  See also incarnation
"Jesus Loves Me" (Warner), 81
"Jezebel," 190, 193
Jim Crow, 127, 216
Jimmy Swaggart Telecast, The, 117
John Street Methodist Church (New York), 83, 126
Johnson, Alonzo, 24, 33
Johnson, Charles S., 131
Johnson, James Weldon, 30, 131, 132–33
Jones, Absalom, 81–82, 107
Jones, Charles Price, 84, 129
Jones, Nathan, 63–64, 67–69
Jones, Robert R., 125, 126
Jones, Watson, III, xvii, 150
Jordan, Meagan, 152–53
Joy Baptist Church (Boston), 77
Jubilee Year, 166
"jumping the broom." *See* marriage
Jumping the Broom (dir. Akil), 92
Jungmann, Josef A., xii
Junior, Nyasha, 203
"Just As I Am" (Elliott), 81
justice,
  defined, 10
  See also liturgy, and justice

Katie's Canon (Cannon), 28
Kellogg, Paul, 131
Kendi, Ibram X., 95, 102
Kiefer, Ralph, 15
King, Martin Luther, Jr., 117, 138, 140, 215
King, Rodney, 216
kinship, xiii, 17–18, 25–27, 63, 68, 213, 221
Kirk-Duggan, Cheryl, 186, 199
Ku Klux Klan, 127

labor, 136
Lathrop, Gordon, 4, 167
Lemann, Nicholas, 135
Levine, Lawrence, 110–11
liberation, xi, xiii, xv, xvii, 21, 36–37, 59–61, 66, 124–25, 148–49, 160, 199–203
Liberator, The, 125–26
Liele, George, 77
"Lift Every Voice and Sing" (Johnson), 132
Lincoln, C. Eric, 44, 72, 136–37
liturgy,
  defined, xii–xiii, 3–5, 6–10
  functions of, 6–7
  and justice, xii–xiv, 8–9, 10–12, 124–41, 142, 149, 220–21
  liturgical elements, 34–48, 74, 85, 170
  liturgical seasons, 170
  study of, 172
  See also worship
Locke, Alain, 62, 131–32
Long, Charles H., 182
Long, Eddie, 120
Lord's Prayer, 146
love, 70, 211, 212–13, 217–18
"Love Lifted Me" (Rowe), 81
Lovejoy, Elijah Parish, 11

mainline Protestantism, xi
Mamiya, Lawrence, 44, 136–37
"Mammy," 190
March on Washington Movement (MOWM), 137
Marks, Morton, 71, 73
marriage, 92–93
Martin, Clarice J., 201, 204

Martin, Trayvon, 150, 216
Marx, Karl, 203
Mary Mary, 159
Mason, Babbie, 120
Mason, Charles Harrison, 84, 129
Massie, Ishrael, 58
Mather, Cotton, 94–96, 99, 106
Mather, Richard, 95
Maultsby, Portia, 78
Mbiti, John, 16–18, 20, 24–25, 26, 35–36, 38, 41, 88, 92–93, 176, 183
McClain, William B., xi, xiv, 7, 10, 169, 171, 219
McGready, James, 113
Meade, William, 98–99
meaning, 167–68
memory. *See* anamnesis
Methodist Episcopal Church, 82
Methodist Episcopal Church, South, 83
Micah (prophet), 142–43
Michaux, Elder Solomon Lightfoot, 118–19
Miracle Temple (Boston), 119
missions, 99
Mitchell, Henry, 40
monogamy, 93
monotheism, 16–17
Montesquieu, 96
Montgomery Improvement Assocation (MIA), 138, 139–40
Moody, Dwight Lyman, 80–81, 86, 109, 113
Moorish Science Temple of America, 114
Moral Majority, 117
Morris, Aldon D., xvii–xviii, 138, 140, 141
Mother Emmanuel Nine, 216
Moton, Robert Russa, 110
Moyd, Olin, 40–41
Mt. Sinai Holy Church of America, 115
music, 41–47, 76, 78, 86, 108–11

NAACP, 130, 132, 138
Nation of Islam, 114
National Association of Evangelicals (NAE), 115
National Baptist Convention, USA, 127–28
National Baptist Magazine, The, 128
National Convention of Gospel Choirs and Choruses Workshop of America, 86
Native Americans, 99, 216
"Near the Cross and Pass Me Not" (Crosby), 81
Negro Convention Movement, 126–27
Neo-Pentecostalism, 121
New Negro movement. *See* Harlem Renaissance
New Negro, The (Locke), 131
New Songs of Paradise (Tindley), 86
Nicaea, Council of, 157
Nietzsche, Friedrich, 203
Nix, A. W., 118
Nixon, E. D., 140
non-denominational churches, 5
Norris, Kristopher, 104–5
North Star, 125–26

Oduyoye, Mercy, 19
Ofori-Atta-Thomas, George, 27, 34, 38–40, 48, 55–56, 70, 73
Old Fashioned Radio Hour, The, 115
"Old Rugged Cross, The" (Bernard), 81
Old Time Gospel Hour, The, 117
"On Christ the Solid Rock I Stand" (Mote), 81
Opportunity, 131

Pacific Coast Apostolic Faith movement, 128
Paramount Records, 118
Parham, Charles, 84, 128
Paris, Peter J., 20, 21, 28, 181
Parks, Rosa, 215
Parrinder, Geoffrey, 183
paternalism, 100–101, 108
Patterson, Orlando, 187
Payne, Daniel, 43, 82, 108–9
Peace Mission, 115
Pearson, Carlton, 120
pedagogy, 200
Pentecostal Faith Church (New York), 119
Pentecostal Holiness Church, 129
Pentecostalism, 116–17. *See also* Sanctified churches
Perini, Matthew J., 68
Philips, John, 86

Pitts, Walter F., Jr., 77, 79, 109–10
Platonism. *See* dualistic anthropology
portamento, 78
Powell, Adam Clayton, Sr., 131, 133–34
praise/pray's houses, 75–76
prayer, 35–37, 79
preaching, 37–41, 67, 77–78, 121, 220
  prophetic, 40–41, 215
predestination. *See* election, divine
Price, Fred K., 120
Proctor, Jenny, 57
Proctor, Samuel Dewitt, 61
prophetic literature, 9, 10, 142–45, 148, 165–66
Prosser, Gabriel, 60
Protestant Episcopal Church, 99
providence, 98, 108
psalmody, English, 79
psalms, xvi, 45, 79
PTL Club, 117
Puritanism, 79, 94–95, 97–98, 112, 157

Raboteau, Albert, 20–21, 23, 37, 58, 67, 71–72, 91, 113
race records, religious, 118–19
Radio Church of God, 118
Radio Church of God of the Air, 119
radio evangelism. *See* broadcasting ministries
Randolph, A. Philip, 137, 215
Rasor, Stephen C., 214
redlining, 216
resistance, 58–59, 126–29
respectability politics, 65–66, 102, 153, 190–91
resurrection, 4, 24, 171, 183, 196, 207, 218
Revised Common Lectionary, 170
revivalism, 115–16
Reynolds, Thomas E., 194–95
rhythm, 41–42, 56, 76
  cosmic, 19, 67
Rice, Tamir, 216
Richards, Dona Marimba, 87, 88
Ricoeur, Paul, 203
ring shout, 43, 56, 76, 91, 109
ritual, 9–10, 54, 87–93
  defined, 87–88
Roberts, Oral, 116, 119–20
Robertson, Pat, 117, 120
Robinson, Ida, 115
Rodeheaver, Homer A., 81
Ross, Leora, 118
Ross, Rosetta, 187
Rouget, Gilbert, 77–78
Rowe, James, 81
Russell, Letty, 179

sacraments, 14–15
sacred cosmos, xiii, xvi, 18–19, 22, 27–28, 63, 221
Sacred Harp, The (White), 80
Sacred Songs and Solos with Standard Hymns (Sankey and Moody), 109
sainthood, visible, 96–97, 105–6
Salem Baptist Church (Detroit), 119
Saliers, Don, 5, 206–7
Salter McNeil, Brenda, 150
salvation, 179
Samaritan woman, 145, 147
same-gender sexuality, 152, 193
Sanctified Church, The (Hurston), 85
Sanctified churches, 84–87, 128–30
Sanders, Cheryl, 84, 85, 129
Sankey, Ira, 80–81, 86, 109
schizophrenia, liturgical, 14
Schüssler Fiorenza, Elisabeth, 202, 203–4
Scopes trial, 115
scripture, 9, 10, 15, 19, 20, 60, 79, 82, 142–49, 165–66, 184
  and justice, 142–49
sermons. *See* preaching
Sernett, Milton, 135
servanthood, 178
sexism, 150, 151, 166, 188, 194. *See also* misogyny; "Mammy"; "Jezebel"
Seymour, William, 84, 128
"Shackles (Praise You)" (Mary Mary), 159–60
shape-note singing, 80
shouting, 42–43, 47–48. *See also* ring shout
signification, 67
Silver Bluff Baptist Church (Beech Island, SC), 77
Silver, Harvey, 68
  slavery, 16, 21, 25–27, 189
  slave rebellions, 75

slave religion, 20, 21, 32–34, 56–62, 72–74
See also abolitionism
Smith, Harmon L., 5, 11, 14
Smith, Kelly Miller, 221
Smith, Mitzi J., 203
Smith, Theophus, 54, 62, 70–73, 87
Sobel, Mechal, 25, 41, 59, 90–91, 93, 105
Society for the Propagation of Christian Knowledge (SPCK), 99
Society for the Propagation of the Gospel in Foreign Parts (SPG), 45, 99, 111
songbooks, 80
Soul Echoes (Tindley), 86
Souls of Black Folk, The (Du Bois), 102, 131
Southern Christian Leadership Conference (SCLC), 138, 140
Southern, Eileen, 43–45, 47
Spencer, Jon Michael, 42, 56
spirit possession, 24–25, 41, 47–48, 54, 64, 72, 74, 91, 111–12
Spiritual Movement, xvi
spirituality, 63–64, 184–86
womanist, 209, 213, 217
spirituals (songs), 43–45, 47, 72, 76, 79, 108
Spurrier, Rebecca, 195n95
St. George's Methodist Episcopal Church (Philadelphia), 81, 107
Stanton School (Jacksonville, FL), 132
Stearns, Shubal, 77
Stewart, Carlyle Fielding, III, 89, 184–85, 210, 215
Student Nonviolent Coordinating Committee (SNCC), 138
style-switching, 71–72
Sunday, Billy, 81, 113
Sundays, 169–70, 171
Survey, 131
survival, 9, 56–58, 61, 173–74, 176, 178, 180, 182, 201
Swaggart, Jimmy, 117
Swann, Darius L., 63, 68, 73
"Sweet Hour of Prayer" (Walford), 81
Synan, Vinson, 84

Taryor, Nya, 54
Taylor, Breonna, 216
televangelism. *See* broadcasting ministries
theology,
Eurocentric, 93–101
liturgical, 167–75, 176–98, 199–218
Till, Emmitt, 216
Till-Mobley, Mamie, 215
Tindley, Charles A., 86
Tinney, James S., 85
"'Tis So Sweet to Trust in Jesus" (Stead), 81
"This I Know" (Crosby), 81
Tometi, Opal, 150
Townes, Emilie M., 177–78, 186, 190, 194, 199, 209, 213, 217
traditionalism, 168–69
transgendered persons, 214
trauma, 159–60
Trible, Phyllis, 202
Trinity Broadcasting Network (TBN), 120
Trinity Church (New York), 45
Trulear, Harold, 207
Truth, Sojourner, 215
Tubman, Harriet, 141, 215
Turman, Eboni Marshall, 205, 208
Turner, Nat, 60, 141
Turner, Victor, 185n60
Tuskegee Institute, 110
TVOne, 120

Ubuntu, 18, 62–63
Underground Railroad, 126
United House of Prayer for All People, 115
United Negro Improvement Association (UNIA), 114

Van Alstyne, Mrs. Alexander. *See* Crosby, Fanny, 81
Vesey, Denmark, 60, 141
Victor Talking Machine Company, 118
visible sainthood. *See* sainthood, visible

Walker, Alice, 158, 173–74, 177
Walker, David, 125
Walker, Wyatt Tee, 138–39, 140
Walker's Appeal, 125–26
Walton, Jonathan L., 118, 121–22
Washington, Booker T., 110
Washington, James Melvin, 127

Washington, Joseph, Jr., 44, 94, 126
Watts, Isaac, 45–46, 76, 78–79
Way Maker, 30. *See also* folklore
Weed, Eric A., 100
Weems, Renita J., 202, 204
Weisenfeld, Judith, 114–15, 136–37
Wells-Barnett, Ida B., 128, 215
Wesley, John, 82, 111
West, Cornel, 153–57
Whalum, Wendell, 82
Wheaton College, 116
Whelchel, Love Henry, Jr., 90, 111, 135–36, 155
white supremacy, xi–xii, 106, 216–17. *See also* anti-Blackness
White, Benjamin Franklin, 80
White, James, 4, 10
White, Mingo, 37
Whitefield, George, 111–12
Williams, Delores S., 180, 189–92, 199, 201–2, 204
Williams, Reggie L., 133–34
Williams, W. T. B., 135
Wilmore, Gayraud S., 11, 20, 32, 56–57, 61–62, 64, 72–73, 75–76, 81–84, 86–87, 107, 114, 126, 136
Wimberly, Anne Streaty, 160
Wimberly, Edward P., 7, 160
Winans, BeBe, 120
Winans, CeCe, 120
Wiregrass Singers, 80
wisdom, 19, 28–30, 67–68. *See also* folklore
Wolterstorff, Nicholas, xii, 10
Womack, Edwin B., 3
womanism, xviii–xix, 158–59, 173–75, 176–82, 186, 199–203, 204, 205–9, 221
  defined, 173–74
Women's Rights movement, 154
"Wonderful Words of Life" (Bliss), 81
Word Network, The, 120
Word of Faith, 121, 122
worship,
  authentic, 12–14, 15, 16, 111
  dialectical, 70–72
  embodied, 4
  as eschatological, 6, 7, 44, 69, 147
  planning of, 220
  types of, 4
  See also liturgy
Wright, Richard, 29

Young People's Church of the Air, 115

Zurara, Gomes Eanes de, 95–96